NOR FLAGPOLE MOUNTAIN

A Community Memoir

written by Mike Headley
and the
People of Childersburg, Alabama

Cover design by Kay Epps Headley

First Printing 2016

ISBN-13: 978-1522891710

MAH Books

headlemk@gmail.com

TABLE of CONTENTS

Most can write, some can write well, but, oh, to write where the mind can't wait for the next word to flash before the eye, or have the ability to make the readers mind dance in anticipation of the next word.

To accomplish such would bring a smile to my face. For that my friend is a writer.

Mike Headley

FOREWORD

In the summer of 2015, I got an email from a high school friend, asking that I help Mike Headley with some "stories" for a book about Childersburg. I didn't know Mike at the time, but I contacted him to learn more. Still by email, he explained that his book —i.e., THIS BOOK — is a compilation of "remembrances" of Childersburg during the 30-year period of approximately 1953 to 1982, and that he indeed was seeking more input. Mike's objective was to collect memories of funny events and strange events, but also about the routine, every-day life of the era; stories about friends and their cars; stories about teachers, places, activities, exploits, unique experiences, and more. And all as told in the words of the person who had experienced them. But he also strongly emphasized that he was not writing a "kiss and tell" book, which might embarrass someone, not to mention possibly "getting him sued."

I found Mike's concept of many contributors for his book to be intriguing. Also he had already written and published at least twelve children's books, which made me feel that he did know what he was doing, so I signed on. Over the following months, as I recalled some of my own situations that might be of interest, I submitted several short narratives to him.

Most of my contributions he has used, with very little editing. However, one or two he turned down because they might offend a person mentioned. I had not really known Mike in school, but with our discussions back and forth, and our mutual interest in Childersburg, we formed an email friendship. After compiling his material into his publication format, he asked if I would be one of his draft-reviewers, and mark it up for corrections. I readily agreed to his invitation.

He also asked me to write this "Foreword" for his book, which I am pleased and honored to contribute. I found the material very enjoyable to read. That is to be expected when one knows personally many of the persons and/or places being described.

But even if you don't know the participants, you will still be drawn into the popular activities of macho guys of the era — hunting and fishing, fast cars and drag racing, and generally getting into mischief! And you can almost sense a feeling of pride in their accounts of those remembrances. The guys are very open in confessing their rowdy behaviors, with no regrets!

As might be the expected, memories shared by most female contributors tended to be more sedate, such as going to town, favorite stores and shopping, and eating places. Also, the girls' narratives were usually not as detailed as those of many of their male counterparts.

But those with wheels, both guys and gals, had a keen memory of the "cruising" routes — Dairy Queen® to Tastyee-Freez and back, or on a quiet night, over to Sylacauga! And both genders reported a fondness of the traditional date location, the Coosa Theater. Sadly, these latter two locations no longer exist in Childersburg.

Mr. Headley appends a list of the 92 contributors to this work, with their graduation years. Of these, 22 graduated in 1961, '62, or '63, graduation years targeted for providing memories. But only seven contributors graduated in an earlier year while 63 graduated later! Why the big difference? Regretfully it is obvious that there are fewer around to respond from that earlier age group. Someone wanting to do a similar collection or study using students of the 1990s and 2000s — in Childersburg or anywhere — needs to start in the next 10 years.

I foresee that perhaps 20 years or fewer from now, this effort by Mike to collect remembrances will be a great asset to some future social scientist seeking to study a small town and its high school as they were in the 1950s, 1960s and 1970's.

Thanks, Mike, for your efforts and dedication in producing this community memoir.

J. D. Warren, CHS 1961

A SHORT HISTORY
CHILDERSBURG, ALABAMA
1540 THROUGH 1952

Mike Headley, CHS Class of 1962

Northeast of Flagpole Mountain is not a historical documentary.
However, it is a story of Childersburg, Alabama from 1953
through 1982 as seen through the eyes of those who lived in
Childersburg, first as children, then teenagers, and finally as
adults. If one wants to read the history of Childersburg I
recommend the book *Childersburg* by J. Leigh Mathis-Downs.
A history of Childersburg from the time of De Soto's arrival
until the present.

The exact date of the first-known European encounter with
the indigenous people living in Childersburg comes to us
from historical records of the travels of Hernando De Soto
(October 21, 1496 — May 21, 1542). De Soto was born in
Barcarrota, Spain and was a traveler and explorer who
entered the Childersburg area around July 16, 1540 where he
came upon the village named Cosa two miles north of the
present location of the city of Childersburg.

The Coosa Indian Nation covered an area from Northwest
Georgia proceeding in a southwesterly direction through
East Central Alabama to include Talladega County. History
tells us this area had been continually inhabited by Indians
before the arrival of De Soto.

The Indian peoples who occupied the Childersburg area for
many generations were removed either by military force or by
white settlers moving into the area, particularly after 1832.
For generations, Childersburg was just another small
southern farming community with a small number of
businesses.

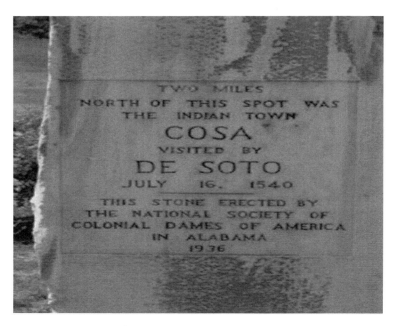

The De Soto Monument

Elaine M. Greer, CHS Class of 1965

The above monument was given to the people of
Childersburg, by The National Society of Colonial Dames of
America in Alabama. And was placed in its location in 1936
where it stands today. The marker can be found on the west
side of US Highway 280 and south of Alabama State
Highway 76, near the red light on top of the hill a few yards
northeast of where a hotel built by Constantine
Frangopoulos first existed. The building was later used as the
bus station in Childersburg.

A Small Town in Upheaval

Mike Headley, *CHS* Class of 1962

For some, visiting Childersburg for the first time might find it
difficult to fathom what this community endured during the

years from 1941 thru 1945. The large upheaval which changed the community forever started in 1941. World War II affected all states, counties, cities, towns, and people of America, but probably none more than the small town of Childersburg.

The Alabama Ordnance Works (AOW) ammunitions plant was built at a cost of almost forty eight million dollars as a production plant for explosives including NC, TNT, DNT, and smokeless powder. The facility was operated by the DuPont Corporation having a peak production rate of 40 million pounds of munitions per month until the end of World War II. Also as part of this valiant World War II effort, Childersburg had the distinction of contributing to the production of (nuclear) heavy water for the Manhattan Project.

Childersburg, a small community of 500 people in 1941, exploded to a town of 15,000-plus souls in one year. To say the community was whipsawed would be an understatement. There were not enough places to eat, to shop or to live. Families, including mine, had men living in their living rooms and on their front porches. My mother and aunts have told stories of men living in remodeled chicken coops. I've been told men were happy to have any place to live that was out of the weather.

World War II was a time of rationing most products. Looking back today I could not imagine the hardships and shortages people experienced. A number of trailer parks and apartments were added. Childersburg even had a bowling alley at the time.

The population spurt included more students. Each classroom in the old school was partitioned to make four. Mr. A. H. Watwood, the high school principal, was invited to provide testimony to a U. S. Senate Committee which was investigating the impact of rapid population growth in rural areas due to such government facilities as the AOW.

The AOW ceased operation in August, 1945. During the war, the plant covered more than 13,000 acres, and employed 15,000 people.

The Alabama Ordnances Works (AOW)

Post War Childersburg

J.D. Warren, *CHS Class of 1961*

As World War II was winding down, the Alabama Ordnances Works (AOW) was shut down. There were no longer jobs, many people left, and Childersburg was on the verge of insignificance! A committee was formed which included Arnold Hobson Watwood, Dr. Robert P. Stock and a few other prominent men of Talladega County plus several state industrial leaders. This committee arranged with the Department of Defense for the use of some of the munitions plant facilities. Due to this committee's efforts, Coosa River Newsprint and Beaunit Rayon Mill were located in Childersburg.

These industries brought a new growth to the community, replacing much of what had evaporated in the previous two years. This brought my family and that of many others to Childersburg. Mr. Watwood and Dr. Stock were major players in the effort to bring new industry to Childersburg.

Sandra Headley Limbaugh, *SHS Class of 1957*

The period following the end of WWII was a time of optimism for many Americans, a time of peace for our nation, a time of hope for a bright future, a time of prosperity with the great depression a fading memory. It was a time of thankfulness and great growth in Christianity. It was a very good time to grow up in small town Alabama.

Our valiant service men had gone to the terrible war areas of Europe, the Far East, and other war zones. Their fathers and grandfathers had fought in the Great World War and only a generation later, the young men of this generation had given their all to fight to bring peace once again. Many gave their lives, and those who were fortunate enough to come home were more than ready to give their all to get an education using the GI Bill or earn a living and enjoy being a part of the young family they had left behind. Their work ethic was to be admired. They truly were the "greatest generation."

A Changed Community

Mike Headley, *CHS Class of 1962*

When World War II was over Childersburg tried to return to a normal small southern town. But Childersburg had been changed forever. The community had two new housing projects added because of the war effort: Coosa Court and Minor Terrace. Uncle Sam left Childersburg with a recreation center located south of the downtown area; with a clinic across the street; and a daycare center located north of the old Childersburg High School.

It was a time when people received phone calls over a black rotary-dial phone which weighed five pounds and was attached to the wall with a receiver attached by a cord. Some had a party-line telephone which meant you shared a line with several neighbors. Pay phone calls cost a dime, cokes a nickel. A doctor's visit was five dollars.

People had front porches, which provided two experiences. The first was to catch a breeze in warm weather air conditioning was just starting to become popular in stores with only a few found in homes. The second was so you could communicate with your neighbors.

In the mid-1950s the Interstate Highway system was being voted on by congress at the behest of President Eisenhower. While cars had safety glass, they only got around 12 miles to the gallon. A child's car seat was unheard of. Children rode to school in buses without air conditioning only to arrive at Childersburg School (which also had no air conditioning).

We played dodge ball, marbles, kick ball, Red Rover-Red Rover, and tag on the school's playground. Most survived the Polio scare of the early to mid-1950s. We rode our bikes without helmets, knee or elbow pads. Our parents whipped our butts when we did wrong. I remember hearing "just wait until your father gets home" more than once. Man! That made for a long day! I believe it made us better people. Kids today have many conveniences we did not enjoy. There were certainly no computers, internet, Email, cell phones, texting, I Pads, or I Pods.

We were taught to respect our flag, country, elders, neighbors, parents, and leaders. Yes, a simpler time, but we, now grandparents, and great-grandparents, have survived.

PREFACE

Dedication

Mike Headley, *CHS Class of 1962*

To my wife, Kay Epps Headley, for helping to rewrite, edit, compile, and publish the memoir, *Northeast of Flagpole Mountain.* Thank you for not taking my life on the many occasions when I was being a complete pain. Thank you for your creative, artistic mind. You have helped me to be a better writer and publisher.

Acknowledgment

Mike Headley, *CHS Class of 1962*

My thanks to Sherry Machen Atkinson, Childersburg High School class of 1962, for her tireless effort in making sure I had my people, times, and places correct.

Many thanks to J D Warren, Childersburg High School class of 1961, for his editing input (the more eyes the better) and for writing the Foreword for *Northeast of Flagpole Mountain.*

My heartfelt thanks go out to the 92 people who provided stories, blurbs, and photographs. Your stories — some of which brought laughter while others brought tears — make this memoir better than I could have ever hoped. Without your help *Northeast of Flagpole Mountain* would have never been completed. Any edits made to this memoir were made for clarity, flow and better understanding.

While completing this memoir I learned the people of Childersburg, going about their daily lives, have woven a beautiful tapestry that I alone could have never written, and I thank them all.

Explanations

Mike Headley, *CHS Class of 1962*

My first thoughts of writing a community memoir came to me around 1990. Why? I think after 18 months of work, by myself and others, I have the answer. Those who experienced Childersburg had a need to go home. Childersburg is no longer the place where we grew up; however, we can remember a different place and time. I can explain what I, the publisher, and we, the authors of *Northeast of Flagpole Mountain* were attempting to accomplish in this memoir.

Come home, if only for a short while. Come home to your childhood; come home to your youth. Yes, friends, come home to Childersburg. Read and remember a place where we were allowed to be children, teenagers, and adults. Welcome home.

Why the Thirty Years: 1953 -1982?

Why only cover 30 years? This was the period of time which reflects the experiences I and many others had in a place called Childersburg, where we had the good fortune to be children.

I have made every effort to ensure what is written in this memoir is true, and factual to be best of my knowledge. Sherry Machen Atkinson, J. D. Warren, my wife, Kay, and I have spent copious amounts of time to make sure that we besmirched no person or family, either living or dead.

As an independent author/publisher I pay all costs in advance of writing, compilation, editing, printing, and shipping through my publishing company, MAH Books. I am grateful to all who chose to participate in this memoir, whether I was able to use your story or not.

Some may wonder why many of the most famous people who lived in Childersburg during the period from 1953 through 1982 do not appear in the memoir. That's a fair question. Please understand I contacted everyone you might have considered. They either chose not to participate or we were unable to reach agreement as to editorial control.

The Colored People

As you read Chapter 15, I would like for you to know that I reached out to several colored individuals and families who lived and went to Childersburg schools during the 30 years period covered by this memoir. None chose to reply to my requests for stories in their community. What you read in this chapter is from the white perspective only. That was not what I had in mind when I began this memoir or Chapter 15.

Secrets

Mike Headley, *CHS Class of 1962*

Childersburg has its secrets. *Northeast of Flagpole Mountain* is not about secrets, and it's not a "Kiss and Tell."

Chapter 1

STORIES: One

A Childersburg Saturday Morning

Charles 'Turkey" Burke, *CHS Class of 1962*

In 1953 Dad had a baby blue 1950 Oldsmobile where we made the trip to downtown Childersburg for ice and other supplies that Morgan Bridge Inn Cafe needed. The Olds had push button start that has been "re-invented" in recent automobile models. We descended down the hill on 1st. Street S.W. past Hall's TV repair shop on the left into the heart of the city. Parking was free and abundant in those days.

Dad always left the keys in the ignition after parking. No reason to remove them. Our first stop was Ben Hosey's Ice House, the skilled "uniformed ice houseman" used ice tongs to pull the slabs on to the deck and immediately grabbed an ice pick to start the "Solomon" separation procedure.

Daddy let me roam as he had other business to conduct. "Hurry, Son, there's no time to waste" as the melting ice blocks waited in that Oldsmobile's trunk. Walking past Willis Curb Market with stalks of ribbon cane out front; skillfully merchandised, your eye could catch the rows of chickens all crouched in the wire nook where chickens were sold live, legs bound with grass string and fitted to a brown paper sack with a slit cut in the top so the chicken's head would poke out. Brown eggs for all to see were on display.

You could get your groceries, seeds, potato slips, lime, popcorn and hair cut — all under the same roof — at Moody Brothers' all-in-one, one-stop store.

Down the street a preacher was on the corner "Preaching to the 'Saturday-Come-to-Town Bunch'." Sorry, not much in the collection shoe box today.

Folks came to town in various types of transportation. One extended family parked their short wood log truck in the lot next to Moody's. Several children were perched on the truck bed rails carefully clinging to brown paper bags that could be re-cycled as lunch sacks. Not enough room in the truck cab for all because the mother, father, grandpa, grandma and the new baby filled the front seat.

No trip was complete without a visit to Maddox Shoe Repair Shop. Entering, you had a view of the aging Mr. and Mrs. Maddox busy cobbling and buffing on the leather belt line shaft. Several people were sitting barefooted in the lobby, sometimes with mismatched socks, on benches ready to be re-shod. New "brogans" were on display for a few bucks in case one's leather was just too worn and unable to accept new soles. You could see the desperate look and disappointment on their faces when they realized money would have to be spent.

Time to go to Dean's Cafe for the lunch crowd is coming. The streets of Childersburg were crowded this Saturday morning, as I look back through the Olds' rear glass headed to our home near the Coosa River.

A Gas Attack

J. D. Warren, *CHS Class of 1961*

Does anyone remember when CHS came under a chlorine gas attack in the spring of 1961? Even if you were there at that time, you may have sensed it without really knowing what was going on. Here, revealed perhaps for the first time, is the background of that event.

In my senior year, because of a scheduling conflict, my friend Jimmy and I wound up taking a general science course. There was nothing wrong with the course — but it wasn't rocket science. Unfortunately the teacher left and a substitute had to be quickly found for the second semester. I never got the impression that the sub knew much about science. Jimmy and I had taken chemistry the year before, and when the course text came to a section of basic chemistry she seemed happy to let us use the class time for some "demonstrations" of chemical reactions.

The 'science room' was on the ground level of the high school addition made in the mid 1950s, right at the angle of the "L" that was formed by the building. In the back of the room there was actually another small room which provided storage for chemicals, equipment, etc., and enough counter space to set up a small demonstration. There was no exhaust fan in the room or anywhere in the building.

The class ended right before lunch, and Jimmy and I would go to the store room to plan and gather materials for the next day's demonstration. I had a book with instructions for chemical lab experiments which gave us a lot of options. But one day when he had left early, I decided to try one of the procedures which produced chlorine gas.

The reaction I started produced much more gas than I thought and more than my equipment could contain. I started wheezing and coughing. I stopped the reaction as best I could and opened the windows to air out the room. No one was around because it was lunch period.

But when I went upstairs I could still smell it in the main hallway, probably because some of the gas had gotten into the ventilation system. And people were beginning to cough and notice the stink. Fortunately it dissipated pretty fast, but I reported to the office what had happened. Needless to say, that ended our chemistry demonstrations. It did take several

3

hours for me to get over the effects of my exposure — but looking back, it could have been a lot worse!

Too Many Cowboy Movies

Mike Headley, *CHS Class of 1962*

I suppose it had to happen. I had seen too many Hoot Mix cowboy movies on TV. Do you remember when the good guys would pull a bullet apart and take the powder out thus rendering the bad guys' bullets useless? The show never quite got around to explaining just how the bad guys ended up with the useless bullets. When you're eight years old those questions don't seem to be an issue. To my mind the bullet separation seemed like a good thing to do. Having a few 22 caliber rounds lying around I proceeded to pull one apart.

Let me set the scene. Mother was washing clothes on the back porch with that wringer washer going -- it was summer. My sister Sandra was killing flies with a fly swatter. I had spent far too much time trying to separate that copper slug from that brass shell. The pliers were not working like they had for Hoot Mix on the TV. So the only thing left to do was get a hammer. I placed that 22 caliber round on the concrete floor of the back porch. I gave that 22 bullet a good whack ...NOTHING! Perhaps a little harder next time, yea, that will do it.

My second blow must have worked because the round exploded. Sending that copper slug flying past my head and ear crease touching both my head and ear as it passed. The round had a little further to go before it embedded in the wall of our back porch. Before arriving at its final destination it passed between my fly-swatting sister Sandra's legs.

For some odd reason Sandra was not at all happy with my method of bullet separation. Worse, she told mother. When daddy got home from work he was not all that upset. The whole thing must have worked out because I was not told "no more cowboy movies for you."

Miner Cliett, CHS Class of 1962
Childersburg's Skeet-Shooting Gold Medalist

Charles "Turkey" Burke, *CHS Class of 1962*

Miner Henry Cliett was the most famous person from Childersburg during the late 1950s and early 1960s. I remember turning on the TV and catching Miner as a guest on the national Arthur Godfrey Morning Show. The setting was Godfrey's farm, a 1,970 acre Leesburg, VA estate.

After a short introduction, the cameras focused on Miner and his skeet shooting abilities. After a few successful single shots doubles were next. As the trap door opened, Minor missed the first "Clay Pigeon" and hit the second. For the next six or more sequences, Miner nailed the first skeet about five feet from the trap and never missed again.

If you walked into Henry Cliett's hardware store in Childersburg toward the rear of the store, you had a good view of cases of shotgun shells and re-loading equipment behind the tables of pipe fittings. The reloading activity was an integral part of the visit to this old fashioned hardware store.

Going out in the woods with Miner carrying our .22 rifles in hand was an experience. After a few rounds of shooting the necks off bottles, Miner asked me to throw up rocks the size of a 50 cent piece. He demonstrated his skill by hitting most of the rocks pitched up in a 30 foot arc. That was an extremely difficult target to hit. Miner did it with ease.

Miner won a spot on the U.S. International Skeet Shooting Team at the age of 17, competing in Oslo, Norway for the World Moving Target championship in 1961. By breaking 634 targets, Miner shot his way to the gold medal. On Miner's return to Childersburg, Henry Miner's dad bought him a new, beige 1961 Ford Thunderbird. Sadly, Miner passed away in December of 1992 at the age of 44 years.

The Governor Wallace Rally

John Madison (Johnny) Giddens Jr., *CHS Class of 1980*

As a youngster, going to Emery's 5 & 10 was a treat. Some people called it "Emery's." Some called it the "5 and Dime." My family called it the "10-Cent Store." I remember going there and all the toys that I hoped to have one day — everything from G. I. Joe to the Red Raider B. B. Gun that Uncle Sandy would eventually buy me — much to mom's disapproval. The trip to the 10-Cent Store that summer day was not about toys — it was about going to see a legend. This man wanted to be President of the United States. He had already run in 1968 and would run again in 1972. At this particular time, he was running for the state's highest office — he wanted to be governor again in 1970. Having already held the office for one term, George C. Wallace was speaking at downtown Childersburg's busiest corner — 8th Ave & 1st St SW. At the time, all I knew was it was in front of the 10-Cent Store.

Dad, Janie and I went to see the spectacle that day — mom was working at the N. F. Nunnelley State Trade School, which Wallace had helped to dedicate in 1966. All traffic was closed and in the middle of the street was a red, white and blue fabric-draped, tall platform with State Troopers all around. I remember well seeing Governor Wallace that day in person for the first time. He was still standing and was a vibrant statesman — and yes, I was a Wallace fan. As an added bonus, and to bring in a larger crowd, country music star, Jeannie C. Riley was scheduled to sing. She had risen to fame in 1968 with her hit, "Harper Valley PTA." That day, she changed the words and sang it as, "Childersburg PTA." Some wondered what she knew that we didn't! Of course, Wallace won the election for which he was campaigning. After his near-fatal assassination attempt in 1972 while running for President, he again was Alabama's governor for a third and fourth time. When he was in his last term of governor, I met with him as a part of Auburn's Engineering Student Council and told him about seeing him on that summer day many years earlier. His slow, drawn-out response was, "Oh, yes, Childersburg."

A Prank Reversed

Roscoe Limbaugh, *CHS Class of 1953*

In the nineteen seventies when our daughter Allison was in high school, she was hired to work after school for J&J Drugs. It was located next door to Limbaugh's House of Furniture. On her first day of work, Wallace Shoemaker and Royce Warren, both pharmacists, decided to play a trick on her. This was their practice for every new employee. They sent her to Limbaugh Hardware to purchase a "sawdust pump."

As Allison started down the street, she became very suspicious that she was being set up for embarrassment and would look foolish. She came back to the furniture store and asked me how she might turn the trick on Wallace and Royce. I told her to go to the hardware store, and explain the situation to her uncle, Robert Limbaugh, and ask him to send a large bill for the sawdust pump to J& J Drug. She was pleased to get to do this and to tell Wallace and Royce the pump would be delivered that afternoon. The trick was indeed turned around. Of course there was no pump to be delivered. Fun and games between Childersburg businesses continued for years to come.

The Central of Georgia and Southern Rail Roads

Charles "Turkey" Burke, *CHS Class of 1962*

We were happy growing up as children seeing both the Central of Georgia and Southern railroads pass through Childersburg. Many of you remember hearing the distinct train whistles and the arrival of this mass of steel. As children we were excited, when the ground shook under our feet. "Get out of the way — Big Boy is back again." Walking the rails to school, putting a penny on the rail and visiting the train stations are some of my most vivid memories.

The stations were a great place to "hang out" to see freight unloaded and the arrival of "nicely dressed" travelers. My mind's ear again hears the sound of the "colored" crew of men as they sang a song to help their day go by a bit faster, while driving spikes into the hard creosote railroad ties.

Occasionally, my family would board the Central of Georgia for a trip to Birmingham, Alabama. What a thrill for a child, to go through the two tunnels, buy candy from the uniformed attendant and arrive at the Grand Station in Birmingham! Once my mother talked the conductor into stopping the train and letting our family off in the residential area where my relatives lived.

The Milk Machine

Mike Headley, *CHS Class of 1962*

In the early fall of 1953 I was in the fourth grade at Childersburg Grammar School. In those days it was a "grammar school" not an "elementary school." Soon after we started school that year a wonderful thing happened.

Dairies in those days were changing from glass bottles to square shaped paper cartons with a wax coating. One day we received a new cooler in the hall near the principal's office in the old grammar school building. I do not remember the name of the dairy on the side of the box but the chest opened from a chrome top door with a chrome handle. The box colors were blue and white with red letters.

Once the top was raised you could see the milk cartons inside. All lined up in neat rows were half pint cartons of milk. In the early days it was stocked half white and half chocolate milk, as I remember, the ratio quickly changed in a few weeks to only one row of white milk and five rows of chocolate milk. A half pint of milk cost five cents. America in those days was making strides in the area of automation.

The carton of milk could be retrieved by placing your nickel in the coin slot then moving the carton to the left front of the machine through the slots where upon you would pull-up on the milk carton and ... Voila! You had your milk. My choice was always chocolate.

After a few weeks someone figured out how to get milk without paying for it. The offender would simply raise the lid on the cooler lean in while no one was around. Then take a #2 pencil plus a straw from the lunch room, and punch a hole in the milk carton with the pencil and place the lunchroom straw in the hole. Three or four good draws on that lunch room straw and a carton of milk would be emptied quickly.

The principal told us in no uncertain terms whoever was the milk bandit had better stop NOW. To my knowledge no one was ever caught. And no one told their parents.

A Fish Bone

Sandra Headley Limbaugh, *SHS Class of 1957*

An incident I find amazing involves my wonderful friend Martha Golden Sherbert. I believe we were about in the fourth grade when this occurred. In those days the lunchroom served fish every Friday. Oh, how times have changed! The food prepared in the lunchroom by the lunchroom ladies was real food prepared from "scratch," good and nutritious. On this particular Friday, the fish was not boned as meticulously as it could have been.

As we were eating our fish, Martha swallowed a bone, and as luck would have it, it lodged in her throat. The only thing to do was to send Martha to town to Dr. Moody to get the bone out. Now it would not have been prudent to send a nine year old to town (about a mile) alone. So it was my very good fortune to be given the job of accompanying her to Dr. Moody's office.

It was a very pleasant day, and since Martha was not hurting, we were in no great hurry. We enjoyed our walk. When we arrived at the doctor's office, he ushered us in, put Martha on the table, and began the medical procedure of removing the bone. Dr. Moody took a piece of gauze, placed it on the top and bottom of Martha's tongue, and proceeded to pull her tongue out as far as he could. He then had me hold the tongue out of her mouth while he took tweezers and extracted the bone.

This was my only experience of assisting a doctor in his work. Martha became a nurse. I didn't. After the procedure was over, Martha and I returned to school as leisurely as we could. It was a brief respite from our lessons. No legal permission form was signed - just as a need arose, common sense prevailed. I know the world is not as safe for children today, and I feel a great nostalgia for a nicer, safer world for all children.

A Pet Monkey

Betty Jenkins Breedlove, *CHS Class of 1962*

The Finns lived in a house just down the street from the Coosa theater. They had a pet monkey. We would beg mother to take us by to see the monkey every time we started to go somewhere in our car. One particular day we stopped by to see the monkey and Mrs. Finn brought it out to the car, the monkey snatched mother's glasses off and broke them.

Egg Salad Sandwiches

Mike Headley, *CHS Class of 1962*

My cousin, Mary Joe Russell Guy, who was seven at the time, told me if you eat egg salad sandwiches in the hot Alabama summertime," THEY WILL KILL YOU!" Being only five, I believed her.

The only problem I had with what Mary told me was I liked egg salad sandwiches ... a lot ... and still do. So why in this world would my mother and all my aunts want to kill the entire Headley, Dudney and Russell families? After all we were having a lovely family picnic at Kowliga. Since that day I have had a hard time trusting what women tell me, especially seven year old ones.

Fireworks Sales

David Swanger, *CHS Class of 1972*

I remember two curb markets, "That Curb Market" and the "Riverview Curb Market." In 1965 Riverview Curb Market would sell fireworks to anyone if they had money. I bought M80s and Cherry Bombs when I was in the 5th grade. Though I still have all of my fingers, that seems pretty crazy now.

Gravity Hill
N 33° 12.231 W 086° 18.498

Mike Headley, *CHS Class of 1962*

Have you ever wanted to roll up a hill in your car? Well, you can. It's true. Gravity Hill is located between Mile Marker 38 and 39 on US Hwy 280/231 seven miles south of Childersburg 35044 and four miles north of Sylacauga, Alabama 35151.

The road has a green and white road sign clearly marked "Gravity Hill Rd." I can personally attest to this phenomenon. It is not a fake. I am sure you will enjoy the experience. I did this many times as a teenager. Go have some fun.

Walking Home from Church

Carolyn Green Price, *CCHS Class of 1965*

We always walked to church and would come home after dark down the road by the Maddox house. We were never scared until one night a bunch of goats got on some cars in a junk yard (near the prison). Sometimes they would even get into the trees! We thought something was going to get us and we ran like scared rabbits and did not stop until we got inside the Maddox' front door.

Leg Hair

J.D. Warren, *CHS Class of 1961*

One of my earliest memories of my 7th grade English class (1956); Robert Burdick, Edward Brown and I sat in the back of the room. From time to time we would pull up our pants legs to see who had the most hair on our legs. Ed Brown was always the champion. Ed and Robert matured early (physically) and I think both were on the JV Football team in the 7th grade, which was not common.

Raise your hand

Mike Headley, *CHS Class of 1962*

Raise your hand if you ever drank a Buffalo Rock Ginger Ale and had that sucker backfire out your nose. Man, did that ever burn! Buffalo Rock is still bottled and canned in Birmingham, Alabama.

Chapter 2

Cherry Bombs and Old Spice
A 1961 Saturday Night Adventure

Mike Headley, *CHS Class of 1962*

This peculiar Saturday evening started normally. It was the fall of 1961 early November. There was a chill in the air, Halloween had passed and I was out in dad's 1955 white Coup de Ville Cadillac with an aqua blue embroidered cloth and leather interior.

One accessory that most cars of the day did not come equipped with was electric windows; a feature that you will come to understand became a problem later that evening. That Caddy had a rear speaker and a pull down leather arm rest in the back seat which made for a most comfortable ride for the back seat occupant.

Powered by a 331 cubic V8 engine with a Carter 650 cfm double pumper carburetor, dual exhaust, and a 250 horse power engine. Cadillac's of the 1950s tended to be on the heavy side. Lots of metal and chrome, however in spite of the weight, this was one fast car.

That night, as I made my second loop from the Dairy Queen® to Tastyee-Freez and back to the Dairy Queen®, I spotted my best-friend-since-third-grade, Ray Williams. Ray was sitting in his Dad's 1954 blue and white Ford. After pulling alongside, we talked and decided that I had more gas than Ray so we did what any young men with limited funds would do ... we drove the car with the most gas.

Off Ray and I go as the song says "looking for adventure." Where to go, where to go? Of course we would do the Dairy Queen® Tastyee- Freez loop again, or we could take a trip over to Sylacauga to the White Midget. On our second loop we met David Lovingood sitting in a car all alone at the Tastyee - Freez. The Tastyee - Freeze was a good place, just not as cool as the Dairy Queen®. Ray and I invited David to join us. We observed as David arrived he was carrying a brown paper bag the contents of which were a mystery. So far so good, right?

I'm driving, Ray is riding shot gun, and David is holding down the backseat. It was a good thing we were in the Caddy because both of these guys were well over six feet tall and I five foot eleven. It was not long until David divulged the contents of the bag ... Cherry Bombs. They were called Cherry Bombs because they were round and red with a green fuse which stuck out about 1 ¼".

Dad's fast Cadillac, Ray with his trusty Zippo lighter and a full pack of Winston's, and David with a sack of Cherry Bombs: *voila!* What could go wrong? If a forensic pathologist had been available to look at those three teenage brains, I am convinced he would have had a difficult time finding four functioning brain cells among the entire trio.

It did not take long until us as a group determined that the logical thing to do was light off some Cherry Bombs. This made perfect sense to us. Now being the upstanding citizens of the community we considered ourselves, to ignite such a powerful explosion in the city limits seemed well ... *criminal.* So we drove out of the city limits, down the Childersburg/Fayetteville Highway ... again ... "looking for adventure."

I am sure of one fact: we exploded no Cherry Bombs in the city limits of Childersburg. Now Talladega County was quite a different matter. Lighting a Cherry Bomb and throwing them out the window, then listening for the ensuing explosion, did not take long to become boring to our teenage ears. The need to achieve a higher level of excitement was just what the doctor ordered for our teenage fun meters. I am not sure who suggested mail boxes but, looking back, I am sure it was not me, OK?

As I remember there was no objection from the group. As a matter a fact, it seemed at the time a perfectly reasonable thing to do on a November Saturday evening. Yea, destroy some poor family's mail box, that'll work. The only problem with the destruction of mail boxes is that it is a FEDERAL OFFENSE. I assure you that at no time did any of this group ever consider that we might be committing a federal crime. After what we shall call a period of experimentation (two or three explosions) it was determined that to get the maximum bang for the buck, Ray was going to have to close the mail box door to get more than a really loud sound plus a great deal of fire coming from the Rural Federal Delivery (RFD) mail box.

With the mail box door open in the dark the whole thing looked like a cannon firing. If you closed the door of a mail box, the ensuing explosion made the box resemble more the shape of a basketball. The really cool ones blew clean off the post. After several mail boxes were blown we would return to the scene of the crime by driving back down the dirt road to inspect our work.

Not having studied the actual passage of time from lighting the fuse until the explosion takes place we were relying on the dexterity of eighteen-year-old Lowell Ray Williams to deliver the cherry bombs in a timely manner.

A quick study of Google now tells me that the actual time from lighting a Cherry Bomb fuse to explosion is between 3½ to 4 seconds. Thank goodness the US Congress decided the manufacture and distribution of Cherry Bombs and their big brother the M-80s, should be severely limited by federal law in 1966.

Having had a mail box across from our house on Highway US 280, I was quite knowledgeable about the actual construction of a" Rural Federal Delivery "mail box. The trick is, if you want the door to latch you must make sure that the door is completely closed. At this point you have a water resistance metal container which will protect your mail.

As I remember, there was a great many things taking place simultaneously in the old Coup de Ville that evening. I was driving, making sure we were a safe distance from the scene of the crime when the actual explosion took place. David was making sure Ray was well supplied with Cherry Bombs and Ray was operating the Zippo lighter, placing the bombs in the mail box, closing the door and then advising the driver (me) that it was time to get the hell out of Dodge. Throughout all of this the radio was playing far too loud. I don't remember if it was Chuck Berry's *Maybelline* or Little Richard's *Good Golly Miss Molly* but we were having lots of fun.

With Ray riding shotgun and me driving, I suppose David was getting somewhat bored all alone in the back seat. So, David started running the back windows up and down ... down and up. This was not unusual since the electric windows in cars were somewhat of a novelty in Childersburg in 1961.

With this distraction going on, I "politely" ask David to STOP! Right ... like that was going to happen. During all this mayhcm and bccausc it was Novcmbcr the wcathcr was a bit too cool to leave the windows down as we motored from mail to mail box.

I am not sure what possessed David to reach through between Ray's passenger's seat and the front door in order to run Ray's passenger window up! Ray not realized the window was closed, mainly because he was busy lighting a Cherry Bomb. Ray let that Cherry Bomb fly which promptly hit that GM "Body by Fisher" safety light tented window with a "PLINK!" My one brain cell which suddenly began working immediately recognized we were in deep kimchi.

The sound the Cherry Bomb made as it bounced off the window landing in Ray's crotch will be with me as I take my last breath.

OK, at this point my life began to pass before my eyes. I am a dead man, just bury me now. When daddy sees that hole in the seat of his Coup de Ville ... well just use your imagination. Ray, being my best friend, and seeing he was in serious jeopardy of never fathering any children, did the only manly thing he could do; so he flipped that lit Cherry Bomb from his crotch landing under the front seat of daddy's Cadillac, which promptly started burning a hole in the carpet.

As I watched this entire affair (through slow motion) Ray headed for the back seat to join David ... leaving me all alone in the front. I can attest to the fact that Lowell Ray Williams had two sons which means the explosion did not take place in his privates.

Realizing that I was alone in the front seat, I did the only thing left to do: I closed my eyes while rapidly speeding down that Talladega County dirt road. I turned my head to the left and hung on. The language that was used during those three seconds could not be repeated in any church I am aware of. My only thought was, get the four windows down ASAP! As four of my five fingers reached the driver's door window buttons that Cherry Bomb went off.

I don't think any of us could hear much of anything for at least the next 12 hours except ringing. As you might have figured, the fun of blowing mail boxes suddenly had lost its glow. I took Ray and David back to their cars at the Tastyee-Freez around two in the morning then headed home with all the windows down hoping the smell from the explosion would somehow leave dad's Cadillac.

After arriving home, I went in to the house and got a bottle of Old Spice from my room. I then began to sprinkle Old Spice throughout Dad's Cadillac. I left the window in that Coup de

Ville down the rest of the night. Thankfully, it didn't rain because those were the first words out of Daddy's mouth when he saw the windows that Sunday morning.

When Mother, Daddy and I climbed in the Cadillac for our regular Sunday morning fifteen minute ride to the Childersburg Church of Christ (old building down town) Daddy's only comment was "a little heavy with the Old Spice this morning?" "Thank you Lord!" I guess it was a good thing I attended church on a regular basis after all.

David Lovingood and Ray Williams are no longer with us. Rest well old friends, it was a fun night.

Chapter 3

A Childersburg Girl
The Grace McSween Story

Grace McSween 1914-1998

Sherry Machen Atkinson, *CHS Class of 1962*
Jan Machen Minor, *CHS Class of 1967*

Grace Elizabeth Edwards McSween was born October 24, 1914. She was adopted by W. O. and Era Edwards. Grace and her sister, Dot, had a wonderful childhood being raised in Childersburg. Their mother doted on them.

Grace graduated from Childersburg High School and headed to Alabama College, later known as Montevallo University. Grace worked in the dining hall at the college to have spending money. While in college her roommate was Jimmie Wills (Mrs. Henry Moody). Jimmie was the first band director at Childersburg High. They remained lifelong friends until Grace's death. Upon graduation, Grace headed into her teaching career of 34 years. Her first assignment was in a one room school building in Bon Air, Alabama. The room was heated by a potbellied stove. Grace took her four year old niece Carolyn to school with her each day.

Grace met her husband at a candy store in Childersburg. Grace and Mac were married and had one son, William Finley McSween. Mac, Billy's father, was killed in action in Italy during WWII in 1945. Billy was 18 months old when his dad was killed. Grace never remarried.

Grace taught school at Bon Air, Alabama, Childersburg Elementary, Childersburg Middle and Childersburg High Schools.

Grace told us many stories about her career. One that I will never forget was the day Mr. Watwood called Grace to his office and told her a father had sent a letter complaining that Grace had paddled his son and broke his arm during the paddling. Grace was beside herself and told Mr. Watwood they would visit the man after school. When they arrived the man was plowing his garden. The father met with Principal Watwood and Grace. Grace told the man she had never paddled his son. The father called his son outside to face Grace and Mr. Watwood. The boy started to cry and said he had gotten in a fight and the other boy had broken his arm.

His dad gave him a blistering! She told us many stories about her teaching days. Polly Holliday was a favorite of hers. Polly said Grace and Mr. Watwood were key factors in her success in her career. Polly visited with Grace every time she came to Childersburg. They would sit on the porch at Grace's home and talk for hours.

Grace was not only a teacher, she was a community leader. She was a member of the Eastern Stars and a longtime member of the First Baptist Church. Grace was a self-taught piano player, and was an excellent writer. She was a mentor to so many Childersburg students. Many came to her home for help with assignments. She stayed after school to help many struggling students.

When Grace was a fourth grade teacher the students brought nickels, dimes and pennies to class. When enough money was raised, she purchased a canary and cage for their class room. The bird was named "Tweety." Every week a different student was selected to take "Tweety" home for the weekend. She would laugh occasionally in her later years about the children carrying the bird home on the bus each Friday.

Grace was like another mother to her nieces. She bought Carolyn, Gayle, Sherry, and Jan clothes, Christmas gifts and carried them to church. She was affectionately known as "Tee" to her nieces who adored her. Grace passed away on July 2, 1998 at the age of 83. She is buried in the old Childersburg Cemetery.

A Childersburg Hero — Patrick Danforth Miller, Specialist E-5 US Army Corps of Engineers

Billy (Mike) Miller, *CHS Class of 1967*
Brain Miller, *CHS Class of 1969*

William (Billy) Miller moved his family to Childersburg in 1963 from Talladega, Alabama raising his four sons and one step-daughter in the big pink house near the old post office in downtown Childersburg. Bill, Sr. worked at the AOW (Powder Plant) as a Fireman until its closure in the 1970s. Patrick Miller, Specialist E-5 US Army Corps of Engineers, served his country in the Vietnam War — completing three tours. Pat did not graduate from CHS but completed part of his 10th grade year in 1966.

Pat joined the US Army going to Vietnam for his first tour of duty in late 1967 returning to the war again in 1969, and a final tour in 1971. Pats' specialty was that of a heavy equipment operator: cranes, bulldozers, road scrapers, and dump trucks. Pat spent his tours in Vietnam re-building bridges that were being destroyed by the Viet Cong, grading roads, and driving dump trucks. Patrick Miller was discharged from military service in 1974.

Pat never talked openly about the particular incident which is the basis for this story. You need to understand Pat was not, how shall I say, a particularly well-behaved student? A situation Grace McSween understood all too well. Pat was what would be considered a disruptive student, always playing pranks and giving the teachers a hard time, especially Mrs. McSween.

One day Grace was out of the class room for a moment. As she returned she saw Pat standing in the middle of the room, ready to throw a paper airplane out the window. Grace said, "Just throw it, I dare you!" So, not one to pass on a dare, Pat let that airplane fly. For his efforts Pat got a trip to see Principal Williams.

One morning, Pat walked into Grace's classroom; she looked up at him, and said, "Pat, just go on to the office, I don't feel like dealing with you today." So, with a shrug of the shoulders, off Pat goes to the office. Mr. Williams ask him "Pat why are you here? Pat just said "Mrs. McSween." So Mr. Williams "sighed" and told him "just sit there until time for your next class."

Pat returned one more time during the 1970 school year walking into Grace's class room unannounced. Upon his arrival Pat presented Grace with a Vietnamese style Kimono and other gifts from Vietnam. Pat told the students about Vietnam, what they grew and exported what they ate, and how they lived. The last thing Pat told the students was to not give Mrs. McSween a hard time, because he had given her enough trouble to last her a lifetime and he was sorry for way he had acted. Pat told the students he wished he had listened to Grace; he wouldn't have had to go through all the things he had seen and all the bad things he experienced in war. Pat told the students to stay in school and study hard. By this time Grace was crying and fled the classroom in tears.

Pat drove semi-tractor trailer rigs over the road for his livelihood until retirement. Because the chemical Agent Orange had left Pat's body ravaged with lung cancer and skin lesions, this native son of Childersburg, and a genuine American hero was under hospice care living in Talladega, Alabama when this story was written.

Patrick Danforth Miller passed from this life August 27, 2015.

A Field Trip

J. D. Warren, *CHS Class of 1961*

In the very early 1950s Mrs. Grace McSween and her son, Bill, lived on SW 8th Avenue with her mother. Looking at the image on a live street view map I would say her house was about where there is a Frontier Bank building now. It was a large house and there were two larger houses, one on each side.

They had huge oak trees in the yards along the street but the houses and the trees are long gone. Sometime about 1951 my family opened a shoe store on the other side of 8th Avenue, fairly close to the McSween house. Sometimes my mother would work, which meant I was brought along.

As Bill and I are the same age, it was fun for me to be allowed to go across the street to play with him. We must have played "cowboys" and the other boy things, but what I most remember is jumping contests. This was simply taking a running start and making a long jump. I think we used a cane fishing pole to make our measurements.

A little later, in the 1952-53 school years, Mrs. McSween was my 4th Grade teacher. I remember on the morning after the election for president before class started, I stood on a chair in the front of the classroom and announced that Dwight David Eisenhower was elected President of the United States! As I recall, everyone ignored me.

But that election brought about one of my most amazing memories. The Eisenhower inauguration took place in January, 1953. On that morning Mrs. McSween lined up her class and we walked to her house to watch the event on television! Fortunately it was not a real cold day, but I don't recall that any permission slips went home or any volunteers came along to chaperon. The trip was only five blocks from school each way, and we went by way of 4th Avenue so there was not much traffic.

Once at the McSween house we all sat on the floor and watched the "swearing in" and his speech on her Sylvania black and white TV. Then we walked back to school on the same route. Every time I think of that day and compare it to all the things deemed necessary to protect children today, I am truly amazed. That was certainly a simpler time!

Grace Bought My Lunch Ticket

Ollie Pardue, *CHS Class of 1966*

When I first attended school in Childersburg in the seventh grade, in 1959, I was placed in Grace McSween's homeroom. I was dirt poor and scared and very shy. Being poor back then in my case meant having very few clothes and no money for the necessities of life. As I look back I know that God placed me in that class with that fine lady. What a kind lady she was!

Being poorer than most kids, I did not have lunch money. Mrs. McSween noticed that when everyone else was going to lunch I just stayed outside. I guess others noticed it too, but she came to me and talked to me about it. I explained to her that we did not have any money. She also realized that I was very shy and embarrassed, that I felt I could not fit in with the other kids. So she told me that she would get me a lunch ticket every week and I would go through the lunch room line just like everyone else and nobody would know that I was given a free lunch.

Looking back, I see the heart of a fine Christian lady doing God's work. She probably had the most impact on me, other than my own mother, than anyone else during that time of my life. I was truly blessed to have an angel like her to watch over me in such a great time of need. There are others in Childersburg that had a positive influence on me but she is at the top of the list. There has always been a special place in my heart for her and always will be. Although I never told her that I loved her, somehow I think she knew it. She took a shy, prideful, and scared little 7th grader and made him fit in with the crowd and that is so important at that age. I know that God is rewarding her for her good deeds she did here on earth. I am forever grateful.

Grace Elizabeth Edwards
Age 6

A Trip to Kiddieland (Birmingham)

Sherry Machen Atkinson, *CHS Class of 1962*

In 1958 my cousin Bill McSween asked his mother, Grace could some of us go to the Dairy Queen in her car. She agreed to let us go if we would not be gone too long. Bill's friend Don Robinson, his sister Nan and I headed to Birmingham to take a ride on the "Caterpillar" at Kiddieland.

Bill was 15, as was Don, Nan and I were 14, no one in the car was old enough to have a driver's license. We enjoyed our ride to Birmingham in Grace's new Plymouth Plaza and the ride at Kiddieland on the "Caterpillar was great also." It was a fast trip and a quick ride!

When we got back to grandmother's house they were very upset to say the least. "Where have you been? To the Dairy Queen® of course." I never told Aunt Grace until she was almost 80 years old what we had done. Grace said, "I can't believe you and Nan did that!" It was only after I had children that I realized what could have happened to her if we had wrecked her car and hurt someone.

Chapter 4

102 Childersburg Businesses

The Alabama Power Company
A and P Grocery
Beans Barber Shop
Budget Shoes
Bakers Texaco
Bunn's Texaco
Burkhalter's Barber Shop
C and H Store
Childersburg Star News
Cliett's Cotton Gin
Cliett's Dress shop
Cliett Hardware
Cohen's Department Store
Collins Store
Felix Crocker's Garage
Coosa Garment Company
Coosa Motor Company
Del-leans Beauty Shop
Dairy Queen
Daffron's Florists
Dean's Café
Do Do's Restaurant
Dunlap's Florist
Duvy's Men's Store
Dru's Beauty Shop
Economy Gas
Elliot's Fabric
V. J. Elmore's Five and Dime
Emory's Five and Dime
Fullers Grocery
Greens Upholstery
Griers Garage

Hagan's Pharmacy
Hall's TV
Hosey's Flower Shop
Hosey's Ice Plant
Jitney Jungle Grocery
J & J Drug
Joiner's Garage
KFC
Kwik-Check Grocery
Millard W. Lawrence Company
Limbaugh Hardware
Limbaugh House of Furniture
Live Oak's Shoe Shop
Lynn Motel
Mac Veazey's Garage
Marie Taylors Restaurant
Maddox Shoe
Malone's Barber Shop
Martin Furniture
Moody Bro. Grocery
Morgan Bridge Inn
Murphee's Boat Works
Osborne's Curb Market
Parker - Morris TV
Powell Drug
Parsons's Texaco
Preacher Sanders Used Cars
Pure Gas Station
Puttmans Cab Stand
Quality Printing
Red Hare's Pool Hall

River View Curb Market
Rumsey Lumber Company
Sheba's Dress Shop
Smith's Sundries
Storey's Jewelry
Taylor Cleaners
Tastee - Freez
The Southern Bell Café
The Bus Station
The Fair Store
That Curb Market
Dan O' Pattie's Restaurant
The Coosa Theater

Slick Thompson's Garage
Veazey's Gas Station
Veazey's Grocery
Wallace's store
Western Auto
Whaley and Robbins
   Furniture
Wilson Bros. Construction
Wilson Bros Standard Oil
   Gas Station
Winn-Dixie
Willis Curb Market

Closed on Wednesday Afternoon

Betty Jenkins Breedlove, *CHS Class of 1962*

I remember when all the stores and the bank closed at noon on Wednesdays.

Magical Downtown Childersburg

Candy Stephens, *CHS Class of 1972*

I loved going downtown on Saturdays. Mom would be shopping at Kwik-Chek and I would walk around town. I would say hello to Mr. Storey at the jewelry shop, then go to Live Oak's Shoe Shop smelling the leather and shoe polish — I still love that smell. Then to VJ Elmore's 5 and Dime to drive the ladies crazy picking up all the toys, or the little bluebottles of "Evening in Paris." Then I would cross the street to J & J Drug to get a Dr. Pepper that would have ice in it. Then on to Limbaugh's Hardware where I would play in the barrel of metal disks that were used in house roofing. Mr. Robert Limbaugh would always give me one and I would pretend they were silver coins. Across the street and say hello to Slick Thompson at his garage, then into the Western Auto to give Mr. Britches Miller a hug.

On to the First National Bank to speak to Mr. Cleckler, and Mr. Whitaker who would always give me a sucker from the bottom drawer of his desk and a hug. I might go to A & P and speak to Mr. Hussey and back to Lawrence's to say hi to Mrs. Lawrence. Then down to the Texaco to see Mr. Parsons he would always give me a box of candy cigarettes. Then I might go across the street to see Mr. Poole at the Coosa Motor Company, he gave me key chains; I wish I still had those. Down to Sheba's Ladies Dress Shop and speak to Mrs. Spivey and Mrs. Busby.

I would end my wonderful Saturday odyssey at Smith Sundries getting lemonade for a dime and looking at all of the Barbie stuff. That is where Mom would pick me up when she had finished grocery shopping. Saturday's were magical in Childersburg as a child.

Competing Five-&-Dime Stores

Earl Wesson Jr., *CHS Class of 1972*

Emory's 5 & Dime and VJ Elmore's 5 & Dime competed with each another on opposite sides of 1st street. Elmore's preceded J&J Drug in their building. I remember the old wood planking in the VJ Elmore store where it made that distinctive clomping sound when you walked on the wooden floors.

Dianne Hillman Prisoc, *CHS Class of 1972*

Both stores had the ceiling fans and the doors open in the summer.

I remember going into the Emery 5 & Dime and buy the wax teeth and wax bottles with the juice in them and stand out on the corner to watch the homecoming parade. I loved the parades back then, they were a big thing!

The Morgan Bridge Inn 1938
Bloyst E. "Rudy" Burke Owner

Charles "Turkey" Burke, *CHS Class of 1962*

Hitler's panzer divisions invade Poland as World War II was only a faint headline in Childersburg, an emerging farming community coping with the Great Depressions aftermath. Bloyst E. "Rudy" Burke from Sycamore, Alabama had a few dollars in his pocket after selling the "What-Not Inn" East of Childersburg. He talked Gus Frangopoulos who owned the old hotel that turned into the bus station on the top of the hill in Childersburg into selling the fish camp and "vagrant hangout" on the south bank of the Coosa River. The purchase was completed for $2,400 down and $2,400 later.

Rudy met Onzell Thrash, a good looking country girl from Jemison, Alabama who was working at the Avondale Mill in Sylacauga, Alabama. Onzell had worked at the mill since 1932. Rudy and Onzell married in 1940 and transformed the old camp into Morgan Bridge Inn, Café and Gas Station. They lived in a storage building while our house was being built immediately across highway 280/231's east side. The Morgan Bridge Inn was completed as Walter Chancellor's Ferry business, which transported cars and people across the Coosa River, was ending. Rudy and Onzell were a perfect team to make the business a success and as Rudy would say, "Feed'n the Public."

The road in those days was called "The Florida Short Route." For the weary highway traveler and locals, Morgan Bridge

Inn, was a "one-stop-shop" service establishment. The weary traveler could get a tank full of gas, a good meal and spend the night in one of the seven cabins on the hill. The Shell Gas Island was under a canopy that covered the café entrance. Walk into a large open dining area complete with tables, booths, counter, stools and "Juke Box" (a Jewel), playing your favorite six tunes for a quarter. Rudy's favorite was, "Drink-up and Go Home" proceeded by "Your Cheating Heart" and "Ain't That a Shame."

The white-clad-uniformed waitress was busy taking orders and "bussing tables." Open seating, with many selecting the booths, each with a remote juke box tune selector station. The music backdrop was blended with the clatter of heavy café ware and constant chatter from our patrons. The kitchen door swings open and the skilled waitress emerges. Each arm is balancing a load with hot dinner plates. Catfish, steaks, chops, BBQ, hamburgers and regular dinners were delivered.

The neon signs out front were working and the cash register, operated by Daddy, was ringing. All which produced a unique clatter of sounds, while over head the fan blades whisk away the cacophony.

A cement pool was constructed next to the café to hold live catfish that could be selected by the customers for their meal. They were netted, cleaned, cornmeal breaded and deep fried, usually whole. This was an efficient supply chain. The Coosa was plentiful with river cats and the White family who lived down the road was skilled net makers and commercial fisherman. However, as the Coosa River Newsprint begins operations; the effluent discharges contaminated the river's water and produced fish that were not edible. The word "Coosa River" became a term that people used in the pejorative. It was understood if fish came from the Coosa River they could not be eaten, especially catfish no matter the source on the river or its tributaries. The White family continued to be our supplier with fish from the Tennessee River.

As the business increased we were serving over 1000 pounds of catfish every week. The pool that stored live fish was replaced with large ice boxes. The fish were never frozen and the inventory cycle was seven days. It took me several years to redevelop a taste for catfish after a constant exposure to the cleaning and cooking of so many catfish during my childhood. Daddy ordered and stocked rainbow trout for me ... "the spoiled child."

The business went through several transitions from a "Café" to a "Restaurant", and then an "Inn." Rudy realized that serving good food was just part of the business' life. Public perception is important if you are to be successful in marketing your business. The gas service was replaced with an enhanced restaurant entrance and new signs "Hot Coffee" and "Cool Inside." We had air-conditioning in the '50s. We raised hogs from the food scraps and added chickens and pheasants to supplement the menu. Even our family dog "Skipper" was included. He received scraps, usually steak for supper.

The kitchen crew was all black and needed a minimum of supervision to prep and cook the food. Henry Brewster (BBQ and Catfish Cleaner), Mary (Chef) and John Henry (Dish Washer and Slaw Chopper) were responsible for most of the food preparation. John Henry always wore a fashioned paper sack on his head. Deep fat fryers, grill, steam table and the BBQ pit were arranged to provide rapid food production. Patrons could view the fresh meats from a glass-front cooler. The restaurant could serve several hundred folks in one "sitting."

We had several dining rooms that had private entrances. Local families and groups could bring in beer and liquor without being seen. This included the "Church Ladies and Deacons." My sister, Dot, was a waitress. I had the potato-eye-removal detail.

Onzel opened the doors at 6 AM and Rudy closed at 12 midnight week days and 2 AM on weekends. We were open 7 days a week and only closed Christmas. I was part of the maintenance crew; painting, grass cutting, plumbing, and cleaning out the sewers. A strong work ethic was an important part of our family.

Dad and mom added the Burke Motel in 1956 and Rudy leased the restaurant to Buck and Dora Jenkins. The restaurant burned in 1962 and the motel, our home and adjoining property was sold. Rudy and Ouzel built a house and moved to the farm. They both died at 60 years old in 1973 and rest on the cemetery land they once owned.

Willis Curb Market
Mr. and Mrs. Willis owners

Betty Jenkins Breelove, *CHS Class of 1962*

My older brother was in the Air Force and on one of his visits home he brought a horny toad with him. He put the toad in a kitchen matchbox. My younger brother, Johnny, and I set up a table and charged admission to see the horny toad. We charged a penny to see the toad and kids were lined up. We took our money to Willis Curb Market to buy penny candy. The Willis's had the best penny candy selection in Childersburg. Mother shut down our little side show when she discovered what we were doing.

Mike Headley, *CHS Class of 1962*

I have three reasons for including Willis's Curb Market.

1. I have heard others speak of being downtown and going into Willis Curb Market for penny candy.
2. The sawdust on the floor. I know of no other business in Childersburg which had a sawdust floor.

3. The incredible smells of the wonderful fruits and vegetables as you walked through the door. These are still with me 60-plus years later.

The Willis's were our neighbors on Highway 280 four miles south of Childersburg. Their son, Wayne, became a music teacher.

Jitney Jungle Grocery

Sherry Machen Atknision, *CHS Class of 1962*

One week before the new Jitney Jungle grocery opened in the 1950s someone placed dynamite around back of the store and blew a hole in the back wall.

Mike Headley, *CHS Class of 1962*

My earliest recollection of a grocery store was the Jitney Jungle on 1st Street in Childersburg. One day Holsum Bread was giving away tiny loaves of bread at the Jitney Jungle. I can't recall seeing that brand of bread in years now, however it's still around. I must have eaten three or four loaves. Well, they WERE really small. The bread came wrapped in an orange-brown wrapper just like the big loaves.

In those days the Jitney Jungle had a real meat market. The meat market was managed by Frank Nichols; CHS Class of 62's father, Mr. Nichols was the butcher.

The Western Auto Store
Lamar "Britches" Miller, owner

Earl Wesson Jr., *CHS Class of 1972*

Randall Senn told this story to me several times over the years when I was at his home servicing his air conditioning unit. In the early days of his working as manager of the Kwik Check and later Winn-Dixie stores was the time frame of Randall's story. This story gives readers a look into life in the small town of Childersburg many years ago. The local paper mill (Coosa River Newsprint) which was the largest employer in the area paid their employees on Wednesdays. In those days the banks and many businesses closed on Wednesday afternoons.

```
Best Wishes

From

WESTERN AUTO

Phone DR 8-5051

Childersburg, Alabama
```

Randall would gladly cash checks because he knew some of that money would be spent in his store for groceries. However, on this Wednesday Randall got caught without enough cash on hand and knew that many of the paper mill workers would be coming in to get their checks cashed since the banks were closed.

Randall lit out for the Western Auto in search for Lamar (Britches) Miller, the owner. If you knew Mr. Miller, you knew why he was called Britches. He was a big old boy and he wore suspenders to hold those big britches up. Randall explained his cash shortage problem to Mr. Miller. Britches turns and shouts back towards the office to his wife; Jessie

Mae, "Jessie Mae how much cash you got in the safe?" "$5,000," was her reply. Britches told her to get it for Randall. Randall left the store without signing a note of any kind, leaving only his word that he would return the following day when the bank opened.

Randall was able to secure another $5,000 from another business with the same terms and armed with $10,000 in cash, he made the Wednesday rush on the grocery store. Much like the story line in It's a Wonderful Life when the banks failed during the depression.

I've been in business 30 years but I can't walk into a bank in this day and time and walk out with $5,000 without signing over $20,000 in collateral. I miss those days of old when a man's word was his bond and everyone pitched in to help one another.

A $52.00 Western Flyer

Robbie Riddle, CHS Class of 1975

I bought my last bicycle from Western Auto when I was 14 in 1970. It was a Western Flyer. I saved my money from cutting grass and paid $52.00 for that ride. My bike was blue with a banana seat and butterfly handlebars.

The Best Store in Childersburg

Joey Ratliff, *CHS Class of 1972*

Do you remember the store that had everything? It was the Western Auto, owned by a man named Britches Miller. It was the best.

Coosa Motor Company
L.V. Poole, owner

Ron Poole, *THS Class of 1968 (Son)*

L.V. Poole, born in 1929, took over the Coosa Motor Company Ford dealership in 1958 from a previous owner. He operated the business for nine years until a down turn required the closure of the dealership in April of 1967.

By that time my Dad had been in the car business in Ashland and Sylacauga. Both were Chrysler, Plymouth, and Dodge dealerships. I have not met anyone in my professional life that had a passion for cars as my Dad. He was always in the car business, he loved it, and he loved people.

Dad would talk to someone for hours, chewing on a Tampa Nugget cigar, which most of the time he bought at Parsons' Texaco gas station just up the street. The dealership was located in what are now the Childersburg Police and Fire departments.

Most of the adults I knew in Childersburg were directly related to Dad. I knew a lot of adults from the First Baptist Church, but most friendships always circled back to the dealership. Lots of guys hung out there, chewing the fat, talking about what shift they were on at paper mill, or about sports or what was going on in town.

You don't forget the smell of places from your childhood. Each time I stepped in the showroom, it had a scent that said "new automobiles." Once air conditioning was installed, probably 1963, the scent was never the same.

Dad had sales guys that helped out, Charlie and Roy. They were always trying to get folks to buy a car. The shop was always a busy place but at my age, I'm not sure if I understood what busy really was.

Charlie was an elderly gentleman, living in Sylacauga, and always had a good story. He would sit with an unfiltered cigarette hanging from his mouth and tell yarns beyond belief, which mostly I didn't, believe. However, the stories were entertaining.

One day Mr. Charlie thought it would be a good time for me to move a car from the lot to the showroom. Dad was not there, so I could not ask him if it was OK, so I did what Mr. Charlie wanted. The door to move the car into the showroom was not much wider than the car. I was 14, having moved cars on the lot for a year or so, I was sure I had the needed skills to make this work. The doors opened and I began maneuvering that Galaxy 500 onto the showroom floor. Mr. Charlie was behind the car, motioning the way to go, I was going slowly. I pulled it off, Mr. Charlie, thought I did a great job. When Dad returned he didn't think it was so wonderful, never said anything to me but I understand he gave Mr. Charlie an earful. I never moved another car to the showroom.

Once you went through the door to the garage, you knew you had entered an area where men worked hard for a living. The oil, grease, car exhaust, hit you all at once. I saw Joe, Jerry, Scott, Preacher, all those guys sweating with grease up to their elbows.

Ed or Bill ran the parts department and made sure the cars were being worked on as promised. The mechanics would talk while they worked; I hung on every word they said. Scott had been with my Dad since the Ashland days and I felt like he would do anything in the world for me. I worked during the summers and most holidays so I got to know these mechanics well. I knew their children, wives, and what they did during vacation, holidays, and Christmas.

I began my career in the automobile business in the summer of '64. My job was to change the oil, oil filter and grease the cars that came in for service. I ruined a lot of t-shirts in that position, because I could never change the oil in a car without getting it all over me. About 3 times a week I would have to wash the cars, just the new ones. I was earning $10 per week when I started and after four years, still earning $10 per week, decided then and there the car business was not going to be my career.

When the new cars would arrive in August the only place Dad had to store them was in our backyard. Our first home on Quail Wood Drive had a large backyard; our second home on Melba Avenue wasn't as large. As soon as the cars were in our back yard men would start to arrive to look them over. They never knocked on the door or ask if it was okay, they would come all hours of the day. For those three to four weeks our home was very popular. I always enjoyed that time.

The new cars always arrived in Dad's showroom in September and it was always a big event. There would be banners up in the showroom, signs on the showroom windows, a lot of people would pass through the dealership checking out the new models.

Marie Taylor's Restaurant
Marie Taylor, owner

Out-running the Baptists to Sunday Lunch

Mike Headley, *CHS Class of 1962*

Food and I have been the best of friends for many years. In the late 1950s my family, on Sunday after church, would do our best to out-run the Baptists, Methodists and Presbyterians to Taylor's Restaurant.

Marie always ran a Sunday special. The menu (a mimeographed piece of white paper with an odd color and odor printed with a blue ink). Did I mention the smell? These menus changed weekly. The menu always had at least three entrées. You were served a meat and two vegetables, coffee or sweet tea and all the rolls you wanted for 75¢, "Deliver Me!" As I remember desert was not included but for 15¢ more you could have cobbler add a nickel and it arrived with vanilla ice cream on top. For a boy of 12 years I thought we were rich.

```
        Compliments of

     TAYLOR'S DRIVE-IN

        Highway 91

   Childersburg, Alabama
```

Mickey Donahoo, *CHS Class of 1961*

Taylor's Drive-in was a popular restaurant, just go inside, and order a burger and fries. Play your favorite selections on the juke box. Each booth would had its own box to allow you to make your selection just insert your coins. Songs were 5ᶜ each or 6 for a quarter. A quarter sounds cheap but back in those days the same quarter might get you in the movie, get a bag of popcorn and maybe have some change.

These were simple times but glorious ones for a teenager; especially one who had his own "wheels" and his favorite girl sitting close to him. Wow! What a time to be young.

Red Hare's Pool Hall
Red Hare, owner

A Card Game

Jimmy Owens, *CHS Class of 1967*

You're probably from Childersburg if you ever played a game of pool at Red's and saw some guys playing poker in the back of the room.

For Men Only

Glendean Fields Ogle, *CHS Class of 1961*

I cannot tell you anything about Red Hare's Pool Hall, except when we walked past we would try to innocently look through the windows because "ladies" did not dare go into a pool hall. In our days those were only for men. God forbid that we go into a pool hall or even consider playing the game.

A Twenty-Dollar Loss

James Morris, *CHS Class of 1967*

The city pool room or pool hall was truly a one of a kind place. I learned a tough lesson. The $20.00 I lost playing the game "Amos & Andy." That grieved me so that I never gambled for money again.

Unfair!

Candy Stephens, *CHS Class of 1972*

I would try to peek into the pool hall and Mr. Red would shoo me away; I always thought it was unfair that girls couldn't go in!

One-Arm Red

Joey Ratliff, *CHS Class of 1972*

One-arm Red Hare could shoot pool better with one hand (no bridge) than anyone else could with two hands. Red was a one-arm shooter, that's all he had. Avery racked for him.

Nine Ball and a Knife

Billy Hall, *CHS Class of 1962*

We were playing Nine Ball the afternoon before the CHS senior prom. There were three of us playing when this guy from out of town, told us he wanted to get in the game. We told him we had to leave at 6 pm to get ready for the prom that evening. He was probably twice as old as we were. We were playing for $5.00 a game which in those days was good money. We won about $75.00 and at 6 PM I went over and hung my stick.

When I turned around the guy was standing behind me. He wanted to know where I was going with his money. I said it's in my pocket now. He said we weren't leaving with his money, and pulled a knife. Won't say any names but someone hit his arm with a cue stick, and we all ran out the door. I don't think I ever shot pool for money at Red's again.

A Game of Poker

Robbie Riddle, *CHS Class of 1975*

Mother would shop for groceries for the next week at Moody Brothers grocery while Dad could be found playing poker in the back of Reds Pool Hall.

Skipping School to Play Pool

Tom Herndon, *ISHS Class of 1971*

I have so many good memories of growing up in Childersburg. One of the places is Reds Pool Hall, but the adventure began at Wallace's store west of Coosa Court near Childersburg High school. One school day in 1968 after the bus made its morning stop at the Wallace's store so the Childersburg High School senior driving the bus could grab a quick smoke. This gave us bus riders a little time to grab some junk food before going to class, instead of getting back on the bus my buddy Mike Busby and I hid in the back of the store.

After the bus headed for the school, Mike and I left Wallace's Store walking the 3/8 mile west toward downtown to Red Hare's Pool Hall. There we planned to spend the day shooting pool, and hanging out. Our plan was a simple one to be back at Wallace's store catching the bus for our afternoon trip home.

Things were going great, and we were having a good time at Reds. I don't remember exactly why but I left Reds to go across the street to Smith's Sundries. As I was about to cross the street I heard somebody call "MR. HERNDON!!" I turned and there was Coach Cox coming out of Millers Western Auto which was next door to Red Hare's Pool Hall.

Coach Cox only asks one question "Is Mr. Busby in there with you?" Knowing we were caught. I said "Yes, sir." Coach Cox and I walked back into Red's where Mike was leaning over one of the back tables ready to take a shot. Just as Mike was about to make his pool shot Coach Cox in a loud voice said "MR. BUSBY!! "Mike almost ruined the felt on that table with the tip of his cue.

Coach Cox took us back to the High School to the principal Kelly's office. Phone calls were made to our parents. Both our dads worked so it was our mothers who came to pick us up. On the way home mom didn't say too much except that she was a little upset with me for doing what I did. All she said was the worst words any guy could ever hear. Saying, "Just Wait Until Your Father Gets Home." Mike and I were suspended for a week, and I thought I was going to be grounded until I was 21! This was a very valuable lesson learned for both Mike, and me.

SMITH"S SUNDRIES
Emmett Earl and Sal Smith, Owners

```
Best Wishes

From

SMITH'S SUNDRIES

Childersburg, Alabama
```

Comic Books were a Dime

David Swanger, *CHS Class of 1972*

I used to buy comic books at Smith', when I had money.
Comic books cost a dime. I got mad when they went up to
12¢.

Smith's had model cars and airplanes that I wanted. You
glued them together. Some cost a dollar, which was a lot of
money for me at the time. I remember adults often hung out
at Smith's.

Mark's Birthday

Robbie Riddle, *CHS Class of 1975*

The Smiths were good friends of my family. They lived 2
blocks east of the store next door to Dr. Stock's office. The
Smiths were God-Parents to my next oldest brother, Mark.
Mark would get to pick out a comic book from Smith's on his
birthday. I can remember hanging out in Smith Sundries
reading comic books and looking at the model cars and
airplanes. My brother, Chris, helped the Smiths learn the
operation of the Icee machine in 1970.

Smith Sundries was the center of weekly family outings to downtown Childersburg. Smith's Sundries was just a 2-block walk from my grandmother's house. So the Smiths were in the middle of a lot of our family activities on Saturdays.

I especially enjoyed the doughnut floats. I remember the coke box which had cold water in the bottom. Cokes were 8-ounce glass pale green bottles and cost a nickel. Smiths had Buffalo Rock Ginger Ale, a drink which is still canned in Birmingham, Alabama.

In addition to the 7 or 8 counter stools there were 4 yellow booths you could sit in to eat your lunch. Mrs. Smith always made fresh doughnuts on Saturday mornings. Many fun memories were made at Smith's when I was a kid in Childersburg.

Lemon Sours Recipe from Smith's Sundries

Marilyn Alexander Primo, *CHS Class of 1963*

2 ounces lemon juice
20 ounces water
2 tsp salt
Ice
Mix ingredients together, adjust salt and lemon juice to taste. Add ice. Shake up or mix in a blender to make it slushy.

STOREY'S JEWELRY
Robert M Storey, owner

My Parents' Jewelry Store

Peter Storey, *CHS Class of 1975*

Robert M. Storey, Jr. and Mildred Storey purchased the jewelry store from Mr. Cockrell in 1951. My father was a Certified Jeweler and was working in a jewelry store in Columbus, Mississippi. Mr. Britches Miller, who owned the Western Auto store, called him to tell him the store was for sale. My dad was from Ensley, Alabama and mother from Bessemer, Alabama. My parents came to Childersburg and decided to buy the store.

Mother asked my Dad, "Do you think we will ever be able to sell enough watches to support ourselves and our children?" At that time it was only my parents plus Peggy and Robert (Bob). Daddy said "I don't know but we are going to try." The family moved to Childersburg and as they say "the rest is history." Mother and Daddy had 4 more children from 1951 until 1960.

Storey's Jewelry was located in four different buildings with the last location the one that Storey's was in the longest. I would say they were very successful raising 6 children. We all worked in the store at some time or another and especially during the Christmas season. Daddy also hired local teenagers and Mrs. Genie Jones worked for the store during the Christmas season every year.

My parents retired and sold the store in 1980. There has only been one Jewelry store since then and that store closed sometime in the 1990s. There is not a jewelry store in Childersburg today. There are many people around today that tell me they bought their first watch, bracelets and or wedding rings from Storey's Jewelry.

The one thing I saw my Dad do as a business man was to treat every customer with the best customer service he could give. There were many times he would do "little" things for people and never charge them. Childersburg was a "great"" little town to grow up in and to raise a family.

DoDo's Restaurant (Lynn Motel)
DoDo (Idoma) Abernathy, Owner

James Morris, *CHS Class of 1967*

DoDo was a joy to be around, even if you were not in her close circle of friends. Being a customer was enough to be counted as a friend, but that would not get you in the back

```
Compliments of

LYNN MOTEL

Highway 91

Childersburg, Alabama
```

room. The last two of her five children did their homework on the café tables.

DoDo Abernathy was a classic Italian woman in every way except for an accent. DoDo's Cafe was really the Lynn's Motel café located on Alabama Highway 91. I first started going to Dodo's in 1964 after I bought my first car at the ripe old age of 14. I never saw her take a drink but she could get very happy the later it got come Saturday night.

Coffee drinkers had their own table out front, and when you received your coffee the cup it would be filled and refilled until you burst or left. If you sat at DoDo's restaurant you were expected to try any new HOT dish DoDo offered you. You never repeated the word HOT!

From the 1960s to the 1980s DoDo's was the deer hunter's headquarters. Most hunters and some dog drive organizers would stop by for breakfast or to recruit hunters.

There was a time Friday and Saturday nights especially before the big race at Talladega Raceway when the county was dry and those who had had too much to drink came into DoDo's. Years later when the Talladega County was no longer dry Dodo's was the place to go to wind down (in the early hours of the morning after last call.)

Dodo's was home to the hard working people of Childersburg. Many loved DoDo and patronized her café which was open 24 hours a day seven days a week. I am very sad every time I go by and see Dodo's is closed.

DoDo had Five Daughters

Dianne Hillman Prisoc, *CHS Class of 1972*

DoDo had 5 daughters, Anna, Angela, Augusta (Gussie), Amelia (Amy), and Amber. The last two of her five children did their homework on the café tables

The Best Cheeseburgers

John M Giddens Jr, *CHS Class of 1980*

DoDo made the best cheeseburgers in Childersburg Mom and I still talk about them. Lynn's Restaurant was affectionately named "DoDo's."

Millard W. Lawrence Company
Millard Lawrence, Owner

Betty Lawrence Jones, *CHS Class of 1962*

Daddy grew up in Etowah County, Alabama, then graduating from Jacksonville State Teachers College. He obtained a teaching position at Clay County High School where he met mother who was one of his students. I was told that mother said she would not marry Millard Lawrence if he was the "last man on earth." Apparently she changed her mind because they were married May 6, 1939.

Daddy was drafted into the Army in January 1943. There he fought in the Battle of the Bulge in Germany receiving a purple heart for his injuries. Upon his return from WWII our family moved to Coosa Court later moving to Indian Hills in Childersburg. Daddy was employed at the Alabama Ordinance Works (AOW) as a cost accountant.

Daddy later opened his own business as a Public Accountant and Insurance Agent. The business was located upstairs above the Childersburg Fire Department. Many will remember this building as Limbaugh Hardware on 1st street. Daddy's offices were shared with the Coosa Garment Company upstairs.

Daddy had the brick building where the Lawrence's Agency was located at 120 7th Avenue, SW. in 1952. Later he entered into an agreement with the U.S. Postal Service and had the second building which was adjacent to Lawrence's on the north side of his original building. The front of the building was leased to the postal service and the rear of the building was a storage facility for Daddy's use.

If Daddy needed office supplies, he never bought just one... if there was a price break at two dozen... or twelve dozen, he always brought the larger amount. Lawrence's soon became the "go to" place for office supplies because he always bought extra. He gradually began to purchase items that others wanted.

Lawrence's became the school supply place in Childersburg because daddy saw the community had a need. We were your "one stop shop." One could purchase a typewriter, bible, billfolds, real ink fountain pens, crepe paper, greeting cards, a sheet of poster paper, or a box of crayons. And of course all of your business office needs.

Limbaugh Hardware
James, Robert, and George Limbaugh, Owners

My Brothers' Business

Roscoe Limbaugh, *CHS Class of 1953*

As a boy growing up in the late1940s and early 1950s, there were many opportunities for work in Childersburg. In addition to school, sports, and the never ending farm work, I had the chance to earn a little extra by working for my brothers, George, Robert, and James Limbaugh. They decided to go into the hardware business after WWII. They opened a hardware store in Childersburg a town dear to their hearts and one in which they saw great potential.

In addition to hardware they stocked sporting goods, appliances, tires, and later added china, crystal and silver. It was a place to shop for almost anything. Limbaugh's carried everything from "thunder pots" to fine china. They sold and serviced appliances and TVs. It was said that George could sell refrigerators to Eskimos.

The building and construction trade was not to be overlooked by these brothers who were willing to get in on any opportunity to expand their business. They did electrical installations in homes, as well as installing bathroom fixtures, did plumbing work and contract painting. That is where my work at Limbaugh Hardware came in while I was in high school. I did all of these jobs and became quite a skilled handyman. I also learned sales techniques from working with my brothers. This influenced my life's career in sales.

Limbaugh Hardware served many purposes and was a place where members of the community came by to visit, talk over current events and even sometimes carry on city business. Robert Limbaugh was mayor for 16 years, and people in Childersburg would often come by and discuss problems or ideas they might have. It was also an after school gathering place for the Limbaugh children and grandchildren. It was a second home for me as well as many other family members.

Robert Limbaugh 1950's

Sandra and I brought our children, Greg, Allison and Stephanie to be weighed on the nail scales. There was a convenient Coca Cola sign in the back of the store with inches marked off where we could measure our children's heights. Since my Father had died when I was quite young, these brothers, as well as my other three brothers, served as both brothers and father to me.

Limbaugh Hardware had originally served as a fire station, a jail, and a sewing factory (Coosa Garment Company) plus Millard Lawrence had his accounting business upstairs in the late 1940s and early 1950s. When it became available, the brothers bought the upstairs and renovated it which provided more room for their expanding business.

After the remodeling, a Grand Opening was planned. The grand opening proved to be quite an affair for both Childersburg and Talladega County. There were door prizes such as a refrigerator, TV and many other things of value. Everyone was given a vase and a station was set up so that the vase could be personalized by swirling it in various colors of paint. Footsteps were painted on the sidewalks all leading to Limbaugh Hardware. It was indeed a "grand" opening and drew many people from the town as well as the surrounding counties.

The Limbaugh Brothers thought big and their business reflected their optimism for Childersburg as well as America.

Del-leans Beauty Shop

Seventy years of continuous service to the women of Childersburg, Alabama

Linda Justice Simpson, *CHS Class of 1962*

In 1958 Olean Justice, Dell Justice and Margaret Harkins made the decision to attend Birmingham Beauty College to become hairdressers.

Most of us remember the treacherous two-lane highway through the narrows they would travel every day, and the best I remember there was almost nothing between Harpersville and Birmingham at that time. As a child it was scary to me riding through the narrows. During the cold winter months long icicles would hang for days on the rocks along the side of the road, in addition to the danger of icy patches since it was shady and ice took a long time to melt. These ladies enjoyed the school and the trip wasn't bad when they had each other to laugh and talk with. Occasionally on Saturday one or more of their children would go with them and the owner would "hire" them to empty the trash and do some clean up.

After completion of the course and obtaining their state licenses, Olean and Margaret started work at Dru's Beauty

Shop located on First Street across from The Fair Store and Dell started work at Beth's Beauty Shop, in Grove Park. Later Margaret Harkins opened a shop in her house and then later moved it to the Giant Foods Shopping Center.

Dru Jobe had a well-established shop having opened it at this same location in 1945. She and her husband Terry Paul had moved to Childersburg from Mississippi in 1940 when they started work at the Alabama Ordinance Works. After a brief move to San Diego in 1944, they returned to Childersburg in 1945 and she opened Dru's Beauty Shop. Mary Jane Rognelson was one of the hairdressers at Dru's in the early 1950s and Myra Tinsley also worked there in the mid-1950s. Dru's husband owned a barber shop in Sylacauga which later became Machen Barber Shop. In the summer of 1961 after her son, Ernest, graduated from high school, Dru and her family made the decision to move back to Corinth, Mississippi, and Dell and Olean took a giant leap of faith and bought Dru's shop. They renamed it *Del-Lean's Beauty Shop* but remained at the same location. Margie Hobbs worked there for a while and Sandra Tanner started training in Cosmetology under Dell and Olean. Gail Armstrong Allen also worked there during the mid-1960s before moving to Florida. Jimmy Sharbutt's law office was next door and when he decided to relocate, Dell and Olean expanded the shop to add a Merle Norman Cosmetics Studio.

In the late 1960s Olean and Dell decided to relocate the beauty shop to a larger building up the street next to Taylor's Cleaners. Carrie Butts Gore moved to the location with them, and within a few weeks Carolyn Upton Miller joined the team. Sandra Tanner Butts also worked a few years during that time. Gail Commander, Phyllis Gray, Debbie Williamson, and Karen Haynes also worked there for short periods of time. Following small town traditions this was more than weekly shampoos, haircuts, permanents and manicures. Lasting friendships were formed between the hairdressers and their customers, they got to know their families and close, life long bonds of love and friendship were established. They supported each other during good times and bad as is the way of small town culture and values.

For health reasons Dell decided to retire in 1982 and Olean bought her half of the business continuing at the same location. Carrie Butts Gore and Carolyn Upton Miller continued working for Olean as well as Cyndi Houston Sims who had joined them in 1978 and Pam Lester Storey who started work in 1982. In 1990 Olean decided to go into semi-retirement and sold the shop to Carrie Butts Gore and the name was changed to *Carrie's Beauty Shop* but remained at the same location. Olean continued to work two days a week for several years then retired.

Shirley Hamilton, Kathy Levesque, and Zona Jennings worked at Carrie's during the 1990s and Rebecca Nortego came to work a short time before Carrie sold the shop to Pam Lester Storey in December 1999. Pam changed the name to *Pam's Hair Heaven* but remained at the same location and the shop is still in operation in 2015. Shirley Hamilton, Rebecca Nortego, Debra Crowe Epperson, Jessica Crowe Pilkington, Tracey Guy King, Devin Raines, Lindsey Jones Bolt, and Cathy Hill Green, have worked for Pam over the years and Jessica Ferguson and Morgan Kelly are presently working for Pam.

Through the years with each transfer of ownership the core values remained the same, old friendships were kept and nurtured as new friendships were formed. It is noteworthy to add that this beauty shop has been in continuous operation in downtown Childersburg for 70 years (1945-2015), at two locations with five different owners and four different names. I hope it will continue to thrive and prosper and remain an integral part of Childersburg for another 70 years.

Dianne Hillman Prisoc, *CHS Class of 1972*

My mother had her hair done every Friday at Del-lean's. I was about 3 the first time I saw a hair dryer. I had a fit when they put my mother under it. I thought they were electrocuting her.

Allison Teague Bell, *TCHS Class of 1983*
I spent many hours at that beauty shop! Nanny would pay me a quarter for collecting the Coke bottles from around the dryers. I thought I was so rich then.

Elliot's Fabric Store
Margaret Elliot Owner

Phyllis Jinks Boyett, CHS Class of 1980

A fond memory of Childersburg was when my Mom took me to Elliot's Fabric Store and she would buy a Barbie doll dress for my Barbie doll.

Margaret Elliot made Barbie dresses out of fabric remnants, and I thought they were beautiful! I think they were 50¢ to $1.00 each. They were in a box beside the cash register. What a great memory.

Chapter 5

Swimming Pools and Swimmin' Holes

Swimming Pools

The (old 1950s) Childersburg Swimming Pool

Mickey Donahoo, *CHS Class of 1961*

As summer would come to Alabama in the 1950s and the temperatures increased in Childersburg, kids would look for ways to keep cool and we would head for Mr. Yarborough's swimming pool on our bikes. The first pool in Childersburg was owned by Mr. Fred Yarbrough and was located near the Central of Georgia Rail Road tracks east of downtown, and northwest of the present Limbaugh Center. The street which ran on the pool's north side was known as Alabama State Highway 76; today the Desoto Cravens Parkway, but in the 50s and 60s that road was called the Winterboro Highway. The pool had two diving boards located at the east end of the pool. It cost a dime in the early 1950s to swim. However, a dime was not always easy to come by.

Just before school was out, Mr. Yarborough would invite some of us boys down to his pool. He would run some water in the pool and hand us scrub brushes to clean off whatever had come to live on the pool walls during the winter. As a payment (as if playing in the water weren't enough), each kid-cleaner could put his name in the hat and the "lucky one" would draw a free pass to all the summer swimming he could stand.

I say "lucky one" but that was not always the case. Some hard earned advice, if you won a free pass to Mr. Yarborough's pool and have an older brother, don't run home bragging about "your" pass because you may no longer have a "free pass" but a bloody nose for all you're scrubbing.

Linda Justice Simpson, *CHS Class of 1962*

We had fun in the summer swimming at Mr. Fred Yarbrough's pool located on the eastside of downtown just after the overpass going east on the Winterboro highway.

Jackson's Lake/Butler Springs

Stuck in the Mud

Marilyn Alexander Primero, *CHS Class of 1963*

I got the family car for a Sunday afternoon; it was a Black 1956 Dodge and would just fly! Anyway, I pick up a car load of friends. Leslie McInnish was my best buddy since 6th grade. Leslie was riding shotgun and I was driving. We drove to Jackson Lake near Vincent first, and then we were going to Lakeview near Harpersville. We were just making a big circle.

We got to Jackson Lake and cruised around. We needed to turn the car around and go back to the main road. It had been raining most of the week so the ground was wet. Leslie said "just drive out there, and turn around." So, I did! The car was so loaded with all of my friends, the ground was softer than what it looked like and I buried that Dodge. We couldn't even get the doors open!

Leslie climbed out the window to go get help! It took two big tractors to pull us out! They thought they were going to have to get a tow truck, but thanks to Southern ingenuity and determination they got us out of the mud! Needless to say, we didn't go to Lakeview that day. We had to find a place to wash that mud off the car! It was a mess! My dad never knew about that little escapade — I don't think!

One day daddy was having lunch with one of his coworkers. The guy asked my dad, "Connie, how fast will that Dodge go?" My dad said, "Oh, 50 or 60 I guess." The guy laughed and said, "Hell, man, it passed me the other night going to Sylacauga doing at least 80 miles an hour!" Guess who was driving?

I don't know how I lived through all the dangerous things I did! Like riding a motorcycle with Adrian Young out Winterboro highway wide open! Amazing!

Mike Headley, *CHS Class of 1962*

The Jackson's Lake/Butler Springs swimming pool was located between Vincent and Sterrett, Alabama northeast of Childersburg. Jackson's Lake was a bit nicer than Wyatt's Lake plus it had a water slide lots of parking and a large dance floor. The price for a song was the same at all the different places, one song was $.10 but you could get three for a quarter. We did some dancing in those days.

Jim Reeder, *CHS Class of 1975*

Butler Springs was in Vincent. I remember the big elephant ears plant there. I swam there many times.

SWIMMIN' HOLES

Bon Air Pond (Rhoden Spring)
Bon Air, Alabama

Dwain Adams, *CHS Class of 1962*

A cousin of mine born on the same day and year as I was, loved to leave his big city home in Dallas, Texas and come to visit me during the summers here in Childersburg.

I was 12 years old at that the time and as luck would have it, Dad was out of town during the week on his job driving a truck and Mother worked at the Bon Air Cotton Mill during the day. Left to my own devices I really knew how to entertain a big-city kid. One day Mother told me to take my bike to the First National Bank of Childersburg and make a deposit. So my cousin and I got on my bike (riding double) all the way down to the bank and back.

The rest of the day my cousin and I were out to have some fun. I got the great idea that we should take a number two washtub to Bon Air Pond and float around. Why I had the bright idea a number two wash tub would make a great boat is another matter. Now coming from my house there was a dirt road on the left. It's about a mile and a half to the Bon Air pond. Its right before you cross the railroad tracks going southeast in to Bon Air. So off we went walking, and carrying that number two wash tub. When we arrived at the pond we stripped off our clothes, and left them on the bank along with mother's bank book. It was hot, I mean Alabama hot. So we decided to go swimming. Anyway the tub didn't work very well, and the pond was full of glass so we quickly tired of that adventure.

Down the road on the left as you entered Bon Air was an old home place where there just happened to be two pear trees which had pears ready to eat. So my cousin and I headed out in search of those pears. After enjoying the pears, and easily bored we headed back to Bon Air Pond to get our shirts, and mother's bank book.

While on the way back we looked up to see a man driving an old pickup coming toward us. He pulled alongside and said, "Hey, did you know two boys drowned in the Bon Air Pond today? There's a big crowd gathered there now." I said, "NO KIDDING! We're headed back there ourselves." He looked puzzled, then said, "Say, aren't you the Adams kid?"

Turns out someone went to the pond and seeing our clothes, plus mother's bank book, figured we had drowned. One policeman, if I remember correctly was Odell Ellison, cut his feet badly wading in looking for our bodies. Someone finally called Mother at the Bon Air Mill to let her know about the drowning, and mother said, "Not my boy, he knows there's glass in that pond."

The next day my cousin and I were off on yet a whole new adventure. My cousin and I were the talk of Childersburg for days. My cousin had lots of tales to tell his friends when he returned to Dallas.

Wyatt's Lake / Lake View

Marilyn Alexander Primero, *CHS Class of 1963*

Lakeview was such a cool place. I loved the original "Zip line" across the lake — but was it really a lake or a 'man-made' lake!? My dad was buds with Mr. Wyatt; they were such nice people and one of my favorite swimming memories.

Mike Headley, *CHS Class of 1962*

Wyatt's Lake swimming hole was located near Harpersville, Alabama. Wyatt's Lake had a skating rink, a dance floor and a quarter-mile dirt race track. The entire complex was reached by driving down a dirt road. The skating, dancing, swimming, and racing at Wyatt's lake were lots of fun.

If there was a downside to the skating the only thing I can remember was that after 55 other guys had sweated in the same shoes, they got a little ripe. I got my own skates for Christmas 1956. Man, was that was a blessing!

The Skating Rink had different colored lights which were turned on and off, up and down depending on the mood which the operator was trying to convey. For instance there were several moods as follows. All Skate, Couples Only, Skate Backwards, Girls only, Boys only — which usually turned into see who can skate the fastest.

When the operator announced "Boys only" we would set up what was called "The Whip." For The Whip to work really well you would need at least 10 guys. Holding hands we skated around the rink as fast as possible then a big guy would anchor himself at the top of the curve, while the rest of the guys would skate past. The last guy in the whip was doing about 50 miles an hour while trying to hang on as the group went around. As one might imagine the last one or two guys would lose their grip which would send them flying into the rail. This made the girls scream, which I suppose was our intent in the first place. No one was ever seriously hurt, well maybe a slight concussion from time to time. During those days none of us had ever heard of lawsuits, much less tort law.

The dance floor was located on the North side of the skating rink. The structure had a roof and hand rails around three sides which kept dancers from falling into the lake. A coin-fed Juke Box kept the dance music going. You paid 5¢ for one song or three for a dime. Around the ripe old age of fourteen, I started to spend more time on the dance floor than in the skating rink. I had become a better dancer and also that's where the older girls were.

The Swimming Hole was the first thing I noticed when arriving at the age of eight. Usually I went to Wyatt's Lake with older sisters, and cousins. As I grew older I drove myself, spending more time at the skating rink and dance floor, not to mention the race track. The water was spring fed, which helped. But the water was not as clean as at Butler Springs. Wyatt's Lake had three different diving board heights. The boards had no spring, just a rough cut slab of oak wood from which one could try to dive, or jump.

I must admit I heard the word marijuana for the first time at Wyatt's Lake. It was a Saturday summer evening about 1959. There was a guy riding a new Harley Davidson Speedster motorcycle. It seems that if one was so disposed one could buy marijuana from a certain restaurateur in Childersburg. A year later the restaurateur went away to spend some time with the State of Alabama prison system.

Mickey Donahoo, *CHS Class of 1961*

Mr. Wyatt dug out a hole with a spring near Harpersville, Alabama and opened Wyatt's Lake to the public. It was complete with a trolley, diving boards, swings, skating rink, and dance floor. This was obviously a pretty good representation of heaven.

The thing that really stands out in my mind were the diving boards—not the 10 foot one but the 42 footer. If you were brave enough to climb up there, Mr. Wyatt would get on the loud speaker and draw everyone's attention to you. You may have just climbed up there to see what it looked like with no intention of diving or jumping. However, with everyone's eyes on you, you would probably experience you first encounter with peer pressure. You were expected to leave the board by air, not the steps.

Well with everyone looking at you, especially the girls (otherwise no girl of worth would look at a 6 foot, 135 pound Charles Atlas) you are expected to do something so it became easier to jump or dive rather than climb down. The jumping scared me most so I chose to dive.

Later, for no other reason than the attention, I would make the climb, await the announcement and dive. I never liked diving, but did it to save face. I hated every second of it. Later, when I became a little more comfortable (that is a stretch) with the dive it became a little easier. However, all was not glory (as it was short lived) because Larry McCarrick would climb right up behind me and do a backward flip—such was my short lived glory.

I took those swimming holes for granted back then, but have since come to thank God for those men who added so much to my early life.

My Bathing Suites Got a Hole in It

Sue Ellison Mc Duffy CHS Class of 1961

Wyatt's Lake was near Harpersville where the slide was in the water. Mother bought me a nice swimsuit at Sheba's in Childersburg. I wore a hole in it very quickly.

The Blue Hole

Sherry Machen Atkinson, *CHS Class of 1962*

My mother told me her parents W. O. and Era Edwards, her sister, Grace McSween, and the Caldwell family would go to the Blue Hold once a year on vacation! Granddaddy would hitch the mule to the wagon and tie Betsy, the milk cow, to the back and off they would go.

Grandmother, mother and my aunt would sleep in the wagon. Mother said they, along with the Caldwell family, would stay a week. Granddaddy took the cow so they would have fresh milk while on "Vacation!" I was in awe when she told me this story. Billy's cousin and his wife own the Blue Hole property now.

Herb Haynes, *CHS Class of 1973*

I will never forget the Blue Hole. There were many hot summer days we would visit. It very much lived up to its name. The water was crystal clear and very blue in color. We would pack in someone's car or van and head out to the Blue Hole. We always challenged each other to jump in first. After the first one jumped, the rest were sure to follow. The water was so cold even in the middle of a hot summer day. When jumping in, it felt as though you had just jumped into a large blue slushy. You could literally feel the ice in that ice cold water. After a short swim and when getting out, not only was the water blue, but so were we. I sure miss those days!

James Morris, *CHS Class of 1967*

There are three mounds of sand on the bottom of Blue Hole. They look like ant hills with water spewing sand out the top. There are some old brick at the outlet that raises the waters to about 16 feet deep. A thermometer under the water said the temperature is 56 degrees. At one time a steel cable was strung across the blue hole between two trees. A rope was tied about halfway across. Boards where nailed on the near side tree so to gain enough elevation to swing out over the cold water and make it back to the top of the bank. Otherwise if you launched from the bank you would not make it back to dry ground.

I've seen many a poor soul swing and miss the top, eventually come to a complete stop dead center above the Blue Hole. Most begged for mercy, and then reluctantly drop from the rope into the icy blue water. I've seen water melons, Coke and a beer floating all at one time, to stay cold. For most folks one dip was enough. You could climb out up a muddy bank or walk a log out to dry ground. This was hard because the cold water affected your balance. Two dips meant you were dared or you got pushed in. Three times meant someone had thrown your car keys in the Blue Hole and the only way you were going home was to dive down in the icy water to retrieve them. I remember the water in the Blue Hole was warmer than the air on a cold winter day.

Four Mile Creek

Noodling

Mike Headley, *CHS Class of 1962*

Four Mile Creek flows from the base of Flagpole Mountain, east then turns north to enter the Coosa River just north of Coosa Pines Road which we referred to as the "Plant Road" in the 1950s, 1960s and 1970s.

Many a summer day my cousins and friends would ride our bikes north down the Old Sylacauga Highway toward Childersburg on what was then a dirt road to a wooden bridge just north of Bill Breedlove's dad's farm. There was a short dirt trail leading down to the creek.

For those who are unfamiliar with noodling allow me to explain. I was first introduced to the manly art of noodling at the ripe old age of nine. Picture this; a big fat catfish is in a hole under the bank. You simply walk along the creek bottom, bare foot (of course) in chest deep water where you run your hand in the holes looking for a cat fish. That, my city friends, is what was known in the South as "noodling."

There are certain hazards associated with "Noodling." For example: snakes, which we had unfortunate encounters with a few times. When you're 12 years old, and a boy who is 15 tells you that snakes can't bite you underwater YOU BELIEVE IT!I don't ever remember going to the creek when we did not see snakes. Mostly Cottonmouths, its Alabama — in the summer — believe me folks we had snakes.

Why we never had to run to Mr. and Mrs. Breedloves's farm Betty Jenkins Breedlove's (CHS Class of 1962) in-laws a quarter-mile away with someone snake bitten, I have no idea. If we had, occasion to do so we would have been in good hands because Mrs. Breedlove was a nurse at Beaunit Mills.

Swimming (boys only)

My cousins, Robert and Frank Russell, and I, plus Bill Breedlove and the Williams brothers' swam a lot in Four Mile Creek. We would ride our bikes down those dirt roads just a mile East of Flagpole Mountain as fast as we could go. Fast bike travel created two things, dust and sweat which seemed to collect on our shirtless bodies.

During the summer there was a great deal of vegetation which grew along that dirt road (Talladega County road 45 /

Old Sylacauga Highway) which crossed a wooden plank bridge which raddled as car came across. This bridge crossed Four Mile Creek (one half mile south of Mountain View Cross Roads. If someone was so inclined to cool off a bit on a hot summer afternoon, and you did not have swimming trunks, plus the cars that came by were few and far between well ... we skinny dipped a lot.

Kowliga and Wind Creek

Mike Headley CHS Class of 1962

I traveled to Kowliga and Wind Creek with family, relatives and friends on many occasions to picnic, swim and water ski. From Childersburg, to reach Wind Creek you travel south on US Highway 280 through Alexander City, Alabama a distance of a little over 45 miles and pulling my speed boat, it only took around and hour to arrive at the boat ramp.

A Trip to Wind Creek

Dianne Hillman Prisoc, *CHS Class of 1972*

Those of us that went to First United Methodist remember our youth trips to Winn Creek, some of us rode in the back of a pickup truck with wooden slat rails, and Billie Ann Reagan was our youth leader.

Kowliga

Mike Headley, CHS Class of 1962

Before there was a Wind Creek State Park, my family, friends and relatives spent many a fun day at Kowliga Beach 45 miles south of Childersburg near Alexander City, Alabama.

I don't know who came up with one of the most unpleasant rules ever to torture a seven year old boy? That would be the Wiseinstine that said "you had to wait one hour after eating before going swimming." I can assure you my mother and aunts thought that law was created in the heaven. On numerous occasions there I sat wasting my life away and longing to be swimming and playing in the water. I was not allowed as much as a toe to enter the water. Friends, that gave a new meaning to the term "Water Torture."

I know my older sisters; Bettye, Sandra and cousins, Robert, and Frank Russell plus Cousin Brenda Dudney would sneak off and swim before the hour was up. How could I see these things? When your seven years old you have X ray eyes, which I received from watching Flash Gordon on TV. Leaving cousin's Mary Joe Russell Guy, and Marie Dudney Stewart and I at the water's edge alone.

Panama City Beach

The Hangout

Mike Headley, *CHS Class of 1962*

As I got older I followed my sisters and cousins to the dance floor at the "Hangout. The Hangout was the place to be after the sun went down on the beach at Panama City, Florida. You could, listen to the music, dance, buy a coke for 10¢, and check out the girls. The beach was next to the dance floor so you could walk right out on to the beach holding hands with a girl you had just met if you were lucky. Enjoying a moonlight hand-in-hand walk on the beach with a girl from Huntsville or Dothan, Alabama on the Gulf of Mexico — a summer romance.

The Redneck Riviera

Mike Headley, CHS Class of 1962

Many from Childersburg, Alabama spent summer vacations on Panama City Beach at what some people refer today as the Redneck Riviera. Through the years usually with one uncle and three or four aunts, our mothers and 15 cousins in one three-bedroom cabin (on the beach) where we would stay for a week. My uncle and aunts would drive all night from Childersburg, arriving at Panama City Beach the next morning.

We would spend from early morning until sun down in the water and on the sand. We had cereal with milk for breakfast, bologna sandwiches with mayo on white bread and Cool Aid for lunch. Our evening meal consisted of local fish with French fries and sweet ice tea. One vivid memory of Panama City Beach was going to the gift shops which sold the most tacky tourist stuff. One day we stopped at a shop where they had a giant clam shell out front, must have been three feet across — that made an impression on this nine year old.

If there was a down side to PCB vacation was our mothers made us stand under a shower (outside) before coming in the cabin because each of us kids were carrying about a pound of sand on our bodies. I remember no better times as a kid.

On the Beach at Panama City, Florida

Chapter 6

The Coosa Theater
Donald Jenkins Manager

The Coosa Theater under Construction 1941

A Place We Went As Kids, Then Teenagers

Mike Headley, *CHS Class of 1962*

The Coosa Theater was built in 1941 during the great influx of people who came to Childersburg because of the war effort. My first memories of the Coosa Theater started in 1954. It was a large two story dark red building with the marquee facing to the south. There was a single door entrance on the south side of the building under the marquee to allow the colored people to enter the theater with a set of stairs up to the second floor balcony so that the colored people could sit and watch the movie separate from the whites.

75

My Family Moved to Childersburg

Betty Jenkins Breedlove, *CHS Class of 1962*

We moved to Childersburg in November of 1953 from Atmore, Alabama — daddy, mother and three kids. My dad was transferred to Childersburg by Martin Theaters to be the manager of the Coosa Theater. Our old Studebaker broke down three miles south of Childersburg at Casey Holt store. I remember the first time I saw the theater it looked like a barn.

We moved into the one bedroom apartment inside the theater. To get to the kitchen we had to walk behind the large movie screen, walking over huge cords, in pitch black darkness because any light could be seen through the screens. My mother's brother was a carpenter and he made several trips to Childersburg to build two addition bedrooms behind the screen.

All the sounds from the theater could be heard in our apartment from the laughter or screams of the audience to the sounds of the music or gunshots from the movie. To this day I cannot watch a scary movie without having a nightmare. I wasn't allowed to stay up till the movies were over, so especially on school nights; I had to try to go to sleep hearing the scary scenes of a horror movie. I still sleep with the T.V. on.

A ticket to get in the movie cost 15¢; popcorn and sodas were a nickel each. Mother always said she was the cheapest babysitter in town. On Saturday a double feature and a cartoon feature as well as a serial would be shown. Parents would drop off their children early and pick them up later. Lots of kids would stay all day. Many children and some adults rode bikes to the movie. The theater had a bicycle rack out front and it was usually full on Saturdays and Sundays.

Daddy put all of his children to work in the theatre. I learned to make change and wait on customers very young. I was not tall enough to reach over the counter so daddy turned a couple of soft drink wooden crates upside down for me to stand on.

A Two Seater

During World War II, when the AOW was booming, the theater sold out every movie. Daddy said they would stop the show between movies and make everyone leave since people would buy a ticket to sleep there because of the housing shortage in Childersburg. I imagine the big two-seater seats would have sold for a premium during that time. There were only a few of these seats on the end of the first few rows. I took many naps in one of those two-seaters.

I Still Love Popcorn

I still love popcorn and could eat it every day. Popcorn and drinks were inventoried by the bag and cup. I could have all I wanted in a glass from our kitchen and a candy box or shoebox worked great for the popcorn. I also had many friends at school recess because I brought the leftover popcorn to school in a large paper bag every morning for midmorning snack.

I remember once the theater flooded. The floor sloped toward the screens and we had to wade in the water about knee deep to get out of our apartment. The employees opened the side doors, then with big brooms and buckets, swept the water out and turned on big fans to dry the floors.

The Coosa Theater was a center of activity for the community. The Childersburg merchants had a fashion show once. The 'Childersburg Star News' covered all the events and a lot of the advertising for the Theatre and other local merchants.

I Want a Chicken Leg!

Once a little boy came to the concession stand and asked for a Chicken Leg. My sister Jean told him we didn't have any chicken legs. He kept insisting that he wanted a chicken leg. He finally pointed to a picture on the ice cream freezer box, what he wanted was a Drumstick Ice Cream Bar.

Phoenix City Story (a movie)

Many movies were sold out for every showing. *White Christmas, Seven Year Itch, Rebel without a Cause,* is a few I remember. The most controversial and biggest sell out, was the *Phoenix City Story*. All the films came in by delivery and had to be ready to be shipped out on schedule. It was difficult to hold a film over but the *Phoenix City Story* was one of the times it was held over for two days. Daddy had to deliver the film to Anniston for the next showing.

Projectors, Posters, Promotions and Parties

The projector machines were huge and burned long thin carbon rods. The projector room had two of these machines and movies were more than one reel long so the movie would be switched in the middle. I have wished so many times that my family had saved all the advertisement posters. So many of them are valuable now and they sure held a lot of memories for me.

From time to time the theater would have promotions and giveaways. One of the giveaways was a little car similar in size of a Kawasaki Mule (four wheeler) It was red; and we drove it around the parking lot. I surely hated the night of the drawing. I don't remember who won it.

I had a birthday party on my 10th birthday and invited all the kids from my fourth grade class. The party was held inside the theater. Tables and chairs were set up between the first row of seats and the screen. Daddy showed us a movie. I was so excited.

A Dog and a Pony

A trick dog show came to the theater. The man that owned the dogs gave Johnny a Jack Russell Terrier that was elderly and in bad health. The dog's name was Danny. Danny and Johnny put on dog shows for the neighborhood kids but didn't charge admission.

In 1955 Daddy bought us a pony. We boarded the pony at Doctor Hagan's Veterinarian clinic on the west side of Highway 280 across from the theater where Wesson Electric is located now. The pony was blind in one eye. Johnny and I would walk to the pasture, saddle the pony and bring it back to the theater to ride. We were not allowed to ride it across the highway. One day we decided to ride it across the highway, someone told Dad, we were not allowed to go get the pony alone anymore.

Riding the Aisles of the Coosa Theater

Christmas of 1954 my brother Johnny and I both got bicycles for Christmas and we learned to ride them up and down the aisles of the theater. We also roller skated inside the theater.

Homesick

In the summer of 1957 Martin Theaters transferred Dad to Sand Mountain, Alabama. We were all so homesick for Childersburg that Dad quit his job in less than a month and we moved back. Dad sold insurance on our return to

I Was Amazed

Ollie Pardue, *CHS Class of 1966*
At age 13 I collected bottles; I could make a few cents on each and eventually got enough money to go to the Coosa Theater. Going to the movie for the first time in my life, needless to say I was amazed.

A 15¢ Movie

Carolyn Green, *CCHS Class of 1965*

Sandy, Linda Maddox and I would walk the 20 minutes to town on Saturday mornings going to the Coosa Theater downtown. It cost 15 cents to get in. That was back when Elvis had made a big hit, *Heart Break Hotel* and was very popular.

The Concession Stand

Mike Headley, *CHS Class of 1962*

The cokes, popcorn and candy were sold to the left of the front doors. Your coke did not come in a glass bottle or aluminum can. It was made when you ordered. There was a machine that dispensed syrup and carbonated water. The attendant would get a black plastic cup holder; then place a white paper cone shaped cup in the holder. Placing the cup under the coke dispenser they would pull the lever one direction and coke syrup would be added. Then the lever was moved in the opposite direction and carbonated water would be added. Last a scoop of ice would go into your cup. The coke was served with a straw that had no covering.

The best smell was the coconut oil the popcorn was cooked in. The popcorn was served in a white paper bag with red writing printed on it. I always had popcorn and a coke. At that point I was ready to sit down and watch the movie.

The She-Wolf of London

Sandra Headley Limbaugh, *SHS Class of 1957*

I remember being allowed to walk with my sister Bettye and other children living in Minor Terrace to the Coosa Theater at night to watch a movie. I was seven at the time we went to see *The She-Wolf of London*. It was about vampires and the night was very dark as we were returning home. I was very scared, and that is probably why the memory is so vivid. There were no ratings and if a movie came out we watched it. Most movies were okay. The Coosa Theater was a big part of our lives and entertainment. There we had Saturday matinees with Roy Rogers and Dale Evans, or my favorite, the Lone Ranger. The movie, Cokes and a popcorn were 20¢ and always to be enjoyed. Friends met for an afternoon of fun.

Jailhouse Rock

Marilyn Primero, *CHS Class of 1963*

I saw *Jailhouse Rock* at the Coosa Theater, back in the 1960s

The Saturday Picture Show

Mike Headley, *CHS Class of 1962*

Each week on Saturday morning there was a serial. The serial piqued our interest bringing us back the next Saturday morning. Usually Buck Rogers stuff. I would not miss those serials for the world. Next we would see the *Movie Tone News* a short film which showed news from around the world which had occurred over the last few days. We did not have much TV or any internet in those days so *Movie Tone News* was a way we had of learning what was going on in the world. All of this was followed by a cartoon. I liked Foghorn Leghorn ("I say, I say, Boy") the best. Then the week's main feature was shown.

We only had the one screen so our choice of movies was what was showing, no 12 screens here. The total cost for a Saturday's entertainment in 1954 was 25¢ which included popcorn, a soda and the movie. What does movie popcorn and coke for two cost today? — Way too much!

I Cried

Joey Ratliff, *CHS Class of 1972*

The Coosa Theater was where the new Veterans Clinic is now but closer to the RR tracks. The first movie I ever saw was *Ole Yeller*! I cried when Travis shot his dog! That was a long time ago.

From Buck Rogers to NASA

Mickey Donahoo, *CHS Class of 1961*

Living in a small town such as Childersburg we were limited in the types of recreation available to us in the mid-1950s. One place we could go on Saturday mornings was the Coosa Theater downtown. The Saturday line-up consisted of some world news reel, a cartoon (usually Bugs Bunny, Tom & Jerry, or another equally good selection) and two main

82

features. One feature would be some movie, seemingly selected at random and the other feature might be Superman, Batman, a western, Robin Hood, or Buck Rogers. This last feature would likely shape the rest of our day—especially for the boys. We boys would leave the movie house and assume the role of our hero.

If the movie had been Robin Hood, we would cut a limb for a bow and make arrows from a straight golden rod stalk. If the movie was a western, we would choose up sides for cowboys and Indians or good guys and bad guys. This playing would last well into the afternoon.

If you were lucky there might be a pretty young lass to share the movies with. If you were, really lucky, you might share one of the "love seats." If things went well you might end up holding hands or putting your arm around her—it couldn't get any better than that! However, after the movies were over, the boys would leave and do boy-things and your favorite girl would just go her way. Obviously, we had a lot of things right but botched some others.

For this Childersburg kid Buck Rogers was my favorite hero. Some kids might dream of being a cowboy or Robin Hood or some other hero. But I dared not dream of being Buck Rogers because that stuff was the product of the vivid imagination of some dreamer spending his time on something that could never be.

I eventually absorbed all of the knowledge I could about rockets, Sputnik, and space travel without knowing it was shaping my future. I would only realize it after NASA offered me a job and my unconscious dream became reality.

I never flew in space but I became a part of one of the greatest adventures ever undertaken by the United States of America. I am in my seventies now, and a realization comes to my mind, that I had been blessed to have been a part of a dream I once had as a kid growing up in Childersburg.

Date Night and a Movie

Earl Wesson Jr., *CHS Class of 1972*

Date night was usually a movie at the Coosa Theater but when you got off work at 6:00 PM and had to eat and get a bath and to the movie by 7:00 PM, and my date had to be home by 9:30. Plus we always had to go to "Hollywood" for some recreation .... well; we were married before we saw a complete movie unless we went on Sunday afternoon

Chapter 7

The Dairy Queen®
Steven Garrett Stephens, Owner

Mike Headley, *CHS Class of 1962*

Steve Garrett Stephens, Owner and a franchisee of the Dairy Queen in Childersburg had three different locations in the 50 years of service to the community. Steve's first Dairy Queen, built in 1955, was a standard Dairy Queen, a white building with blue trim and two sliding windows, walk up style on the front. You would walk up to the window and place your order, and wait... which would not be long. Steve's second Dairy Queen was a small red brick building downtown next door to Storeys Jewelry.

Around 1960 Steve moved to his third and final location on the west side of highway 280 just east of Grove Park. Most would say his best, and by far his largest store which included a dining room. The building is still there today but no longer a Dairy Queen. It was occupied by a restaurant owned by his granddaughter, Robin, for several years. However, it is now closed.

Many days I would ride the three miles north from my home on US 280 to the DQ^{TM} on my 1957 Black Cushman Eagle Motorcycle stopping for a cone, sundae, or banana split. If you ordered a banana split it would come in a plastic red or blue container with a curl on one end, the whole thing looked like a little boat.

A Day That Changed My Life

If we are lucky we witness one or two events which change our lives forever. One of those events happened to me at the ripe old age of 10 years in the summer of 1954. I had been to Steve's original Dairy Queen with my family on numerous occasions. So that had little to do with the event which changed my life. As I stepped up to order, there was a big guy with a white paper hat on his head slightly cocked to one side, plus wearing a white shirt with short sleeves, white slacks and white shoes. As the window slid open I looked up to see one Steven Garrett Stevens.

Steve was the consummate Dairy Queen entrepreneur. Just as I started to speak, Steve, with that big smile, asked "what can I get for you?" Since I had never ordered for myself before, this was a big deal. The weather was hot. — think Central Alabama in August — so I wanted something cool. I said with my best "grown-up voice "I would like a medium cone, however; may I have it dipped in chocolate, please?" This was my first time to have such a special desert. Oh, I had had a banana split with the three mounds of soft serve ice cream covered with chocolate, strawberry, and pineapple toppings with nuts sprinkled on top, and the whipped cream, with a cherry. All served in one of those red or blue plastic Dairy

Queen boats. However, today I was looking for something different. I had been told by my friend Ray Williams a special cone could be had with either chocolate or caramel covering.

I hadn't studied physics, but I knew about Isaac Newton, and I also knew that the ice cream in that cone was going to end up swimming in that stainless steel bowl if Steve turned that cone upside down while attempting to cover it with chocolate.

When you are 10 you just know certain things. I had discussed this very subject during church with Ray. We had decided some things in life you could not do. It simply could not be done. After all one does not mess with Mother Nature. Steve was wrong and I would have a great laugh and tell all my friends of his mishap.

As you might understand Steve presented me with a medium size Dairy Queen Soft Serve cone covered with that hardened milk chocolate coating. My life was changed forever. For a 10-year-old boy, it was apparent something's were inexplicable. I was speechless. Steve Stephens was either a magician or a wizard. Fact is he may have been both. Either that or someone was lying about this Newton guy. It was all a bit much for a 10-year-old boy on a hot August day in Childersburg, Alabama.

The Good Old Days

Chuck McMillian, *CHS Class of 1974*

Those were the good old days back when Steve would close up the Dairy Queen and leave us all there in the parking lot. He never worried about someone robbing him or someone breaking into the store. Steve knew almost all of us. I wish things were still like that today. America as we know it will never be like that again ... and that's sad.

Two Dairy Queen Specials

Earl Wesson, Jr., *CHS Class of 1972*

When I was ten years old the DQ had 2 specials painted on the front windows. #1 was burger, fries and shake for 49¢ and #2 was 2 burgers, fries and shake for 99¢. In the 1960s and 1970s the DQ was the place to be Friday and Saturday nights, it took forever to drive through. Where did the "good old days" go?

Tony Butts, the Dairy Queen's Pied Piper

Tony Butts, *CHS Class of 1960*

I worked for Steve driving a three wheeled Dairy Queen Cushman Truckster to all the neighborhoods of Childersburg including Camp Childersburg the prison on the North West side of town. I was the ice cream pied piper for the children of Childersburg for several summers.

Steve's Third and Last Dairy Queen

David Swanger, *CHS Class of 1972*

In my youth in Childersburg there weren't a lot of chain restaurants in the area. In 1960 Steve built his third and final Dairy Queen restaurant north of the swimming pool. My entire family went for the Dairy Queen grand opening. It seemed like half of Childersburg showed up; there was a lot of excitement in the air. Steve gave toys to all the children that evening; I remember getting a whistle shaped like an ice cream cone plus a coin bank shaped like a Dairy Queen building. We ate some ice cream but I mostly remember the toys and huge crowd. It was a different time. I'm not sure what it would take to get a large crowd to show for the opening of a fast food restaurant these days.

My grandparents lived on the old Sylacauga highway so my parents had to drive past the Dairy Queen twice when we visited. We kids begged mom and dad to stop at the Dairy Queen and it was a big treat to get to stop.

In my teen years, the Dairy Queen was a hangout for a lot of my classmates and me. Often we'd sit in cars and not go inside, trying to be cool. Hey, there weren't many places to go in Childersburg back then.

My brother-in-law, Russell Justice, claimed he was friends with people who worked at the Dairy Queen that may have helped. I liked their burgers but for me I liked their foot long chili dogs the most (not counting the ice cream). Before I had a driver's license, I would sometimes ride my bike south from Lakeside Drive to the Dairy Queen and get a foot long chili dog (paid for from my paper route). I moved from Childersburg in the early 1970s and the last time I drove south on Highway 280 I noticed the Dairy Queen Building was still there, but it's a Robins Restaurant now.

A Free Dilly Bar™

David Swanger, *CHS Class of 1972*

Living in Grove Park the Dairy Queen seemed like part of our neighborhood and I was down there all the time. When I had no money Steve would give me a cup of ice water and that ice was perfect to cool off a kid riding a bicycle on a hot summer day.

Sometimes a treat would come in the form of a Dilly Bar which were made on site but would not pass Steve's inspection. If you played your cards right you might get a free one.

M-80s and 18 Wheelers

Joe Peerson, *CHS Class of 1968*

One rainy Sunday afternoon James Lloyd Donahoo and Jimmy Herndon were throwing M-80s onto the highway from the Dairy Queen parking lot, which were landing under the tires of 18 wheelers as they rolled by. The noise was like a tire blow out so the 18 wheelers would stop to check their tires. This activity produced a good bit of laughter from all of us.

James Lloyd had a beautiful red 1968 Pontiac GTO, all clean and shiny. When he left to go home Jimmy Herndon threw three or four M-80s towards the highway, aiming for the roadway under the GTO. However, the M-80s landed in the area between the windshield and the hood of that GTO causing a fair amount of damage. I don't remember what happened after that.

A Yard Dog with Milk

Sue Brannon, *CHS Class of 1963*

Porky went to work at the mill in Bon Air as a young man. When payday came the first place Porky and his friends would head after their shift was to the Dairy Queen. Steve would wait for them to come after they got off at 10:00 p.m. Several guys would be in that hungry group, Nolen could really eat as a young man and would order three foot-long hot dogs and milk. After several trips Steve would see Porky coming and would order three foot-long hot dogs for him. Steve named it the "yard dog."

Porky Brannon and Garland Justice would always take their ball teams for a treat at the Dairy Queen when they won a big game Porky and Garland coached a lot of kid's baseball teams, and treated them often at the D.Q.

The Place to Be Seen on the Weekend

Earl Wesson Jr., *CHS Class of 1972*

The Dairy Queen was the place to be on the weekend, a constant flow of traffic through Steve's Dairy Queen parking lot. If you were lucky, a parking spot would open up; you could back in and watch the parade of cars passing by through your windshield or from the hood of your car. Many nights we circled the Dairy Queen as all our friends did.

A Long Walk

Linda Justice Simpson, *CHS Class of 1962*

One time a group which included my mother and sister, Patti Shannon and her mother, and others from Coosa Court walked from our house to the Dairy Queen when it was across from the Lynn Motel on Highway 280 south of town.

This was a long walk for us. Dilly Bars from the Dairy Queen were the best!

Dairy Queen Whistle

Peter Wallenfang, *CHS Class of 1972*

These whistles were given away during Steve's grand opening of his third and final Dairy Queen. I still have mine.

The 200 pound Rock at the Dairy Queen

James Morris, *CHS Class of 1967*

Did you ever help put the 200 pound rock at the Dairy Queen in the back seat of someone's car?

Chapter 8

Neighborhoods and Memories

Curfew was the street lights, and my mother did not call my cell phone, she yelled "time to come in!" I played outside with my friends, not on line. Yes, television was new but not many people had one. Radio or the telephone was the way most people got their news. If I didn't eat what my mother fixed for dinner, then I didn't eat. Hand sanitizer didn't exist, but you could get your mouth washed out with soap. I rode my bike without a helmet, elbow, or knee pads. Getting dirty was OK. I drank water from a garden hose and survived.

Author unknown (modified)

Coosa Court

Linda Justice Simpson, *CHS Class of 1962*

We moved to Coosa Court a middle class neighborhood, and I was welcomed by the neighborhood kids. We played outside all day in the summer and roamed the woods behind the house, played in tree houses, had rope swings in the trees and looked for arrowheads in the fields.

A Kindergarten in Coosa Court

Sandra Headley Limbaugh, *SHS Class of 1957*

I grew up during the late 1940s and 1950s. I have fond memories of those years and warm feelings for wonderful friends. I started to kindergarten in 1944 at a school located in Coosa Court —a group of hastily built houses located just off the Childersburg School campus. I do not think it was a part of the public school system, but I was allowed to ride the school bus anyway with my sister, Bettye, who was in the third grade. This begins my story of how greatly times have changed. Rules were more relaxed and common sense prevailed. Thus, even though I was not a student in the public school system I could ride the bus with my sister. It just made sense. We lived near Flag Pole Mountain, and we had to walk about a mile before reaching the bus stop. That big yellow school bus was certainly a welcome sight on cold mornings. My kindergarten experience was short-lived as my family moved to Oak Ridge, Tennessee for our father to work at the nuclear plant. We then returned to Childersburg just in time for my first grade.

In those days almost all children were what are being referred to now as "free range" children. It was just a way of life in our schools and in our homes. It probably made us more self-assured and confident.

Pinewood Terrace

A Trip Down Memory Lane

George Gilbert, *CHS Class of 1961*

When my brother, sister and I were in Childersburg for a visit, we turned left off the Plant Road after we crossed the railroad bridge. We remembered the friends we knew all those years ago on Lakeside Drive. On the left lived Billy, on the right were Leon and Annette and next door lived Sarah, Jimmy and Carrol; across the street lived Charlie. Half way down the steep hill lived Linda and next door Clara, across the street lived Coach Cox.

In the circle lived Larry and Mary Alice and two doors down Jimmy Ray. Exiting the circle on the left lived Corky, next door lived Hugo. Across the street lived Jimmy Ray. Down the road lived Coach Dean, and next door Coach Price. Bert Carson lived at 45 Lakeside and we lived at 47, and across the street lived JoAnne. Billy and Mike lived on the right and Bobby, Annette and Charley lived across the street. Down the street on the right lived Livaughn. Next door to Livaughn lived Sandy, Paul and Doug, and next door Barbara. Across the street on the left lived Kay and Joey. Down the road lived Pat, Bitsy and Buddy, across the street Tommy, Malley and Ann. Back on the right lived Audrey and Johnny. We rode bus # 37 to school, fished and swam in the creek and river, played hide and seek, kick the can, soft ball, and some of us Little League and Pony league. We have many pleasant memories growing up in Pinewood Terrace. Also we had many friends who lived in Pine Crest.

Walking to That Curb Market

David Swanger, *CHS Class of 1972*

When I was 5 and my brother was 4, we walked from Lakeside Drive to "That Curb Market" and bought some candy. Maybe a one-mile walk each way. We crossed US Highway 280 twice. We were nearly home when Minister Perry spotted us and told our parents. I couldn't understand why Mom and Dad were so upset. We weren't allowed to leave the yard without supervision for a long time.

Going to Grandmother's

Dianne Fuller Harrelson, *CHS Class of 1972*

When we visited my grandparents I would always ask if I could go play with Candy Stevens or Pam Cobb. My grandparents lived on the other end of Lakeside Drive. Their house was the second on the right after turning off the plant road. Granddaddy always had rose bushes in his front yard. I remember when Teresa Polk moved from Grove Park to Pinewood Terrace. Made me sad because I could no longer walk the 'Brownie Hut road' to go and play with her.

Cutting Grass

David Swanger, *CHS Class of 1972*

I used to mow lawns on Lakeside Drive and one time the Hardin's had a leaky water pipe in their front yard and their grass grew like crazy. They had me mowing their lawn on a regular basis until they fixed the leaky pipe. I was just a kid but they were very nice to me.

My Family Home

J.D. Warren, *CHS Class of 1961*

The new plants brought a mini-population boom to Childersburg, which had lost population with the closing of the AOW after World War II. Pinewood Terrace and Grove Park were built to accommodate the influx in new families. Soon we moved to Lake Shore Drive in Pinewood Terrace. That was my "family home" even after I left Childersburg and had my own house and family until my mother passed away a few years ago.

Forest Hills

Moving to Forest Hills

Robbie Riddle, *CHS Class of 1975*

My family of six moved to Forest Hills in 1960 from Minor Terrace. This was the "new" neighborhood with homes built in the late 1950s. They were all brick homes. Forest Hills was a great place to grow up. Our address was 341 Forrest Hills Drive. I can remember the phone number as 378-7248. We had a black rotary phone that was in the hallway of our three bedroom home with two bathrooms. Frank never lived in this house. The four youngest brothers did. Three of us slept in one bedroom with bunk beds. No air conditioning, just a big attic fan for the entire house. My brothers and I all had a paper route from 1962 to 1970. The Birmingham News was an afternoon paper with a larger Sunday-morning paper. My Mom split the routes up between the four of us covering Forrest Hills and the Pine Crest neighborhoods. We had over a hundred customers and delivered all 100 papers on our bicycles. We rode our bikes to Childersburg Elementary it was always a race to see who could get there first.

My Western Flyer bike had a huge basket on the front. Every day after school we would deliver the papers rain or shine. On Sunday mornings before church we had the luxury of mom taking us on our paper routes in Mark's 1965 Corvair. We also had to make monthly collections for the paper of $2.71 per month. We knew every family in Forrest Hills and in Pine Crest and had been inside all the homes when collecting for the paper. I cannot remember how much money I made but I always had change in my pocket. A lot of great families raised their kids in Forest Hills.

To this day I can still name the majority of the folks that lived in the neighborhood. We played and hunted in the woods behind our house; built forts out of pine tops and would camp out on the weekends and attempted to stay out of mischief. Dad always had a garden in our backyard alongside the rest of our neighbors. Mom lived there until her passing in 1989.

Grove Park

Judi J Headrick, *CHS Class of 1972*

The gang from Grove Park rode ours bikes everywhere. We rode them every school day even in the winter. The only time we did not was when it was raining hard, and then Catherine Washam would drive us to school. This was before girls could wear pants to school. We rode our bicycles to town whenever we wanted.

We Had Freedom

Candy Stephens, *CHS Class of 1975*

I remember back and think of the freedom as children to roam our neighborhoods at will, like walking the Brownie Hut road, I walked many times without a thought of danger, and I think how sad it is for our grandchildren that they can't even play in their yards without an adult to keep them safe.

Minor Terrace

Dlaine Pogue, *CHS Class of 1984*

I grew up in Minor Terrace. I lived there the first 20 years of my life and I have the best memories from that neighborhood. I had so much fun you just wouldn't believe it. Do you remember walking thru the trails and riding your bike at "clay banks?" I sure wish I could go back to that time in my life.

Playing Under the Streetlights

Brenda Williamson, *CHS Class of 1966*

My family lived at 52 Minor Terrace. Next door to the Carpenters on one side and the Webster's on the other. We played games under the street light after supper in summer with the Burdick's, Brenda and Eddie Slaten, Brenda Jones and Rebecca Hare. I remember the Ivey's, Dillard's, Riley's, and Deloach's store.

George Gilbert's 1950's Library Card

Our home near Highway 280

Ollie Pardue, *CHS Class of 1966*

In 1959 my parents divorced. It sounds bad but it was the best thing that could happen to me considering the situation. The good news was that I moved to Childersburg; Mom and all of us kids moved into a small house near Highway 280. We had to rely on my older brothers to provide for the bare necessities. All other needs had to be put on the back burner. The thing I found in Childersburg was a community that cared. I experienced a friendship with someone that would last for a lifetime.

Childersburg, I learned, was a town that cared about its youth. The support for the football team was unbelievable. Everyone wanted to be a part of it and attend the games. I too wanted to attend the games. I somehow found a way to get into the games without a ticket, which I could not afford. If you are traveling from town heading east to the old high school and as you went under the railroad viaduct (it's the road that Mrs. Grace McSween lived on). If you take the first left after the railroad via duct you would be at the stadium just across from the high school. Immediately after taking that left turn there would be a lower parking lot on the right. Running under that road near the parking lot is a small drain pipe. I learned that the pipe started at the roadside and drained out on the inside of the fence near the stadium.

Later, our family was able to move into the government housing project, Desoto Court. We moved right across from, you guessed it, Newton. Newton's dad, Jack Sanders, was a barber in Childersburg. His mother Jesse was one of the finest ladies I have ever met. She was one of the people in the neighborhood that took a personal interest in all of us kids. Jack was like a father to many of us. Newton and I have been friends since that night we sneaked into the football game. I have never had a better friend.

Together with other friends, Newton and I started a little group that we called the "Minor Terrace Angels." It sounds bad, like a gang, but we were harmless (somewhat).

To sum up my experience, Because of the people in Childersburg, and the influence people had on me I turned out pretty well. From a family of thirteen children, eleven that lived, by the grace of God the nurture of a loving community and a mother that had true faith in God, I was the only one to finish high school.

Staring at the TV

June Melton Lassiter, *CHS Class of 1967*

I remember sitting and watching the test pattern on our TV screen waiting for Saturday morning cartoons.

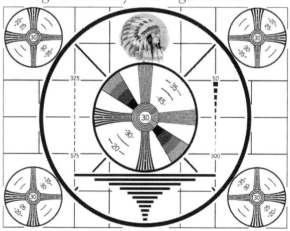

Comic Books

Sherry Machen Atkinson, *CHS Class of 1962*

Do you remember the News Stand? I bought many comic books there. We would trade with our friends and get ones we had not read.

Children Played Outside

Linda Justice Simpson, *CHS Class of 1962*

A time when people did not lock their cars and children played outside without fear. Crime was almost non-existent; however, we did not have air conditioning, clothes dryers, lap tops, cell phones, car seat belts, children's car seats, or fast food restaurants.

As kids growing up in Childersburg we had a gallon of this stuff swabbed on us.

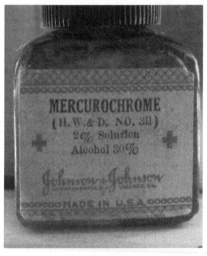

We did not have cell phones and only went back to the house to go to the bath room or eat lunch, and sometimes we even took a sandwich with us and ate in the woods. At night we played under the street lights and ran all over the neighborhood playing hide and seek and kick the can.

I remember hiding in a neighbor's detached garage. We skated with our skate key skates on the sidewalks and rode our bicycles yes, in the streets. I walked to school except when it rained. We walked downtown to the Coosa Theater on Saturday mornings and watched all the good westerns with Roy Rogers and Dale Evans, plus Gene Autry and the Lone Ranger. I could see the movie, buy popcorn, a coke, and milk duds for 30 cents AND we could stay and watch the movie more than once!

We went to Sunday school and church on Sunday at the First Baptist church and then went to visit our grandmothers on Sunday afternoon

These were the days of black and white televisions with *The Mickey Mouse Club*, *I Love Lucy*, *The Ed Sullivan Show*, *Gun smoke*, *Wagon Train*, *Wyatt Earp*, *Davy Crockett* , *Jackie Gleason* (the honeymooners), *Tennessee Ernie Ford* (Sixteen Tons), *Leave it to Beaver*, *Father Knows Best*, *Red Skelton*, *Rawhide* and many others.

We had two TV channels coming from Birmingham and no remote, that's right we actually had to get up and manually adjust the volume and change channels. The music we listened to could be understood, we had Elvis one of the great entertainers of all time and perhaps the best entertainer there has ever been.

The Sidewalks Were Brick

Sherry Atkinson, CHS Class of 1962

Do you remember when the sidewalks in downtown Childersburg were brick? I loved it when they concreted them so I could skate on the concrete. I wish they were back to the original brick. I think the brick is still under the concrete.

The Recreation Center (USO)
Built in the early 1940s

Mark Riddle, *CHS Class of 1966*

The Troggs — "Wild Thing" played, Susan and I won a dance contest that night and got their single as the prize. We had a lot of good times at the old Rec Center between 1964 and 1969.

Dianne Hillman Prisoc, *CHS Class of 1972*

I remember "My Girl" was the first song I ever slow-danced to. Carroll Gulledge had taught me to dance in our den, so the first time a boy asked me to dance at the Rec Center I was so scared I said, "No." Carroll was watching, he came over and took me by the hand and told me NOT to turn another dance request down. So the next song up was "My Girl." When I was asked again, I looked over at Carroll and he was nodding 'go ahead,' so I did and I remember stepping all over that poor boy's feet.

A 75¢ Simplicity Pattern

My mother made this outfit for me; and I wore it on Friday nights at the Childersburg Rec Center. ROCK ON!

The Viaduct on 3 Street South West

Elaine M Greer, *CHS Class of 1965*

Remember walking to and from Childersburg High School under the viaduct. I lived on 5th street then. The old viaduct looks the same, except there's lots of writing on it now.

Jane Watwood Gibbs, CHS Class of 1958

Lucinda Newman and I used to play "house" in the space on the north side (left) under the viaduct. Sweet memories!

James Morris, CHS Class of 1967

My mother told me workers slept under the Viaduct when the Alabama Ordnance Works was being built during the early 1940s because there were no places to live.

Cousin Cliff's Clubhouse, WAPI TV
(Birmingham)
1929 -2008, Korean War Veteran

Dianne Hillman Prisoc, CHS Class of 1972

I remember Rita Lucas being on the Cousin Cliff Show. She was about ten, and she lived across the street from us. We all gathered around the television to watch her.

A Fast Coke

Nancy Pressley Beckham, CHS Class of 1966

Our family would drive around Talladega County on Sunday afternoons and Daddy would stop at one of the country stores and get everyone a coke. Daddy, however, insisted I drink the coke quickly so he could leave the bottle at the store. Daddy never liked coke bottles rolling around in our car's floorboard. Do you know how difficult it is to drink a cold coke from a bottle, in a hurry, When You're Six Years Old!?

This activity took place between Sunday morning church and Sunday night church because on Sunday afternoon we were on our way to or from, one of our relatives homes, because that's what you did on Sunday afternoons in those days.

I Grew Up In Childersburg

Linda Justice Simpson, *CHS Class of 1962*

I grew up in Childersburg. Lifelong friendships were formed and I could not have had a better foundation for my life. I did not realize it at the time I had an ideal childhood, by today's standards some might say ... boring.

Malcolm Bates CHS Class of 1983

Coosa Court, Bowen Drive, Desoto Court, Lakeside Drive, and Minor Terrace were all places we hung out and lived. They were great neighborhoods in those days and I met lifelong friends there.

The Hodges Meteor Strike

Mike Headley, CHS Class of 1962

November 30, 1954 at 1:46 p.m. a meteor weighing 8.5 pounds came through the roof of Ann Elizabeth Hodges home. The meteor first struck a radio then hit Mrs. Hodge's in the side. Legal problems between the home owner and the Hodges (renters) were so great that Mrs. Hodges mental and physical health suffered. She and her husband divorced, and she died of kidney failure in 1972. The home was located seven miles south of Childersburg in the Oak Grove community.

Bicycles

Mickey Donahoo, *CHS Class of 1961*

Today, bicycles are taken for granted by most kids—I mean brand-new ones with all the bells and whistles. This was not always the case in the '1950s. I don't remember a kid that had a new bike; however, there must have been some because there were bike parts to be bought and sold by this ten year old.

I would look for "used bike" parts and pick them up through swaps or trades. I had usually spent all of my cash at the Coosa Theater on the Saturday movies (especially if you were fortunate enough to sit with a girl who always needed" a coke and popcorn so cash for bike parts was hard to come by.

You would sometimes trade for a part you really didn't need because you knew some boy that needed that part. If you were lucky, he would also have the part you needed. Over time bike parts were obtained and you could eventually assemble the bike you wanted. Later, you could trade for other parts to upgrade your ride.

This system of barter would later in life serve us well us as it made mechanics out of many boys. When we got old enough to drive at 14 years old, I would found myself employing the same strategy to get car parts to fix my car or make it run a little faster.

Today I drive down the streets and marvel at what people leave on the curb for the garbage pick-up. It may be a bike with an "unfixable" bent rim or maybe a perfectly good bike that someone had out grown. These finds would have been a gold mine back in our younger days.

As my wife and I travel parts of the world, especially Africa, I am taken back to my youth as I see young men riding bikes obviously build from parts as we had done. In Africa, Mexico and other countries with so much poverty, these few "bike" owners are looked upon with envy by the ones who must walk. In America we are truly blessed.

A Trip to a Watermelon Patch

Mickey Donahoo, *CHS Class of 1961*

If there was a group of teenagers at the Dairy Queen, or Tastee Freeze who were looking for a little excitement, and the time of year were right, a group would hop into the back of a pickup truck and head off in the dark of night to a watermelon patch for a raid.

The crew would take only enough melons to eat and share. The rest of the patch went unmolested. However, if the owner was warned a shotgun blast could be heard in the black of night, and almost anything could happen. At least once a raid resulted in a meeting of parents and their sons at the police station.

A Different Time

Mike Headley, *CHS Class of 1962*

Most children today have no idea how much fun we had without spending lots of money. Mainly because our parents did not have much money after the bills were paid. We still had a wonderful time just being children.

1953 Prices

House: $17,500
Gas: 29¢ per gallon
Bread: 16¢ per loaf
Gallon of Milk: 94¢
US Postage Stamp: 3¢

Girl Scouts, 1953

1953 Cooky Mints (see the box, that's how they were spelled!)

Cub Scouts, 1953

The first Cub Scout Pine Wood Derby was held in Manhattan, CA in 1953

Do You Remember These?

Mike Headley, *CHS Class of 1962*

Read each statement, then close your eyes and remember a simpler time. A time when people knew their neighbor, attended church, and believed in America.

Cooties
I double-dog dare you
Eeny, meeny, miny, moe
Hide and Seek
You're it!!
Red Rover, Red Rover, send someone right over!
Take one giant step, May I
Simon Says
The Monkey Bars near Coosa Court
Dodge Ball, Hop Scotch, and Jump Rope

Hot Potato
Kick Ball
Marbles
Pickup Sticks,
JAX's
Lincoln Logs
Chinese checkers
Hula Hoops
Metal Roller Skates with leather straps, and a key
Porky Pig cartoons
Foghorn Leghorn cartoons
Bugs Bunny cartoons
The Road Runner cartoons
Donald Duck cartoons
Mickey Mouse cartoons
The Cisco Kid
Hop along Cassidy
The Lone Ranger, on the radio (before he was on TV)
Roy Rogers and Dale Evans
The Mickey Mouse Club (TV)
Howdy Doody, Buffalo Bob, and Clarabelle the Clown
Cousin Cliff Holman
The Popeye Club WAPI-TV (Birmingham)
Circle Six Ranch with Benny Carle (WBRC-TV
     Birmingham)
Joe Rumore WVOK 50,000 Watts Radio (Birmingham)
Shower of Stars Shows, Birmingham Auditorium
Sky King (TV)
Flash Gordon
The Little Rascals
The Adventures of Rin-Tin-Tin
Gilligan's Island
Cereal boxes with prizes
Captain Midnight secret decoder ring
Jack in the Box prizes, real prizes, unlike the paper ones
     today
Attaching wooden clothespins to your bike making a noise as
     you rode down the street
Hearing crickets

Running through the sprinkler in the summer
Drinking from a garden hose
Wallowing in the sheets in August because your family had
    no A/C
Waiting for an hour after eating before going swimming
Laying on your back trying to pick out shapes in the clouds
Spinning around until you're too dizzy to stand up
Catching Lightnin' Bugs at night in a Mason jar
Riding on your friend's bicycle handlebars (with no helmet)
Being picked last for a team ☹
The Twist
Elvis Presley's hit song "Heartbreak Hotel"
45rpm records
Your first kiss
New shoes for the first day of school
Coonskin Caps
Letter Sweaters
Poodle Skirts
Black chalk boards and being sent outside to beat the erasers
Wooden school desk that weighed 60 pounds
Your mother was home when you came in from school
A double-pop icicle, which you shared half with a friend
"Toddy", a chocolate drink only sold at the Comet Drive-In
Kool Aid was the drink of summer
Candy Corn at Halloween
Wax false teeth
Bubble gum with a cartoon on the wrapper
Pink Bubble Gum Cigars
Candy cigarettes
Pouring peanuts in your RC Cola or Dr. Pepper
Buffalo Rock Ginger Ale (still make in Birmingham,
    Alabama)
5¢ Cokes in a pale green glass bottle (8 oz.)
Tom's peanuts and candy
Black Jack Chewing gum (licorice)
Chef Boyardee Pizza (in a box)
TV dinners in aluminum foil trays
Burma Shave signs 1923 - 1965, See Rock City
Your mother was the most beautiful woman you knew

Being tucked in bed with bed time kisses, and prayers
Clothes lines and clothes pins in the bag that slid along the
    line
Green Stamps
Sputnik
Free road maps at the gas stations
Riding in a car with no seat belts or child seats
Car Hops and Curb Service
President John Kennedy's assassination
George Wallace was Governor of Alabama
Alaska and Hawaii became the 49th and 50th states
Elevators had people operators
The Fuller Brush Man
Brylcreem
"Ding-Dong, Avon Calling"
Blue Flash Blubs
Metal Ice Trays (with levelers)
Timmy and Lassie
Aluminum Christmas Trees
Penny candy
Erector Sets
Tinker Toys
View Master (viewers)

Minor Terrace

Dlaine Pogue, CHS Class of 1984

I grew up in Minor Terrace. I lived there the first 20 years of my life and I have the best memories from that neighborhood. I had so much fun you just wouldn't believe it. Do you remember walking thru the trails and riding your bike at "clay banks"? I sure wish I could go back to that time in my life.

PRESIDENT · · · · · · · · · · · · · · · MICKEY DONAHOO
VICE PRESIDENT · · · · · · · · · · · · ·MARVIN SHAW
SECRETARY · · · · · · · · · · · · · · HILDA BUMGARNER
TREASURER · · · · · · · · · · · · · · · J. D. WARREN
REPORTER · · · · · · · · · · · · · · · CARRIE BUTTS

SENIORS

WAYLAND ADAMS
CARY ALLEN
JAMES AMOS
LEON ARMBRESTER
GAIL ARMSTRONG
MARY BARNETT
BOBBY BELL
ERNEST BOARTFIELD
JERRY BRANNON
BARBARA BROOKINS
TOMMY BROWN
HILDA BUMGARNER
YVONNE BURDETTE
ROBERT BURDICK
BOBBIE BURNHAM
RONNIE BUSBY
CARRIE BUTTS
JOE BUTTS
EUGENE CARVER
JIMMY CHAMBLESS
JIMMY CLECKLER
SANDRA COSPER
PAUL DILLARD
MICKEY DONAHOO
BRENDA DUDNEY
REBECCA EDWARDS
SUE ELLISON
GLENDEAN FIELDS
KAY FISHER
GARY FRANKS
WILLIAM FREAR
JERRILYN GARRIGUS
BETTY GIDDENS
JANICE GIDDENS
GEORGE GILBERT
BARBARA GREEN
TOMMY GREEN
DONNIE GRIFFITT
JEROME HALL
BITSY HARDIN
SANDRA HARRELL
THURSTON HARRIS
CAROL SUE HAY
CARSON HEATH

DICK JACOBSON
ERNEST JOBE
BETTY JOHNSON
JIMMY KING
MARY LOUISE LAIRD
JIMMY LAKE
EARL LANCASTER
CAROLYN LIPSEY
MARTHA LITTLETON
DON MADDOX
DONALD MALONE
PAT MEYERS
BETTY MIMS
BILL MCSWEEN
JERRY NIX
FERRELL NOWLAND
SANDRA NORRELL
GAIL OVERTON
JOE PARKER
MARY ALICE PARSONS
LARON PENNINGTON
JOYCE PRICE
PATRICIA RAY
MARTHA RESTER
RAY REEVES
FRANKLIN RIDLEY
CAROLYN RILEY
FRANCIS ROWLAND
JERRY SANDERS
LINDA RUDDY
JO ANN SEAY
MARVIN SHAW
GAYLE SIMPSON
JACKIE SIMPSON
EUGENE SKELTON
MARGRETTE STANLEY
PHILLIP STEPHENS
ROBERT TERRILL
JACK WALLACE
J. D. WARREN
BRENDA WHEELER
REBECCA WHITTEN
CONNIE WILSON
ADRIAN YOUNG

SENIOR SPONSORS

MR. DONALD WILLIAMS

MRS. MARY LAIRD

MRS. MARVENA HAMMONDS

CHS Class of 1961

Childersburg's Home Town paper in the 1950s and 1960s

THE CHILDERSBURG NEWS

"Your Own Home Newspaper"
Published Weekly

E. E. ROZELLE
Editor and Publisher

Phone DR 8-6206

Chapter 9

Stories: Two

A Duel in Forest Hills

Bubba Cleckler, *ISHS Class of 1958*

It was a lazy summer night in 1957. Our group was hanging out at the Recreation Center for the weekly Friday night dance. We were sort of shy with the girls but we enjoyed listening to the music and dreaming. The group consisted of Eston Lovingood, Hugh Frank Riddle, Pat Hardin and me, plus a couple of other want-to-be duck hunters.

A heated discussion broke out between some of the group as to how far the pellets in our shotgun shells would travel. Estimates ranged from 50 to 80 yards. I, of course, was a proponent of the 80 yard faction even though I knew it was impossible.

The discussion raged on until someone suggested we run a test to determine who was correct. But what sort of test? Discussion on the subject was slow to develop until one in the group suggested a shootout. There was a long silence. Gradually we began discussing the possibility and finally decided that Eston and Hugh Frank would be the shooters and the rest of us would add support — sort of.

We divided into two groups and each went home to get their shotguns and shells. To the guns and shells they added all the heavy clothes they could find. We met on Forest Hill Drive separating the two shooters by approximately 60 yards. The "seconds" moved the two cars behind the shooters to silhouette them in the headlights. The seconds were safely hiding in the vehicles while the shooters were on their own.

At the sound of a car horn both shooters fired three shells and jumped in the back of the cars. Off we went in case someone reported the shots to the police.

After the shotguns and extra clothing were safely back home we met back at the Recreation Center. Eston, who of course was unhurt, decided to put Band-Aids all over his face and hands so that everyone would think he was hurt bad.

When we entered the Rec center, Hugh Frank though he had actually seriously hurt Eston, we kept telling everyone (who would listen) how badly Eston had bled and what terrible pain he was in.

It was not long until we could no longer maintain our straight faces and began to laugh. Hugh Frank was a little mad at being tricked but got over it quickly. We laughed about the "DUEL in Forest Hills."

My Years in Childersburg

J. D. Warren, *CHS Class of 1961*

I grew up in Childersburg. My parents, along with me and my new-born sister, moved there from Alex City, Alabama in 1948. I started to Childersburg School in the fall of 1949. There was only one school then — all grades on the same campus

At the time we came, my father worked as a shipping clerk at the Central of Georgia depot. But the construction for Coosa River Newsprint and Beaunit Mills Rayon plant were nearing completion. My dad soon started to work at Beaunit Mills as a shipping clerk, and eventually became part of management.

I love Childersburg, though I never returned for visits as frequently as my mother would have liked, and even less often now. I guess my feelings for Childersburg boils down to high school being a happy and carefree time. I have happy memories of my school years in Childersburg.

Rope Twirling at the CHS Auditorium

Patsy Cobb Willis Jones, *CHS Class of 1971*

Mrs. Campbell's 1962 dance class

Left to right Ferron Mayfield, Pam Cobb, Patsy Cobb, Jane Elliott, Myrtle Milliner, Marion Perkins, Pattie Whitlock, Susan Vincent, & Donnie Milliner

Our First TV: a 14" Dumont

Mike Headley, *CHS Class of 1962*

On a winter Friday evening in 1955 Daddy came home from working in Birmingham with a new TV. He would share a ride with some other guys in the area, and in the back of that 1954 Ford with the trunk lid up came our very first television.

A Dumont T.V. with a mahogany cabinet displaying a 14" screen, and two large knobs on the front almost as big as a teacup.

It was not the first time I had seen a television. That event had taken place two years earlier. Our family went to the home of some friends to watch a very snowy 10"screen. All I can remember was I saw a train and lots of snow. The reception was not that good even though the family lived at the base of Merkle Mountain.

If we were going to watch the TV stations in Birmingham we were going to need to get the antenna on the roof. The commotion took place on the following somewhat cool and definitely windy Saturday morning. With mother in front of the TV in the den shouting "yes —no ", me in the yard as the relay messenger and daddy on the roof we started.

Daddy proceeded to twist and turn that TV antenna towards the two stations on Red Mountain located on the south side of Birmingham amid a fair amount of miscommunication. The stations we were attempting to reach were channel 6 WBRC and channel 13 WAPI. After a good bit of shouting, hand waving, and general mayhem we managed to have one of the stations appear on that 14" Dumont TV screen.

It was not long until I was watching *Flash Gordon, Hop along Cassidy*, and *Howdy Doody* with Buffalo Bob. I had heard *The Lone Ranger* on the radio for several years in the afternoons when I came home from school, now I could SEE the Lone Ranger and Tonto in real life on the TV. Life was good.

Good Friends — and Fried Squirrel

Bettye Headley Donahoo, *CHS Class of 1954*

On occasion Kathleen Golden, one of my two best friends (the other being Polly Holiday) would spend the night with my family. I remember Kathleen asking me one time if we had fried squirrel every night for dinner. We didn't, of course, but must have had it often, because at that time she had never had anything else to eat for dinner at our house. Mother's fried squirrel and gravy was quite tasty, as well as fried rabbit and gravy which showed up at our table on a regular basis. Daddy hunted and fished a good bit thus supplemented our diet with food from the woods and the Coosa River.

Fund-Raising Projects

J. D. Warren, *CHS Class of 1961*

Most of us needed funds so that we could go on the senior trip. The whole class had a project taking orders for the sale of brooms and mops. I'm sure a lot of people got tired of seniors knocking on their door peddling brooms and mops. I remember going to Harpersville to sell. People would be supportive when you told them the reason you were selling, but would back out of their purchase if they found you were from Childersburg rather than a local kid.

Many of us had other fund raising projects. I took orders for greeting cards from my neighbors. Several of us also took orders for a dozen fresh Krispy Kreme donuts, delivered fresh and hot on Saturday morning to the customers' door. We would go early in the morning to the bakery in Sylacauga to get our orders at wholesale prices then deliver as promised.

Many of the class of 1961 participated in what was called a rummage sale. We were allowed to set up in a vacant building on 1st Street downtown Childersburg. If you wanted to participate you brought clothes, dishes, etc. You also had to work your shifts in the rummage store. We put people's names on the price tickets to divvy up the sales. The sale went on every weekend for weeks. Business wasn't that great, but it was fun to hang out all day with friends and classmates.

A Memorial plate sold by CHS
students for a 1953 fund raising event.

Burning the Trash

Mike Headley, *CHS Class of 1962*

When I was the ripe old age of nine years I was sent by my
mother to do what was known in the 1950s as "burning the
trash." Because we had no trash pickup it was my job to carry
the trash from the house about 100 feet behind our home and
burn it every three days. About once each month I would
take a wheel borrow and load the leftover ashes for a trip of
200 yards over the hill from our house to a small ravine where
we had a trash dump.

I don't remember checking either the direction or the speed
of the wind prior to lighting the trash on fire. After the fire
had swept across several acers of Barely Do, I was able to

determine the wind was blowing at least 20 miles per hour, and out of the South East.

Mother called the Forest Service, who by that time had seen the fire from the fire tower at Flag Pole Mountain. The forest service arrived quickly, which was good because the fire had started to leave Barely Do burning in a northwest direction across Mr. Green's land and fences. It was amazing just how quickly a pine fence post will burn in August. Despite the best efforts of mother, grandmother (all 5'0" of her), granddaddy, plus me, we were losing the battle.

When the Fire Service arrived they quickly started to cross Barely Do with a tractor pulling a rather unique plow. That plow would cut a shallow trench throwing the dirt to the sides. It looked as though things were starting to finally improve, when I noticed another Fire Service guy following the guy on the tractor. Well great, while we were trying to put the fire out, this nut had a little burner thing, and HE WAS LIGHTING MORE FIRES! Not knowing at ten years old what a back fire was, I was very upset.

Long story short, let's just say daddy did not have much of a fruit crop that year, or any other year after that. I suppose it turned out ok because I was not all that fond of picking fruit anyway. The fire did not burn that many trees on Mr. Green's land. As for Mr. Green's fences, daddy paid to have them repaired. The ones burned by my trash-burning fire, plus the ones knocked down by the Forest Service tractor. So you see "all's well that ends well."

Playing Marbles

Mickey Donahoo, *CHS Class of 1961*

When the spring weather turned fine, especially after school was out, there was no better place for a young boy to live than Childersburg. In the early 1950s there was TV in very

123

few homes so we boys had to create our own schedule for the day. For a lot of us, we would head for the local movie house long before the first picture was to begin.

First, we would look under the bed where we kept our marbles in a tin cheese container. We would gather up a sack of marbles that we could afford to lose if things didn't go well. Of course, we would take along our favorite "taw" because we could shoot it well and it would bring us luck. Usually, our favorite marble was a cat's eye while some would use a steel ball or a log roller. We usually steered clear of the guys who shot those.

Usually any empty dirt lot would do if the ground weren't rutted from recent rains. The movie house had a large dirt parking lot and you could usually find a smooth place to draw a circle. First, we would challenge a couple of guys to shoot marbles and settle on the rules. Then we would draw a line in the dirt and lag to see which shooter got the first shot. Now it was time to line all the marbles in the center of the circle and the shooting would begin.

As long as you knocked a marble out of the circle and your toy stayed in, you could keep shooting. You had to beware of some of the finer points such as "roundance", "slippance", ventures and other techniques you might need as the game progressed.

We would shoot marbles for hours and when we finished and it was time to go we would bag up our marbles, if we had any left, and head home, to see a movie, or over to a friend's house to play. After all it was summer. What a fun time to be a kid in Childersburg.

A Lateral Pass, a Forward Purse, and a Dentist Visit

Mike Headley, *CHS Class of 1962*

This story started on a Friday morning in the fall of 1954. My cousin, Dr. Jones, had just hung out his shingle announcing to the good people near Five Point's south in Birmingham of his services as a dentist when the following incident occurred.

Mrs. McCaffry's fifth grade class was on the playground on the west side of the school near the principal's office along with several other classes. This was in the days before they installed a loop drive in front of the school. I am not sure how I came to be in the middle of a game of Keep-Away, but there I was. The game had started without me, however; it came my way because games of Keep-Away tend to move all over the playground in a hurry.

By then fifth grade girls began to carry purses and were very proud of that step in becoming ladies. However, boys, being of a prepubescent nature at the age of ten, do not have a clue or for that matter no more than three brain cells working at the same time, so we did not see the importance that fifth grade girls had placed on their new found accessory. A group of boys had purloined a girl's black folding purse and were having a grand time playing Keep-Away with it

The game of Keep-Away is accompanied by a great amount of screaming and squealing on the girl's part and a good bit of shouting by boys. All of this is accompanied by a great deal of running around the playground by both sexes while the teacher's sort of half watched.

I cannot tell you which girl's purse someone had taken. However, I remember it was a fold over black patent leather model with a snap. The game had been going on for at least a minute when I became involved.

A boy shouted to me, then gave me a lateral purse pass. Not being the athletic type I did my best. I looked to my left to see a boy going long for a reception. I let fling with that black clutch on a long pass, which was caught by the receiver, I was so proud! Having completed the pass, thus avoiding the thundering herd of fifth grade females which were quickly approaching I was rather happy with myself.

At this point things got interesting. While I had made a quality pass, my game of Keep-Away had just gotten a little more serious. While I threw the purse with my right hand my body turned a bit to the left. At that point I recovered by turning back to my right with a slight grin on my face.

At that point I caught a rock square in the mouth which broke my left front tooth in half and gave me a fat lip; however, there was not too much blood. The fifth grader who threw the rock was Childersburg's one and only Terry Kay (Penton) Cleckler, CHS Class of 1962. Terry Kay apologized as I walked to the principal's office holding half of my front tooth in my right hand. Mother was called; thank goodness we had just received our new party line house phone, which had recently been installed in our home on Highway 280 four miles south of Childersburg.

I do not remember how I got home early that day (normally I rode Mr. Greens bus #21 — second load). We only had one car in those days, and daddy used it to get to work so mother could not come to the school to pick me up so Mrs. McCaffry must have carried me home.

Just a side note: in 1955 running on the playground was allowed, and considered wholesome, even encouraged by the staff so that when you returned to the class room you would be less likely to be disruptive, well for boys anyway. So, we all went back to our class rooms after recess stinking like a herd of wet goats. There was no air conditioning in our school in 1955 so we all stank. The olfactory nerves got a work out in those days.

126

I went to see my cousin, the dentist in Birmingham, on Saturday morning. My family did not sue the Talladega County school board, the principal or the Pentons. That was not the way things were handled in those days. My father paid all my dental expenses until I married in 1965. Through the years I have had several crowns on my left front tooth — all because of a game of Keep-Away in 1955.

Hunting and Fishing

Mickey Donahoo, *CHS Class of 1961*

Hunting and fishing were activities available to young boys that knew where to go. Some places were common knowledge to be avoided but other than those few, the creeks, ponds, rivers, fields and forests were wide open.

If you had an after school trip planned, it was not unusual for the student to bring his gun or fishing equipment to school in his vehicle — try that today. If it were a weekend excursion, you could start out in the morning and hunt the fields and woods all day without little mind to fences or boundaries. We would often start out rabbit hunting in the morning with a couple of guys and maybe one "rabbit" dog. As we made our day long circuit, we would "gather" up more guys and dogs until we had a formidable group by day's end. A few bad acts by some guys, such as gates left open where cattle got out, or damage to someone's fence plus the concern for landowner liability brought our time of free roaming to an end. It was good while it lasted.

Coke Bottles for Cash

June Melton Lassiter, *CHS Class of 1967*

Does anybody remember returning Coke bottles for cash? We were the first recycle generation.

James Morris, *CHS Class of 1967*

Mother would give me a dime to do some chores around the house. Back in late 50s early 60s about half the good people of Childersburg kept their soda bottles on the back porch. I had a path from the back of Grove Park through all the back yards over and under all the fences then across the branch to the old country store on the eastside of Mr. Bunns Texaco station on Highway 280.

Redeeming the 3¢ deposit per bottle would add up quickly. I would then take my new found wealth over to the Dairy Queen. If it was Saturday I might walk on downtown to the Coosa Theater to see a movie. That is if I could make it past Emory's Five and Dime store.

Randall Fields, *CHS Class of 1967*

When I was ten I would walk to town picking up coke bottles on the side of the road. My route to town took me between the two Childersburg cemeteries. By the time I got downtown I had enough money to buy something cheap, maybe a comic book. It was a tough way for a kid to make a living because some of those bottles were covered with fire ants.

Robbie Riddle, *CHS Class of 1975*

I traded my coke bottles in at Moody Brothers grocery for three cents each. I kept Forrest Hills bottle-free for years. The large basket attached to my bike which I used on my paper route came in handy to collect those coke bottles.

Joe Peerson, CHS Class of 1968

I bought lots of Mars Bars with that bottle deposit money.

Sand-lot Sports

Mickey Donahoo, CHS Class of 1961

There wasn't much sand around Childersburg but there was plenty of red dirt to play our games. There were often touch (two hands anywhere except when the occasional girl played) football games in a vacant lot especially during the football season when our beloved Tigers played.

Little attention was paid to whether the "field" was dry or muddy—game on! We had a playbook with one play in it—all of you go long except you and you will stay and block. This was our precursor to one day being a Tiger and playing for Coaches Cox, Shell, Dean, or Ingram. Then we had Coach Billingsly fondly known as "The Butcher "with occasional help from Bobby Overton, and Bill Kallenback.

In the summer out came the baseball, gloves (if you had one) plus bats. Sometimes we would choose sides and play a "real game" but most of the time we did not have enough players for two teams. So we would play "flies and skinners" or "shove-up." These were not team efforts but still honed our skills to one day be a baseball Tiger.

Other non-school sports activities would include basketball and speedball. Speedball was especially interesting as it combined football and soccer into one sport. As may well be expected, the list of things you couldn't do to each other was much shorter than the list of can-dos. As I watched a Rugby game in South Africa a while back it brought back happy recollections of speed-ball.

Also, included in sand-lot sports would be several variations of marble games along with "mumble-peg." Mumble-Peg was a favorite game at recess. Just try to bring a knife to school today.

The game was a type of follow-the-leader in that the first player would perform some feat with his pocket knife that ended with it stuck in the ground. The next participant must perform the same feat with his knife, also stuck in the ground or else, he was out of the game. Innovation and practice were the keys.

The pocket knife could be used to play splits. This consisted of two players facing each other about 4 feet apart. One would throw his knife just outside his opponent's foot but missing the foot by less than six inches. If the knife stuck in the ground then the guy's foot was moved out to touch the knife. Each took turns until one could "split" no farther, or until the knife stuck in the other's guy's foot. If this happened the "sticker" lost to the "stick-ee."

Good Friends

Bettye Headley Donahoo, CHS Class of 1954

On occasion Kathleen Golden one of my two best friends, the other being Polly Holiday, would spend the night with my family. I remember Kathleen asking me one time if we had fried squirrel every night for dinner. We didn't, of course, but must have had it often, because at that time she had never had anything else to eat for dinner at our house. Mother's fried squirrel and gravy was quite tasty, as well as fried rabbit and gravy which showed up at our table on a regular basis. Daddy hunted and fished a good bit thus supplemented our diet with food from the woods and the Coosa river.

Chapter 10

Childersburg Holidays

Christmas Parade 1961

Santa must have worked at the Western Auto

Dianne Hillman Prisoc, CHS Class of 1972

My family went to the Western Auto store often because the Millers lived right across the street from us and daddy bought almost everything we needed from Mr. Miller. I realize now when I was a little girl that Santa stopped there to get my toys.

Was Santa at Osborne's Market?

Joy Burton Lawson, CHS Class of 1972

I remember daddy, mommy, and all five of us kids going to the A & P Grocery one Christmas Eve running into Milton and Nina Mattox with their boys. We were so excited because Santa was coming that night. Daddy would go to Osborne's Curb Market every Christmas buying fruit, nuts and candy. When we got up Christmas morning in our stockings we found, you guessed it, the fruit, nuts and candy from Osborne's market. All of us kids swore that Santa brought it.

Christmas 1955: A Fairway Flyer

Mike Headley, *CHS Class of 1962*

I stopped every time I passed by the window of the Western Auto on 8th Avenue from Thanksgiving until Christmas, 1955. The window of the Western Auto was decorated with Christmas lights by Mrs. Miller. In the window was a beautiful Western Auto "Fairway Flyer" bicycle with a black frame and chrome fenders and handle bars with white grips. A chrome headlight powered by a generator attached to the rear wheel, hand brakes (on the handle bars) for both front and rear brakes and a chrome air pump if I ever needed to pump up a tire. This was the first time I had ever seen a bicycle with 3 speeds. It had those skinny tires (very British). All my friends had bikes but nothing like this.

Most bikes in those days had heavy frames with a regular foot brake. I begged my parents to get this bike for me for Christmas. It must have worked because on Christmas morning there it was between the fire place and the Christmas tree. I thought I was the coolest kid on the planet.

The problem this eleven-year-old suffered from in the months of early 1956 was that I had seen my future Christmas bike thru a pair of very rose-colored glasses. That Western Auto" Fairway Flyer" was great on paved streets (and fast). However, I lived in the country with the only paved road being US Highway 280/231 which was not safe to ride a bike on because the road was very narrow at that time not to mention the speed of the cars.

My friends were riding those old heavy fat tire relics, not me. I was riding on the latest English styled three-speed, narrow-tired racer. Most of my travels were on dirt/gravel roads where the dust would fly when a car passed spewing dust — and the components of an English-styled racer which I had been so proud of Christmas morning was not compatible. The dust ground into the working parts and maintenance became a problem. When you are 11 years old, it's hard to see the future, especially when Christmas is on the way.

A Christmas Gift Prank

Roscoe Limbaugh, *CHS Class of 1953*

All was not hard work and serious business with the Limbaugh brothers or the other merchants in Childersburg. Good-natured pranks and sometimes a little mischief were practiced. The Limbaugh brothers took great delight in pulling pranks on each other. James and Robert were both married and had children at the time. George was very much the debonair single man with a quick eye for a pretty girl. He had as the object of his affection one of the loveliest ladies in Childersburg. It was the Christmas season, and George had carefully selected a very expensive Bulova watch to give her as a present. He had it wrapped beautifully and hid it at the store until the big day to give it to her arrived.

Robert and James saw an opportunity to embarrass George and took it. They purchased a child's inexpensive Mickey Mouse watch, wrapped to exactly match George's gift, and waited to see the results. As George presented his gift, he was greatly chagrined and embarrassed as she opened the box and pulled out the Mickey Mouse watch. George had much explaining to do. After having their fun, James and Robert did confess what they had done.

How could a town with merchants with such names as Chuggy Moody, Britches Miller, and Sonny Salloway behave seriously all the time? The fun and pranks continued.

Cracker Balls in the Hall at CHS

Danny Wiginton, *CHS Class of 1965*

I was never one to get in trouble in school, but I had a streak of mischievousness in me from time to time. It was the last day of school before Christmas break 1964 and I thought 'why not stir things up a bit?'. We had just changed principals from James Williams to J.L. Kelley, who was a strict disciplinarian and who ruled with an iron hand.

I brought about 40 cracker balls which explode with a loud pop when stepped on. I gave Max Cantrell half of the balls and both of us started dropping them in the hallways during a break between classes. When the first 1 or 2 balls exploded, our fellow students started looking for the balls on the floor to step on.

Max and I met in the center of the hallway and watched the fireworks. Teachers got angry, bringing paddles to the doorways of their class rooms. They really did not know what to do except threaten students not to step on any more balls. Finally all the cracker balls had been stepped on and order was again restored. During the next class, Mr. Kelley instructed all the trouble makers "come to his office." To this day, no one knew who was responsible — until now.

Christmas 1971

Earl Wesson Jr., *CHS Class of 1972*

Christmas was always a special time downtown Childersburg when I was growing up. I loved the Western Auto Mr. Miller owned next to Red Hare's pool hall. Then there was Smith Sundries, plus two5&10 stores, Cohens, C&H store, Limbaugh and Cliett Hardware stores. Plus Mr. Millard Lawrence's Office Supply where we got our pencils, paper, tablets and fountain pens. So many sights and sounds to remember. "Merry Christmas Childersburg, Merry Christmas."

Dewey Lockhart
Childersburg's Santa Clause

Santa Clause

Earl Wesson, Jr., *CHS Class of 1972*

Santa WAS Dewey Lockhart and Mr. Lockhart WAS Santa! Dewey could always be found walking the downtown sidewalks most weekends and was always at Mrs. Hosey's Flower Shop for pictures after the Christmas Parade.

I worked at A&P grocery from 1970 through 1974 and remember Dewey Lockhart was Santa Clause walking the streets and sidewalks of Childersburg during Christmas, dressed as the jolly old elf himself. Dewey would stop at the A&P; buy a coke, rest a little before resuming his appointed rounds of all the stores in Childersburg, visiting with all the children he could meet as Santa Clause.

When Dewey passed away, I was moved to write a letter to the editor of the local paper and they published it. I can't remember all of what I said but I recalled one Christmas when Dewy was really sick and he should have been at home in bed. Someone questioned why he didn't go home? But Dewey asked "what would the children do?" They expected Santa Clause to be there and Dewey Lockhart wasn't about to let them down. Dewey always walked the streets and had a photo shoot at Hosey's Flower Shop every Christmas. Christmas just never seemed the same after Santa (Dewey Lockhart) passed away.

A Christmas Play

Marilyn Brown Lawson, *CHS Class of 1970*

Do you remember being in a Christmas plays in elementary school that depicted the nativity? The one that sticks in my mind was the year that we had girls dressed as angels, we had a girl dressed as Mary, and me ... well I was a SHEEP. I had to wear some kind of a white getup and crawl around the manger. Not one of my most proud moments. The entire time I was thinking, why was I not chosen as an angel?

Cohen's Department Store, Christmas 1970

Brenda Solley Brown, *CHS Class of 1960*
Marilyn Brown Lawson, *CHS Class of 1970*

When I, Marilyn, was a teenager, my brother's wife, Brenda Solley Brown was able to get us both jobs working at Cohen's Department Store during the holiday season. Brenda had worked at Cohen's previously, as well as Winn Dixie prior to marrying my brother. The idea of earning any kind of money was very appealing to me, because my father had a massive stroke prior to my junior year and was disabled. I jumped at the chance to earn a paycheck.

Neither of us had transportation to work, but my mother came to the rescue by offering up her VW Bug for us to use. Brenda recalled when she worked at Cohen's previously; Mr. Crowley would leave to take the daily deposit to the First National Bank, walking through downtown Childersburg flanked on both sides by a couple of salesladies for protection

We worked from 8:00 a.m. to 6:00 p.m. with an hour for lunch. Since we were sharing a car, we took lunch breaks at the same time and running over to the Dairy Queen to get their daily special. In those days, we did not wear slacks to work or school - you wore dresses. This was the style in those days. Being the holiday season, I started out as a gift wrapper (it was a courtesy offered if you shopped at Cohen's). There was a gift wrapping window in the back, and that is where customers took their merchandise to be wrapped for Christmas.

On my first day, at work Mr. Crowley demonstrated exactly how to roll off just the right amount of gift paper (no waste allowed) and we were to use ONLY three pieces of tape per package. I can honestly say that particular Christmas I knew exactly what just about every woman in Childersburg and surrounding areas was getting as a gift; because not only did I wrap it - I tried it on to see if it would fit.

Men would stop by the store on their way home from working the midnight shift at Beaunit Mills, Kimberly Clark paper mill, and Avondale Mills, to do their Christmas shopping on the way home. They would look around for a saleslady approximately the same size as their wife, say "about her size" and we would try on garments to make sure they were the right fit. It being a small town, oftentimes the salesladies knew right off the bat what size the women being shopped for wore, because we knew most of the women in the area.

At night when I got off work, sometimes I couldn't feel my feet from standing on them all day, and I made $8.00 a day before taxes. On the last day of my temporary job, Christmas Eve, Mr. Crowley called us all to the front of the store one by one and told us how much he appreciated us working that holiday season, and told us to pick out a pair of hose from the display for a Christmas gift. I remember thinking that sure was a nice gesture on his part for a Christmas present.

I will never forget my first job and the excitement of working that holiday season and earning some much needed money. I remember a few years later when Cohen's went the way of most small town stores - they closed. I, along with my two small children, went to their "going out of business sale" and I remember the wave of nostalgia that I felt that day - and I still do to this day. If I am driving through Childersburg with one of my grandchildren, I point out Cohen's Department Store and tell them that Maw-Maw once worked at Cohen's for $8.00 a day.

An Easter egg Hunt at the Russell's Farm 1949

Mike Headley, *CHS Class of 1962*

The Russell's farm was located on 40 acres of land about one mile south of Center Hill Methodist Church, right off the south side of the old Sylacauga Highway, Talladega County road 45. Because we did not own an automobile at that time my family, daddy, mother, Bettye, Sandra, and myself, walked the 1½ miles to the Russell farm from our house on Highway US 280.

Mr. and Mrs. Russell, from the late 1940s until I got too old to hunt Easter eggs sometime around 1956, had a big Easter egg hunt on their farm each Easter after church services and people had eaten lunch. There was an unwritten rule at Miss. Sally Ross's Easter egg hunt. If you had gotten so big that you could easily out run the younger children, and get lots of eggs, before the little ones had an opportunity, you were too big to participate. However, the good news was that you could help your dad along with the other men hide eggs if you were a male. This meant you were no longer considered a child.

There we lots of eggs in many colors; thousands, in fact. If the usual number of people came, there would be hundreds. There were many families with grandmothers, grandfathers, mothers, fathers, brothers, sisters, aunts, uncles, and cousins; with children of all ages and sizes in attendance. Strollers were not the rage in those days so parents or older siblings actually carried small children in their arms.

Trees were budding out and flowers were in bloom on the Russell's farm. All in all a great day for an Easter egg hunt. There was ice cold lemonade for all, plus cakes and pies (after the hunt). All set on boards with saw horse tables and covered with white table clothes waving in the slight breeze. The day was full of sunshine with few clouds in the sky. The scene was one of happy people and children from the Center Hill and sounding communities enjoying the spring weather.

There was only one problem. On most of these occasions I was accompanied by my mother, father and two older sisters; Bettye would have been 12; Sandra 10. When you are 5 years old, you're at the Easter egg hunt to have a good time, right? Here I was dressed in my white knee shorts, white socks, white shirt, white shoes, and pale blue blazer. All around me

I see Miss. Sally Ross's farm with acres, and acres of land, trees, barns, tractors, and fun. I ask you — what could possibly go wrong? Well to start with Bettye and Sandra were constantly following me around to see that my whites stayed white. This was no way to run an Easter egg hunt.

Miss. Sally would give the final instruction as to the rules which we all had to follow. Like I cared, I was five. Soon the men and older boys were off to hide the eggs. I could not wait. Finally we were off; the first rule was no running. I quickly broke rule number one. I personally saw my cousin, Frank Russell, who was 3 years older than me, RUNNING. I guess it helps if your grandmother is Mrs. Sally Ross Russell plus when the hunt is on your grandmother's farm...... connections help, even when you live in the country.

Off I go with mother in hot pursuit. It was going well; I had an oversized Easter basket, that sucker must have been two feet tall. I had found about 15 eggs at this point, and then the trouble started. Mother found an egg that someone had stepped on. No flattened egg was going in my Easter basket period. Mother tried to explain that stepped on eggs would count just like a real, un-stepped-on egg. Nope, I was not interested in a smashed egg. That egg was not about to rest it's flat self on that purple fake grass which mother had purchased at the Elmore's Five & Dime in Childersburg on Saturday afternoon. Besides I had a Chocolate bunny in a see thru box in the basket — no — way! A man's got to do, what a man's got to-do. Seeing I was losing this argument. I had no choice, so I manned up and started to cry.

Long story short I did not find the golden egg, nor did I win for most eggs found. I think I got some third place prize for the second most eggs found in my age group ..... Great!

After the hunt was over everyone gathered around the tables for ice cold lemonade, cake, and pie. The ladies wore their big Easter hats and new dresses, followed by their teenage daughters with their new dresses and hats but smaller, then last, the youngest girls with their new dresses, and even smaller hats.

The men and older boys always wore slacks with long sleeve white shirts rolled to above their elbows. No ties (well maybe the preacher from the Center Hill Methodist Church) but he would be the only one. After all, we lived in the country.

I attended many more Easter egg hunts at Mrs. Sally Ross and Grandpa Russell's farm. As the years went by I moved further and further from the all-seeing eyes of my mother and sisters.

I don't remember if Miss. Sally refrained from partaking of her snuff box during the Easter egg hunts or not. You see, Mrs. Sally did enjoy a good dip under her lip —"it settled the nerves." As for Grandpa Russell he never refrained from his tobacco habit on Easter, or any other holiday for that matter.

I later learned the real reason for Easter, and that made the day even better. Christ has risen. I don't hunt Easter eggs much anymore, but I will hide a few if you'll let me.

A Childersburg Labor Day

Joyce Mayfield Allen, *CHS Class of 1962*

Long ago and far away in a land called Childersburg, Labor Day was a very important holiday. That was a long time ago, and the celebrations we once enjoyed are now relegated to the forgotten culture of our youth. I remember the parades with the beauty queens perfecting their waves as they rode past on the decorated floats. There were floats representing various unions, there were clowns and there was such a spirit of joy! The happy throng continued to stay together after the parade ended; the celebration moved onward. We could follow the wafting aroma of Bar-B-Que that led us to the work in progress, a feast was being prepared.

There were no parades on this Labor Day 2015; no clowns to make the children smile. Memories are all we have of those days gone by, the days when our parents were with us and we thought it would always be that way. I really never bothered to imagine not being YOUNG!

Halloween Night 1959

Mike Headley, *CHS Class of 1962*

I have talked with people and some have pleaded ignorance, with a bit of twinkle in their eyes as to the events of that particular Halloween. That's OK, however, if you are reading this story and you know someone who graduated from CHS during the years between 1958 and 1963 you might want to ask them again. Late October in central Alabama brings many delightful experiences. Football games, the first frost which starts to make the leaves turn and hunting would have started by this time of year. Rabbit, squirrel, and turkey seasons would have been in full swing. Deer hunting was just starting to return to Alabama in the late 1950s so it was not as popular as it is today.

Halloween would mean that the CHS Home Coming football game with its parade and blue and white decorated floats along with the band, majorettes, cheerleaders, and the football players would now be a happy memory for this year.

October 31, 1959, Halloween night, was a Saturday evening not all that different from Halloweens which I had enjoyed in the past. True this happened to be the fifth Saturday evening of the month. I suppose being a Saturday evening meant that more kids were out that night. Being late October as I recall the temperature was not all that cold.

I was driving in my 1956 Chevrolet hard-top convertible with a two-tone paint job, Roman Red with Indian Ivory and twin antennas — one on each rear fender. Fender skirts covered the rear wheels and a continental kit on the rear bumper. In the late 1950's that was considered a cool car.

As I remember we communicated our intentions, by talking at school, each other's homes, over our party line phones, or the Dairy Queen or in the Tastyee-Freeze parking lot. That way we could meet and enjoy each other's company. Yea, I know it would be considered ancient by today's standards.

Not living in town, Halloween was a bit of a special experience. I mean, it's not easy Trick-or-Treating when the closest neighbor's house is a quarter-mile away.

As I remember the whole incident started innocently enough. Word got around that people were gathering in front of the Jitney Jungle Grocery store on First Street Southwest. The JJ had closed earlier so the time must have been around 10:30 PM. I was just driving by and happened to see all the kids.

The total number of kids in front of the Jitney Jungle was maybe 35 or 40 at the most. During that time, someone went to their Dad's chicken farm and brought back hundreds of eggs. Soon after that the words "free eggs" passed my teenage ears. Now I ask you ... 30 plus kids, Halloween night, 11:00 pm, with cars passing by on First Street, what could go wrong? As I remember the entire matter to my 16-year-old brain seemed to be a perfect combination of events, the stars had aligned, we were blessed.

As I remember, the first car that was egged was a car someone recognized as kids from Sylacauga. I mean, why were they in our town? Everyone knew they had no right to ride through Childersburg; it's obvious they were there to cause trouble.

Soon it mattered little what town, county, state, or nation you were from, if you were driving east down First Street in front of the Jitney Jungle in Childersburg, Alabama on Halloween Night 1959 you were a target.

As any thinking person would reason it would not be long until the good citizens of Childersburg would take exception to our juvenile behavior. It was not long before Chief Jinright arrived in his new 1960 two-door solid black Ford. During those days the Childersburg police cars did not have identification on the side, just a plain black car. But, why a two-door police car? Perhaps that's all the city of Childersburg in the fall of 1959 could afford.

Anyway, the Chief arrived alone, with his cigar jabbed firmly in his mouth. I assume during those days he was the only law enforcement officer on duty that late October evening. At this point the remaining eggs disappeared back to wherever they had come from.

The Chief, seeing the need to take charge of the situation, stepped up and inquire as to who was throwing eggs? Someone (you know who you are), gave the Chief some lip. The Chief then decided to make an arrest. Looking back, I have no idea what a person would be charged with today, perhaps lip giving?

After the Chief had hand cuffed the lip giver, he opened the driver's door of that new two-door Ford, and proceeded to place the culprit in the back seat of the police car. Due to the Chief's substantial girth he had to reposition his side arm to the right. Then one of CHS' finest sons decided this would be a most fortuitous time with which to remove the Chief's pistol. I myself never touched the pistol, however, I have talked to persons who did, but would prefer their families not be made aware of their conduct on Halloween night more than 57 years later. No one to this day is willing to admit to the offence; however, I had a conversation with a fellow who told me the person's name. A person living in the Childersburg area with the initials B. H. might be persuaded to divulge who the pistol-lifter was; after all it was a very long time ago.

144

Just as you would imagine, things could have not gotten much worse — they did! The Chief was not happy to have been relieved of his weapon. At this point the Chief was explaining in his most vociferous voice, that in no uncertain terms his pistol had better return to his possession, post haste.

No sooner had those words left the Chief's mouth when a 10 pound bag of flower was launched from the roof of the Jitney Jungle. Where it landed in the center of the Chief's new Ford police car, with a Ka-BOOM! Upon making contact with the car's roof, the bag of flower exploded with the Chief standing beside the car. The Chief's blue uniform, while still a deep blue, had become covered with a heavy coating of Martha White's finest self-rising.

At this point the Chief was becoming (how shall I say this nicely) a very "un-fun" person, considering it was Halloween. Bottom line the Chief was ruining what had been up until his arrival a fun evening. I don't remember a lot of what happened after leaving the Jitney Jungle that Halloween night. I suppose I took the loop from the Dairy Queen up to the Tastyee-Freeze and back one more time, and then headed south toward home. So much for a fun Trick-or-Treat night.

Fall Festival 1971; A. H. Watwood Elementary School

Denise Crawford Maul, *CHS Class of 1982*

Did you ever have your picture taken with DoDo Abernathy, Queen of the Witches at the A.H. Watwood Fall Festival? I fondly remember the Fall Festivals at A.H. Watwood Elementary School. The event was always held the Saturday night prior to Halloween. There were cake walks, fishing for prizes, baked goods competitions, costume contests, and oh yes, the Haunted Houses. It was always a fun family affair; back then, the parents would mostly "park" in the lunchroom and the kids could roam freely throughout the event. It was certainly one of the "social events" of the community each year!

One of my favorite memories is of Queen Witch DoDo Abernathy arriving in the lunchroom. DoDo operated the diner at the local Lynn Motel. But on Halloween, DoDo was "The Queen Witch." I recall such great secrecy surrounding her identity that we were never allowed to talk about it to her at the diner. She would pretend that she had no knowledge of this Queen Witch, which of course, increased the intrigue!

DoDo made such an impression on me; I've dressed as a witch about 90% of the Halloweens in which I've participated.

DoDo Abernathy Queen of the Witches And Denise Crawford Maul in 1971

Chapter 11

Principals and Teachers

A.H. WATWOOD ELEMENTARY

Principals

A. H. Watwood

J.D. Warren, *CHS Class of 1961*

Arnold Hobson Watwood had a much larger influence on Childersburg history than many realize. Mr. Watwood was the principal of Childersburg High School at least from 1936 until 1957. I actually have relatively few memories that are specifically about him, but from things I have learned in the past few years I have become very appreciative of his contributions to the town of Childersburg. Arnold Hobson Watwood was born on April 4, 1898 (in Tallapoosa County), and died on August 22, 1969. He married Juanita Little in 1933, in Jefferson County, Alabama. Ms. Juanita Little Watwood was born in 1904 and died in 1993. Mr. Watwood went by his middle name, Hobson, in most of the early records, including the 1910 and 1920 Alabama census.

Hobson, Juanita, and 2-year old John Watwood are listed in the Childersburg census for 1940 and may be listed prior to that date but that record is unavailable. Hobson's occupation at that time is shown as school principal.

The school at that time was known as Childersburg Consolidated School and included grades 1 — 12. An immediate impact of the war plant construction was, of course, a large increase in students. The registration (for all grades) had been just over 500 in the 1940-41 school-years. That number had increased to over 1,200 in the 1941-42 school year.

Mr. Watwood also described, for a Senate Committee early in the war, some of the changes he made to try to cope with the school's increases. The school auditorium was divided into six rooms and the regular classrooms were also divided. This was happening at the "old" Childersburg School site located at 4th Ave. S. E. This was in the buildings where most of us went to elementary school — the one that burned in 1957. The additional building which became the high school wing wasn't completed until late 1942, and relieved some of the overcrowding. Now elementary schools and an even newer high school are in other parts of Childersburg. Adding classroom space wasn't the only problem Mr. Watwood had to deal with during World War II.

In related testimony before the government committee Mr. Watwood stated that all of his teachers, except four, resigned before or soon after the beginning of the 1941-42 school year. They left because better paying jobs became available with the rapidly expanding defense plant, the "Alabama Ordnance Works". Nine additional teachers left during the school year, requiring even more efforts to find replacements. When he hired a replacement teacher, often they couldn't find housing in Childersburg. He had teachers who commuted daily from as far as Birmingham and Alexander City to teach in Childersburg.

Space, teachers, school buses, bus drivers, office staff — all were challenges for Mr. Watwood during World War Two. No wonder the man's hair was white by the time our generation came along!

I think it worthwhile to recognize that A. H. Watwood was a major community leader as well as the school principal. Mr. Watwood retired in 1957. I never experienced one, but I know from others' accounts that he could administer a pretty good paddling! And I do remember that when I was somewhat younger, I saw "Old Man Watwood" (and some dirty words) spray-painted on one of the concrete railroad overpasses.

In J. Leigh Mathis-Downs' published pictorial history of Childersburg, on page 56 there is a picture of the Childersburg School Class of 1929, showing the 13 graduates, along with a "Mr. Hammack" who is identified as the principal, and three others who must be the faculty, including a tall, distinguished young man identified as "Mr. Watwood."

I'm not sure when Mr. Watwood became the principal, but he certainly could not have previously encountered challenges like those he faced for the 1940-41 and 1941-42 school years. He had to deal with the huge increase in school enrollment associated with the "boomtown" population growth Childersburg experienced in 1941-42 when the World War II munitions plant was built and went into production

We Were Both Afraid

Sherry Machen Atkinson, *CHS Class of 1962*

I had the distinct privilege of having a private conversation with Coach Cox at his home a few years before he died. In that conversation I told Coach that I was so afraid of Mr. Watwood when I was younger. He said, "Heck, I was scared of him too!" I had known Coach Cox from a very young age because Coach Cox boarded with the Fuller's that lived across the street from my grandmother.

Skipping School to Play Pool

Roscoe Limbaugh, *CHS Class of 1953*

Mr. Watwood, long-time principal at Childersburg School, was known to be a strict disciplinarian with an almost bigger-than-life aura for the many students passing through those halls. He was both respected and feared by the faint-hearted. He was known to escort big, burly football players two at a time to the dreaded office. Picking them up by their jacket collars one in each hand their feet only touching the floor occasionally. He was a big man with a big, big heart.

Students at CHS did not defy Mr. Watwood without expecting serious consequences. I do not know what possessed me and my friend Bobby Young, son of the preacher of the First Baptist Church, to come up with such a daring scheme. On the first day of school of our tenth grade as we were signing up for classes, we both realized we had a blank period for study hall. Not being particularly interested in the "study" part of study hall, we decided not to sign up for study hall at all.

Our plan was to skip school and go to the pool hall down town. This establishment was owned by Red Hare and held much more opportunity for fun than study hall. Since I drove an old car, we could easily go and come in time to shoot a game of pool.

This daring plan worked quite well for almost the entire year. The last week of the school year Bobby and I heard of an activity that was of interest to us, and decided to forego the pool hall and stay for the activity in the auditorium. Mr. Watwood saw us and asked, "Roscoe, where are you and Bobby supposed to be?" I answered, "Nowhere." He said, "What do you mean 'nowhere'?" I then explained to him that we had been going to town playing pool every day instead of study hall. He then said in his commanding voice and in a tone of unbelief, "All year?" I said, "Yes sir, all year." He then said, "Go on then, if you have been doing it all year just go on then," as he was gesturing impatiently with his hands. He never mentioned it again and we continued our daily trips to the pool hall! I do not know what he was thinking, but he never punished us in any way. I think he was too stunned and probably a little embarrassed by the two wily young boys who had had a fun year playing pool and not studying. I have great respect and admiration for Mr. Watwood.

Donald Duck, the Principal

J.D. Warren, *CHS Class of 1961*

Many know that Don Maddox, Mickey Donahoo, Jimmy Cleckler and I ran around together a lot. Jimmy's father was killed in World War II, and his mother remarried so that all of his relatives were "Dewberry's." Jimmy had two close relations that graduated the same year we did, but from B.B. Comer High School in Sylacauga. Jimmy wanted to attend the graduation and all four of us went.

After speeches, the diplomas were awarded. They went through the A's and into the B's, when "Billy Billingsley" was read out. That of course was also the name of one of the teachers/assistant coaches then at CHS. Jimmy couldn't contain a short "hoot" which drew dirty looks from those in hearing distance. We shushed him and things remained quiet as the Dewberry's received their diplomas, but a short time later a diploma was awarded to — "Donald Duck." At the reading of the name Jimmy emitted a laugh and we all darted for the exit. I was at Jacksonville State that fall and it turned out one of my classmates was … Donald Duck. I got to know him pretty well and he is a great guy. I once asked if he remembered the laugh at his graduation and he laughed and said, "With a name like Donald Duck, you get used to it." He became assistant principal at Wheatley Middle School. Behind his desk was a big poster of Donald Duck — that is, the Disney Donald Duck.

Sometime while Donald was at Wheatley Middle School, as I was driving past a MacDonald's in Tallahassee, FL, I noticed a school bus with "Talladega County" written on the side. I thought, "Maybe it's a group from Childersburg," and made a U-turn to check it out. As I was going through the door, Donald Duck was rushing across the room to greet me with a big hug. He was helping to chaperone a group of Childersburg students on a field trip.

Donald later was promoted to a high position in the Talladega County Superintendent of Education office. But I know from several reports that he maintained his great sense of humor and that he always had a warm spot in his heart for Childersburg.

Toting Books

Dwain Adams, *CHS class of 1962*

At Mr. Watwood's office, one day, a "student" about my age who was often in trouble was sent to the office. Upon questioning the boy about his grades, Mr. Watwood discovered this student was making failing grades. So he instructed him to take home every single book from every class plus all assignment given every day.

To see that this was accomplished, the boy had to check in each day with the office secretary. About a week later Mr. Watwood ran into the boy carrying all of his books and asks, "Son, what are you doing with all those books?" "Toting 'em, Mr. Watwood, Toting 'em," said the boy. Mr. Watwood reply was, "and by gosh that's all you're doing is toting 'em, I'd venture to say."

Teachers

A Confidence Builder Miss Nellie Glazner, Elementary Teacher

Sandra Headley Limbaugh, *SHS Class of 1957*

In the second grade I was fortunate to have as my teacher Miss Nellie Glazner, affectionately remembered and addressed as "Miss Nellie." Looking back through seven-year-old eyes, I thought her to be ancient, but she probably was quite young.

Miss Nellie lived just off the school grounds. Her elderly father lived with her and needed someone to administer his medicine at about lunchtime every day. Since Miss Nellie could not leave her class, she would send a student to her home to measure out the dosage and give him his medicine. How privileged and important I felt when I was given that honor!

No legal document from home or from the school system was necessary. Common sense prevailed. Today it would probably take an act of Congress to accomplish a simple thing like this. I remember Miss Nellie fondly because of her confidence in me and her encouragement in my interest in art.

The Christmas of my second grade Miss Nellie had everyone draw a Christmas card with a house, chimney, snow, etc. She liked my card so much she had me draw one for every student in my class. Thank you, Miss Nellie for building confidence in a shy little girl of seven.

The Watwoods

J.D. Warren, *CHS Class of 1961*

I do recall things about Mrs. Watwood. My class had her as our math teacher in the seventh grade. I wasn't crazy about her math class, but I do have a particular memory of hearing her in the hallway, proudly telling another teacher that her (their) son, John, had been offered a scholarship to Davidson College. This would have been in 1956-1957, and may have been the first time I ever thought about college coming after high school.

I do have a later memory of Mr. and Mrs. Watwood. In the summer of 1960 several of us went through a period where we would take long bicycle rides in the early morning. In particular I remember Jimmy Cleckler, Vicki Helms (Smith) and myself. Sometimes we would stop by the Watwood's home and sit around their breakfast table and talk. They always seemed happy to see us and interested in whatever activities we had going. They were very nice people. Quite different than only remembering principal Watwood as the "old man" who administered the paddle punishments!

Dean Ingram, Math Teacher

David Swanger, *CHS Class of 1972*

I was never a serious student in high school (I'm ashamed now), but I liked math (sort of). When I was a senior I turned into even more of a slacker and made some Ds in Ms. Ingram's class. I just couldn't find the time to study usually. She didn't give up on me for which I'm grateful now. She helped me a good bit with math, I owe her a lot.

J. D. Warren, *CHS Class of 1961*

In high school my favorite teacher was Ms. Dean Ingram, who taught math. I had her for Plane Geometry, Algebra II, and Solid Geometry/Trigonometry. Those weren't usually large classes, and often, the night before a test a large part of the class, maybe 6 to 10 people, would meet at my house to study. I had a bedroom with a door to the outside, so people could come and go as they wished.

If there was problem or a concept that was puzzling to someone they would say so, and whoever understood it would work with them on it. This would be mostly guys but some girls. I've had people tell me years later that those sessions were the reason they made it through the courses.

Another thing about Ms. Ingram was that she encouraged doing a math project. The best ones would go to the regional science and math fair at Jacksonville State, which I was fortunate to have attended twice. Having some familiarity with Jacksonville State from the fairs, as well as it being closer and more affordable, were big influences on my decision to go to college in Jacksonville, Alabama.

J. D. Warren, *CHS Class of 1961*

Ms. Dean Ingram was a softball pitcher. Some may not know but the Childersburg Quarterback Club for several years hosted a state or regional Women's Fast Pitch Softball Championship tourney. There were some really good teams and some tough women there — I mean good players! Ms. Ingram was a pitcher on the Childersburg team when there was a Childersburg team entry. She could bring the heat! I credit Dean Ingram as being a very positive influence on my later life decisions!

Patsy Cobb Willis Jones, *CHS Class of 1971*

I remember being afraid of Ms. Ingram and would not take her math class until my senior year when I had to. She was precious, and I loved her. She explained everything really well. I wished I could have taken her math class again.

Jennifer Trucks Botta, *CHS Class of 1980*

I had Miss Ingram in the late 1970s and she is one of the greatest teachers I know. She is the reason that I strive for her greatness. If one student felt I was worthy of her then I have accomplished my life's goal! She is one smart lady!

Mrs. Nix, English Teacher

Mike Headley, *CHS Class of 1962*

English the class room subject, not the language. The English language seems reasonable enough, but not the stuff you must learn in school. If someone asks me, "Do you speak, understand, and write, English?" I say." Why yes I do." I never understood why I needed to spend twelve years studying a language which I had pretty much mastered before the first grade. You know what I'm saying?

In the ninth grade I was told if I planned to graduate from high school (which at that point, according to my father was at best 50/50) I would have to endure four additional years of what I had been doing since I was a small child.

Now let me see, hummmm, one hour a day, five days a week, four weeks a month, and nine months a year for 12 years. Holy cow, that's 129,600 minutes of my life which at that point had not even included college. Are you kidding me!? Don't answer that. It's a rhetorical question. What does rhetorical mean? Hey Wisenstein you're the one who just spent 129,600 minutes of your life studying English. Well there's a good chunk of my life I'll never get back.

Funny, the subject of English is not even called English until one reaches the seventh grade. Before that we are told we are in spelling, grammar, reading, or in a writing class. What's the big secret? Helloo, it's called English. I mean are the elementary school teachers afraid to share the truth with us? As I remember the only class in high school I was removed from, thrown out of, asked to leave (you get the picture) was Mrs. Nix's tenth grade English class. I wasn't a bad student I just didn't see the need to spend an inordinate amount of time studying a dangling participle. What is the past pluperfect tense of "break?" 'I believed I _had broken_ my leg.' Hey you're the one who is supposed to know this stuff, not me.

Mrs. Nix at Wallace's Store

Glendean Fields Ogle, *CHS Class of 1961*

My friends and I would sneak off campus and go to Wallace's store across from Coosa Court at lunch time. Miss Nix almost caught us once. The store owner hid us when she saw Miss Nix coming in the door. I sneezed and we almost got caught, but Mr. Wallace kinda blocked her and wouldn't allow her back where we were. My closest friend was Judy Lewis. Everyone was upset with me because I sneezed.

Mrs. Smith, Sixth Grade Teacher

J.D. Warren, *CHS Class 1961*

My favorite teacher from elementary school was Mrs. Evelyn Smith. Every six-week period we had a different science project. One six-week's it was a leaf scrapbook. She took the class to a large wooded area in Shelby County where she knew the owner to help in finding a lot of different species. Another six-week's it would be a mineral collection. She brought some minerals from Kymulga Cave for each person to add to their collection. Other periods it was bird pictures and/or drawings, sea-life scrapbooks, and insect collections, with the specimens collected identified and mounted on pins. I think the sixth one may have been astronomy. I liked these things so much that I retained abilities to identify the different things to this day.

Another thing about her was she read to the class after lunch each day. I remember *The Oregon Trail*, by Francis Parkman, which was a combination of history and true-life adventure. Also a book by and/or about William Beebe, an early naturalist and explorer who made deep sea dives in a device called a bathysphere, and also explored jungles of South America.

It was these things from her class that made me want to become a scientist. Of course my image of a scientist was running through the jungle with a butterfly net to collect new species!

Mike Headley, *CHS Class of 1962*

No teacher had the effect that my sixth grade teacher, Mrs. Evelyn Smith, had on my learning experience. Mrs. Smith lived in Wilsonville, Alabama. I suppose that's why most of the field trips we took were to Shelby County. This lady was the first person who tried to understand my dyslexic mind. Mrs. Smith knew that I needed help. The only other person to do so was my mother, who realized that learning for me was a struggle. Mrs. Smith took the time other teachers did not, helping me with my class work.

It made all the difference in my sixth-grade-school experience. Before Mrs. Smith, school was just a place I went to be amazed at how other kids seemed to "get it" while I could never understand most of what was being taught. Mrs. Evelyn Smith made the sixth grade fun.

Mrs. Laird, English Teacher

Ken Herndon, *CHS Class of 1960*

My favorite teacher was Mary Laird. I was in her class for both junior and senior English. She taught me the beauty of the written word and instilled in me a lifelong love of reading and appreciation for good literature. More importantly, she taught me to believe in myself and to set my sights high in life. For that I am eternally grateful.

J. D. Warren, *CHS Class of 1961*

One of my most personal memories is one that deals with the time my senior year the English teacher helped arrange my date for the Senior Prom! Even in my Senior Year at CHS I had not dated very much. Not that I hadn't wanted to but I didn't drive or have access to a car. I had friends who I could have double dated with, but still I was a "social retard."

In my senior year the prom was just days away and I had not asked anyone. My English class was last period, and the teacher was Mrs. Laird. One day as I came into the room Mrs. Laird asked if I had a date for the prom, I said "no." Then she asked if I knew a certain girl, and I said "yes." She said, after class she will be in a certain room. Go there and ask her to the prom.

I'm pretty sure I didn't get much out of English Class that day. I knew who the girl was, and she was cute. I think she was a sophomore. After class, I made my way to the room and spotted my potential date.. As I approached, a girlfriend of hers seemed to ease away. I'm sure I said "Hello," but shortly got around to asking her to go to the prom. She said "yes!" I had to call her the next day to find out where she lived and what color dress she would be wearing.

I made arrangements to double date with my friend, Mickey. Those days he was driving a 1930-something classic car, so that added glamour to the occasion. Mickey had a regular girl friend at the time so the three of us went by to pick up my date. On the way to the Prom, Mickey's car broke down, but Mickey was able to fix it and we were only a little late to the pre-prom banquet.

The tradition was that the class officers of the Junior and Senior Classes and their dates were introduced then came forward to be featured for the first dance of the night. I survived the evening.

I think Ms. Moody had taught her music classes the box step when I was in the 6th grade. Probably we danced more times than that and somehow we made it through the evening.

After the Prom we went to a party — at Ms. Laird's house. Her daughter, Mary Louise, was also in the Senior Class, and I have suspected over the years that she may have been the one to induce her mother to bring me out of my social cocoon. After conversations and some refreshments I think it was my date's time to be home so we left.

When we reached her house I walked her to the porch steps, took her in my arms, and — No, when we reached the steps she said she had a nice time and scooted up the steps. I returned to the car and Mickey took his girlfriend home.

Later that evening Mickey said we had something to do. So we drove to the water tower where some other senior boys had gathered. Someone climbed the tower and painted in large letters, "Class of 1961." This was a sort of tradition at that time, for graduating classes to let those traveling up or down highway US 280 know who the most important people in town were.

I Did Not Drop Out

Ollie Pardue, *CHS Class of 1966*

I was destined never to finish CHS, but thanks to positive role models in Childersburg. Teachers that cared, people who gave constructive criticism when needed, and love, though the word love might not have been mentioned, it was certainly felt.

I cannot find the words to describe how the teachers in Childersburg High School impacted my life and caused me to grow up to be a responsible adult. Maybe "positive role models" and "love" would be the best description.

Christie Wappello Summers, III
April 20, 1936 — March 14, 2002

Christie Summers served the community of Childersburg and students of Childersburg High School for 16 years.

Cynthia Jane Summers, *PHS Class of 1977*

My father was born in a Florida Methodist parsonage in 1936. He later moved to Georgia then Alabama and graduated from Walker County High School (Jasper, Alabama) in 1954 and the University of Alabama in 1957. Daddy's major at Alabama was music with an emphasis on trombone. Mother (Barbara) and Daddy met while students at University of Alabama. Mother shared her book because dad could not afford to buy one for the class they were taking. Dad played string bass in a dance band to make a little extra money.

My parents were hired to teach at Childersburg High School for the school year 1957-1958. They married that fall. Daddy served as the CHS band/choral director with both groups eventually receiving superior ratings consistently at school music competitions for ten years. He then became principal at CHS for the years 1969 through 1973.

After receiving his E.D. (Doctor of Education) from the University of Alabama he became the Dean of Education at Troy State University-Montgomery.

All My Siblings Were in the CHS Band

June Melton Lassiter, *CHS Class of 1967*

I am one of those kids who chose to pursue my personal interest through the CHS band. I grew up as the youngest of five kids and all of us were in the band.

My oldest brother's first year in the CHS band was under Mr. Christie Summers which happened to be Mr. Summers first year teaching in Childersburg. Mr. Summers was the most pleasant and naturally friendly person; he made it a pleasure to learn music. However, he left CHS before my junior year.

In band I learned music plus developed self-confidence through performing in a group and in front of crowds. For someone who is shy and quiet that was extremely important in my development. Each summer and fall we practiced our routines and marched in the hot Alabama sun, plus practiced music in the evenings. After school we practiced and struggled for practice turf with the football team. We marched in wool uniforms in the Labor Day parades in spite of the heat. Mr. Summers made it fun. Sometimes he would get so frustrated and his face turned beet red. I cannot remember him losing his temper even though some of the band members pushed him to his limit. Band was my extended family; it was a friendship group with a common interest. We traveled and performed together. Six of my school years were spent with the CHS band and I would not take one day of it back.

CHS Memories

Linda Justice Simpson, CHS Class of 1962

Our school had long halls, high ceilings, wooden lockers; an auditorium with a stage where we had "plays" each year, a nice library, and of course the principal's office, and no air conditioning. Now all we have are our memories. I am so thankful.

CHS Senior Class 1972

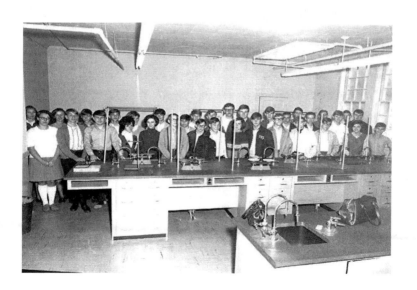

Science Club

166

Chapter 12

Corporal Punishment

This chapter is dedicated to the memory of Leslie McInnish, July 12, 1943 - December 24, 1966. My thanks go to Leslie's family who graciously granted permission for me to write this story.

The Boozer Whipping

Mike Headley, *CHS Class of 1962*

Winter had departed with spring all around and summer was but a month away. The windows were open in Mrs. Nix' English class so I had time to watch the wasps fly in and out of the room through the tall open windows of CHS and bounce along the ceiling. The sweet smell of honeysuckle was wafting on the breeze and the flowers were starting to bloom in Talladega County. Something happened in my 16-year-old brain — I think it had something to do with testosterone.

It was fifth period. Now at that time of day I was not really interested in learning the past perfect tense of anything. I was minding my own business or, more than likely, day dreaming about something while looking out the window. That may have been the reason why the highest grade I ever earned in any high school English class was a D+. My poor departed mother was so happy that I made a D+ she cried.

This incident took place when I was a sophomore at Childersburg High School in the spring of 1960. It involved a friend, Leslie McInnish, I and Mrs. Nix's 10th grade English class.

Childersburg High School in 1960 was in the process of introducing new desks, part wood-part metal, and removing the old solid wood desk that weighed 60 pounds. However, the transition to all new desks took several years to complete; thus causing many classes to have mixed furniture.

Leslie and I had managed to co-exist in Mrs. Nix' 10th grade English class for at least seven months in reasonable harmony when all of a sudden I felt the corner of the desk behind me starting to protrude through the wood slats of my desk into my back.

As "luck" would have it, Leslie had a new desk, while I was sitting in front of him, in an old desk. Being the nice guy I am. I turned and pushed the desk back through the slats and out of my back. Problem solved. Well, that did not last long. I was "intently taking in every word" from Mrs. Nix concerning a dangling participle, when here comes the corner of that desktop again. Thinking that Leslie had simply made a mistake the first time, I now realize that his motives were, shall we say "questionable."

I turned quickly to see Leslie grinning from ear to ear. Realizing that a harsh look had not worked, I turned to Leslie and explained in hushed tones "STOP!" Well maybe not hushed enough, because Mrs. Nix noticed I had "disrupted her fifth period English class."

After my "shout" (as Mrs. Nix described it) Mrs. Nix requested my presence at her desk for a conference, at which point I was told I better not do that again or there would be "consequences." Being duly admonished I returned to my desk. For a short period all was calm. My first thought after being seated at my desk was "maybe it's over." Persistence must have been one of Leslie's stronger traits because the calm did not last long.

Here came that desk corner again. At this point the three cells in my male 16-year-old brain that were functioning told me it was "time for action." Standing quickly, I turned to my left to see Leslie grinning. Placing my hands firmly under the top of Leslie's desk, I lifted the desk with as much strength as

I could muster. Poor Leslie ... desk, books and all went over backwards, with his head thumping the floor like a ripe watermelon. The picture my mind now recalls was something out of a slow-motion movie.

I must admit the whole incident gave me a fair amount of pleasure, at the moment. As Leslie's and the desk's contents spilled onto those hardwood floors Glenn Boots Wilson had worked so hard to polish, I must admit I was amused. To say it created a scene was an understatement.

Leslie was in shock, and, as you could imagine, the class was in total disarray. I don't remember too much other than thinking "this is not going to turn out well." Reflecting on my conduct more than 54 years later, I probably made a poor decision.

Mrs. Nix, with her white hair flying, jumped from behind her desk making a rather futile attempt to control what was left of her 5th period English class, and then told Leslie and me to "go into the hall, NOW!"

The hall outside Mrs. Nix class room was her favorite parking place for her undesirable students. It was not long until Mrs. Nix joined Leslie and me. She wanted to know what had happened. After explaining as best I could it was apparent my pleading was not finding a sympathetic ear.

As I remember, Mrs. Nix sent one of her best and brightest, a girl of course, to fetch Principal Boozer. It was not long until Mr. Boozer arrived. After a short discussion between Mrs. Nix and Principal Boozer, Leslie and I were marched to the principal's office. (We called Principal Boozer "Skunk" because he had a streak of white running down the middle of his mostly black hair, front to back.) After arriving at the office we had to wait for Principal Boozer to return. This is the time you have to reflect on whether a good decision had been reached earlier. In view of what I was about to receive I was starting to have doubts about my earlier decisions.

169

Too late, I don't remember who went first. Punishment of this nature always took place in the Principal's private office. Leslie and I each took five licks. Stung like HELL. That paddle had holes in it! Question, since I did not take physics in high school, "do holes in the paddle increase its speed?"

I can't remember if Leslie made it back to the Principals office before graduation. I know I didn't. Anyone who knew Leslie McInnish would say. "Yep, that's the Leslie we all knew." As you read this, please take a moment, and have a little grin with Leslie, he would like that. Leslie was a nice guy who left us way too soon

Mrs. Williams' Whipping

J.D. Warren, *CHS Class of 1961*

I just happened to be looking when a boy in my first grade class walked up behind one of the girls, took hold of the hem of her skirt, and jerked it up! In the same motion he spun around and casually walked away. While it was certainly cheeky on his part, I don't recall that it was particularly "revealing." What I do remember is that Mrs. Williams, the teacher, also saw it and rushed over and gave him the most severe paddling I have ever seen, right in front of the whole class.

The Watwood Whipping

Dwain Adams, *CHS Class of 1962*

During my younger years I received my fair share of whippings, mostly deserved. None were as memorable and as undeserved as the Watwood whipping. Principal Watwood had huge hands; he was a big man, with lots of experience in dealing with young mischievous boys. Back when I was in the sixth grade, a certain bigger guy who was a bully, decided to pick on me in class. The teacher finally told us to take it outside. The picking continued until I had enough and I swung and hit him right in the face. One of our classmates who were watching from a window hollered, "the little one hit the big one!" The teacher came out and sent us to the office. Mr. Watwood told us to go home and come back in the morning.

That night I thought about the whipping I would surely receive in the morning and talked to my mother. I said I didn't think it was fair and I was going to tell Mr. Watwood exactly that. She thought about it, and then said to do what I felt I should. The next day when we were all in the office and before Mr. Watwood started talking, I asked him if I could say something. He said, "Yes." I said, "Mr. Watwood, I don't think you have the right to whip me." I don't think I could have made him any madder if I had spit in his face. He came out from behind the desk, grabbed me and bounced me off at least three of the four walls in his office, threw me in the hall, turned me over his knee, and hit me three times with that big, ole hand of his. Then he told me to get to class and behave myself.

About noon that day I ran into the other boy, and he said, "I ought to go home and get my gun and shoot you." I said, "What for?" He said, "You made him really mad and he pulled the board out and tore me up! He never bullied me again.

Busted My Butt

Ed Castleberry, *CHS Class of 1965*

Ms. Ingram busted my butt when I was in the 10th grade and it only took one time. I was a quick learner and I had a lot of respect for her after that.

Spit Balls and our First President

Sherry Atkinson, CHS *Class of 1962*

In 1958 Mr. Potts homeroom was a "little unruly" to say the least. There was a large picture of President Washington hanging in Mr. Pott's home room wall.

Spitballs seemed to accumulate on the picture on a daily basis. One day a call came from principal Layton's office to send Mike Braswell, Don Robinson, and Dickey Bean to the office.

Giggling as this trio swaggered into the principal's office, the three young men learned quickly that Mr. Layton was somewhat of an athlete in hurdling. Don told me Principal Layton put one hand on top of his desk and leaped over like Superman," grabbing all three young men at the same time. All three received a blistering that day.

Later in the morning a ladder was brought to Mr. Pott's home room, along with a bucket of water and rags. The immediate cleaning of our first President's picture had begun. I don't remember seeing another spitball on the President's picture, after that day.

I Beat My Best Friends Butt — and Vice-Versa

Ken Herndon, *CHS Class of 1960*

My family moved to Childersburg from Lincoln Park, Michigan in 1953. My dad had taken a job at Alabama Ordnance Works, the old powder plant near Coosa River News Print. We were originally from Alabama so when the job opportunity was offered he jumped right on it. I have always been an active baseball player and my dad had already found a spot for me on Rudy Nelsons Little League team before my mother, younger brother and I even arrived in

Childersburg. I was immediately introduced to Coach Nelson and the other team members, one of them being Jimmy Gulledge.

Jimmy and I were instant friends and we remain close friends even after more than 60 years. He and I hunted rabbits together down in the fields by the Coosa River, and fished the creeks plus rode down the pine trees near the railroad tracks by Pinewood Terrace.

In the spring of 1959 when we were juniors at CHS we were in the same PE class and we played a lot of softball. As a lot of friends are prone to do, we argued and fought but at the end of the day we were still close friends. One day during a PE class softball game Jimmy and I got into an argument over some little thing that I don't even remember. As we were walking back to the school building the argument escalated. First it was loud talk, and that led to a little pushing which, in turn led to a little shoving and poking. Jimmy had the softball in his hand and I had the softball bat as we were walking back up the hill to the school.

I guess he had enough of my loud mouth so he wound up and fired the softball at me and bounced it off my upper arm. Without thinking I let fly the bat fly like a boomerang and it spiraled right around his lower legs and just barely nicked him. At that very moment Coach Cox happened to turn around and see what had happened. He came running down the hill to where we were demanding to know what was going on. There was a lot of "he did it, no, he did it" between Jimmy and myself as we tried to weasel out of the responsibility of who started the fight. After a couple minutes of listening to our lame excuses Coach Cox told us to meet him in the boy's dressing room in the school basement.

When we got there he was waiting for us with his much feared paddle in his hand. He told us if we liked beating on each other so much that he was going to give us an opportunity to do just that. With that being said he had both of us to remove our pants but he was not going to be the one to administer punishment.

Yep, you guessed it, we were. He let us flip a coin to see who would go first and he said there would be no love taps. If he thought we were being too lenient he would do the honors himself. I don't remember who went first but the guy on the receiving end had to bend over and grab his ankles while the other guy swung that paddle with both hands and cracked the other's butt with a resounding smack. When it was over we were both in tears and in some pain.

No reports were written, the principal was not notified and that was the end of it. Jimmy and I maintained our friendship and we never fought or argued again.

The Kelly Whipping

James Morris, *CHS Class of 1967*

Frank Ivey, Hal Butts, and I were caught flipping nickels in study hall at CHS. Principal Kelly walked right up on us, with coins still in the air. We were marched into Mr. Kelly's private office, the one next to the school office, where we each received three licks from that holey paddle. Trust me! Three licks were enough, that lesson was well-learned. I never got caught flipping nickels again!

A Wet Dish Rag

Mike Headley, *CHS Class of 1962*

My much needed attitude adjustment happened in the late spring of 1960. I was 16 years old. This was a school day and I usually got off the school bus around 4:15. That particular afternoon around 5:00 PM my best friend Ray Williams came by our house. Ray wonted me to ride over to Sylacauga with him. I proceeded to "tell" mother I was going to Sylacauga with Ray.

If heaven ever had a more qualified person to enter those Pearly Gates than my Saintly mother I haven't a clue who that person might be. Here's the scenario. Ray was near the kitchen door, left of mother, while I was to her right. Mother was at the kitchen sink looking out the window, washing dishes.

The reason mother objected to my trip to Sylacauga probably had something to do with my recent report card, plus my lack of interest in homework. Anyway mother said "no." At this point I had reached the age where I had become far too big for my britches. Daddy was working out of town so I proceeded to tell mother "I am going anyway."

I remember four thoughts. The first was "what just happened," the second, "why do I taste Palmolive dish soap in my mouth?" The third was "why are my eyes burning" (Palmolive soap would burn your eyes)." And fourth: "why are my face, head, neck, ears and shirt dripping with dish soap?"

It was as if lightning had struck. My mother, the love of my life, my best friend before I met my wife, Kay, had just slapped me across the face with a wet, very soapy dish rag. The humiliation I experienced in front of my very best friend was something I will take to my grave. Needless to say I did not go to Sylacauga that afternoon.

Questions

Mike Headley, CHS Class of 1962

A century comes, and quickly passes away.
Most do not two century's see?
From generation to generation the torch must pass.
Will our fate be to compete, or simply will we go along, never
being complete?
When a hundred years have passed, will the world a better
place be?
Or have we said "as long as I get mind, let other's suffer not
me.
Can I hear mankind's cry, and say "I have not contributed to
the pain."
Have we responsibility to our fellow man?
Are we in this world only passing among this the human
race?
Are we a stone simply passing thru time?
The questions are ours you see, ones which we must answer
or flee.

M. Alton Headley

Chapter 13

Coaches and Sports

John W. Cox
1920 Arab, Alabama - 2002 Childersburg, Alabama

WWII Bronze Star, Presidential Citation
CHS Coach 1947 thru 1979
University of Alabama
George Peabody University
33 years Head Football Coach
Alabama HS AA Hall of Fame 1991

Coach Cox

Sitting With the Man

Sherry Machen Atkinson, CHS Class of 1962

About two years before Coach Cox passed away I had a call from Ruby Cox asking could I come and sit with Coach for a little while so she could run an errand. When I arrived Coach was laying down in the living room.

As we visited coach began to tell me about the first football uniforms that he and Mr. Watwood purchased. They made the trip to Birmingham to Fred Singleton's Sportswear. Mr. Watwood wanted to purchase some less expensive uniforms, but Coach had his eye on the very best. Mr. Watwood told Coach, "These are mighty expensive uniforms John." Coach said, "Mr. Watwood, your son, John, will be playing and I know that you will want your son in the best protective uniform." They went home with the very best in the store. I will never forget that day, and am honored that Ruby asked me to sit with Coach Cox.

Motivation

Charles "Turkey" Burke, *CHS Class of 1962*

It is difficult to find enough words that represent the remarkable motivation that Coach John Cox conveyed to our testosterone encumbered bodies in preparation for the Friday night football game. The grid iron was our stage and we were the performers that our beloved director cast and shaped for the "show down."

Coach Cox became a legend in Childersburg, coaching at CHS for 33 years building a 182-123-13 record. I loved John Cox, along with my fellow teammates. He certainly provided all of us with "The Right Stuff" to find our way to be good citizens in our communities. "With one exception," I remembered our beloved Coach John Cox —This Easter Day of Our Lord, April Six Two Thousand and Fifteen.

Tough Skin

J. D. Warren, *CHS Class of 1961*

Some may not be aware that Coach Cox was also the basketball coach for 13 years and the baseball coach for six years. I was never a very good player, but I did play on the "B" basketball team a couple of years when he was coaching it.

Warming up before one game there was a spray can of something called "Tough Skin," which I called Stick Um, which someone had brought into the gym. This was a product that you could spray on to keep tape from burning your skin. It was in an aerosol can, which was an innovation that was still a novelty at that time. In those days many guys were just starting to use "Right Guard," a spray-deodorant product marketed in a small aerosol can.

While we were warming up I picked up the Tough Skin can and called out to Robert Burdick, one of the other players, "Hey Robert, deodorant!" and gestured like I was spraying it under my arms. Robert laughed and called out to Coach Cox, "Coach, Warren is using the Tough Skin for deodorant." Again, anybody who saw my action knew it was done in jest!

After graduation I was not around Childersburg very much, but after several years I ran into Robert Burdick. He told me that Coach Cox told people that I sprayed the Tough Skin on and stuck my arms down. A few years later I saw Robert again and he said that Coach Cox is now telling the story that he put me in the game and when the ball was thrown to me it hit me in the chest because my arms were stuck to my body with Stick-Um.

Coach Cox passed away a few years after that. I have the highest regard for him. But I will always wonder if before he died, the account of that incident that he seemed to like to tell ever grew to the point where, "... he put me in the game, someone threw the ball to me while my arms were stuck, and the ball hit me in the head and went into the goal for the winning score!" Probably not ... so I guess my chance for "basketball fame" is gone forever.

A CHS Football Game

Roscoe Limbaugh, *CHS Class of 1953*

Once during football season my brothers James, Robert and George Limbaugh (all big CHS football fans) matched to see who would stay at the store (Limbaugh Hardware) to keep it open since it was an afternoon football game. The other two would go to the high school for the big game. George lost! After James and Robert left, George locked the store and headed for the game. George was the first person that James and Robert saw when they arrived. Football (and any other ball) was serious business in the Limbaugh family. At one time Limbaugh Hardware had its own independent basketball team. Brothers Frank and Shealey joined with George on this team.

At the Friday Night Football Game

Mike Headley, *CHS Class of 1962*

I suppose that Tiger Stadium has a different look than when we attended games in the mid to late 1950s through the early 1960s. The field was laid out north to south with the home bleachers on the east side of the field. When you arrived to pay, you were greeted by a teacher from CHS who was happy to have a quick chat while making your change.

If you wanted food or refreshments you had to walk north past the end of the stadium to the area near the boys' dressing rooms where you would find the Coke-a-Cola half trailer attended by the Coke Bottler out of Sylacauga. In those days your Coke came in bottles stacked high in yellow wooden creates with Coke-a-Cola written on the side in red letters. The Coke guy would open the bottle and pour your Coke in a paper cup with ice.

The band was located toward the south end of the stadium so that's where most of the teenagers sat. The parents and grandparents sat in the middle and to the north end. The players, cheerleaders, coaches, and referees plus students all made a most colorful site on a fall Friday night. Rarely did it frost in that part of Alabama before Thanksgiving so the weather was usually cool but pleasant.

Me and Newton Going to the Friday Night Game

Ollie Pardue, *CHS Class of 1966*

As you are aware, a lot of us were poor back in those days. I met my best friend for life Newton Sanders as I was about to sneak into the football game on a Friday night in about 1960. I showed him how to get in without buying a ticket. Here's how we did it. If you are going under the railroad viaduct heading from down town east going towards the school on the same road that Ms. Grace McSween lived on 4thStreet Southeast then you would take your first left towards the football field you were at the spot where we got in to the games. There was a pipe going under the road. This trip was not for the faint of heart. We would crawl under the road through that pipe and come out inside the fence, brush the dirt off our clothes, and head for the bleachers.

The Sylacauga Game

Charles "Turkey" Burke, *CHS Class of 1962*

Skull drills, were presented to us trying to figure out how hard and when Sylacauga was going to hit us was certainly part of the mental game. "O, s***! You mean that Sylacauga tackle weighs 250 pounds and is "quick as a cat". Ok, "Wheel run end-a-round". "They won't know what has hit them, Right? ... Right, Coach?" This was Monday, and by Friday afternoon after the "pep rally" reality had set in and all of us remembered last year's loss. No one wanted to repeat that. We all could picture that giant Sylacauga teams of gladiators with legs like stumps and arms like stove pipes.

Our team was a cast of characters that Coach Cox had selected each of us for the various positions. As in Mrs. Taylor's first grade reading groups, Coach had the "Loins", "Tigers" and the "Bluebirds". Let's say, "The "Serious" "Kind of Serious" and "Bench Warmers." I was in the last group. Coach had to take this motley crew and deliver the motivation component to overcome our deficiencies that would make us winners.

Talking about, "Team Spirit" or as I later learned "esprit de corps" elevated to its highest level. It was Friday night, and the Sylacauga Game was at their stadium. We were undefeated, "on top of the mountain". However, everyone knew the odds and just how difficult a predicament we now found ourselves in. We were "about" to enter the arena with a very capable opponent, plus Sylacauga would have more fans screaming for their side. Coach Cox had used up most of the tools in his motivational tool box.

Using the story "This is Lloyd's last game" we played and beat a tough motivated, Alexander City team. Coach Cox was not new to the game of motivation, and knew how to get us ready for the big Friday night game.

"OK Boys" this one is for you. I know you do not want to go down to the Hagan's Drug store or to the Dairy Queen on Saturday afternoon with your head down. If you lose this one, you might as well enter the city of Childersburg thru the back door." Man what a dose of humility and guilt that each of us could picture in our minds. The disgracing "shame" one would be on display as you entered Childersburg proper, walking past Limbaugh Hardware, trying to find the back door as the critical town people peered and gawked at us.

That alone was enough to send us to the bowels of condemnation.

As Coach Cox was delivering this "guilt laden" sermon, I looked over spotting a spent bundle of ankle wrapping tape that Coach Shell had discarded after wrapping Dickie's and Johnny's ankles. I grabbed the wad and quickly fashioned a white taped "dummy man." Quickly making a "hangman's noose using a shoe string placing it firmly around the "sentenced to death" white effigy. I did the "dead man walking" routine across the table and dropped his lifeless body off the table letting him dangle in space. I repeated this several times as Coach Cox was bringing his speech to its climax. I was able to get the attention of David Dunlap who could "snigger" with the best of them, as David failed to contain himself and almost disrupted the Coach Cox eloquent speech. That was bad because we lost the game. As in Shakespeare's Tragic "Macbeth" — "Out Damn Spot- Out" — Out I say — One — Two, Why? Then this is the time to do it — "Hell is Murky?"

A Transfer to Sylacauga High School

Mike Headley, *CHS Class of 1962*

I never played football at CHS; however, I did play for a short time at Sylacauga High School under Coach Tom Calvin in 1960. Let me explain how that happened. After completing the 7th grade at CHS my parents realized that I had received little education during my 7th grade school year.

This happened due to several factors. Number one; there was little discipline in the school that year. Number two; we had a number of holdovers, young men who had failed for a number of years. In those days the system did not have social promotions. We ended up with five or six 14, 15, and 16 year olds in the 7th grade. They bullied people, and for the most part ran loose. The fact that part of the school burned that year created a certain amount of disruption.

A decision was made by my parents that I would transfer to Sylacauga for my 8th grade school year. After the 8th grade my father was transferred to Miami, Oklahoma for one year to work on a special project for the B.F. Goodrich Company. I completed the 9th grade 1958-1959 in Oklahoma. I then returned to Sylacauga for my 10th grade school year.

I went out for the SHS football team in August of 1960. Later that Fall I broke my collar bone playing football for SHS. Long story short, I had surgery which did not heal, plus an infection that lasted for 6 months. I transferred back to CHS in the late fall of 1960 with my sports career in shambles.

After the Friday Night Game

Beverly Rogers-Dixon Poellnitz, *CHS Class of 1959*

I just remembered how exciting it was back in the late 1950s to wait in the end zone to walk your boyfriend off the field after the football game. That split second when you looked and couldn't find him. Yes, he was dirty sweaty and smelled but you gave him a big hug anyway. Seems like yesterday, a memory I still have. Guess that tradition as well as "going steady "are no longer around. It was a big deal in those days for a boy to ask you to walk him off the field after the game!

We Beat Sylacauga

Linda Joyce Seay Williams, *CHS Class of 1969*

We beat Sylacauga, Coach Tom Calvin's team, for the first time in 13 years in 1969. The next year we beat Sylacauga High School in the rain — in Sylacauga. I heard from a good authority that Coach Calvin said after that game that he thought Lee Carpenter couldn't control the ball in the rain.

But that Carpenter put the ball wherever he wanted. That's a pretty good compliment from Coach Calvin, who was one of the best in SHS history!

Sports Food Science

Mike Headley, *CHS Class of 1962*

One piece of advice head football coach Tom Calvin, SHS (Sylacauga), always gave us after football practice was "go to the Dairy Queen and drink two malted milk shakes." Not milk shakes, MALTED milk shakes. I am sure there was some sports medicine advice in there somewhere. Wow, the 1960s.

1955 CHS Cheerleaders L-R

Linda Hall, Clara Lawler, Lou Ann Elliott, Kay Cleckler, Gayle Williams, Betty Shelton, and Gail Isabel

Patsy Rich Weaver
1961-62

John Watwood (Football Player)

J.D. Warren, *CHS Class of 1961*

John Watwood was tall and muscular, like his father our Principal Mr. Watwood. John was a second-team "All State" Tackle for Childersburg High School in 1956. John graduated from Davidson College in North Carolina, and then went to medical school; John became a surgeon in Alexander City for many years. Sadly, John died in 2015. His funeral had not even taken place as I was writing this piece! It gave me goose bumps!

Mr. A. H. Watwood (Principal) was also a supporter of sports at CHS. In 1947, the school had its first football team, and he hired John W. Cox as the first coach. The team finished with a 2-win and 2-loss record. We all know that Coach Cox remained there for over 33 years and has been entered into the Alabama High School Football Hall of Fame.

CHS Football 1956 (Record 10-0)

First row L-R Alan Mauldin, Gravis Fincher, Bobby Weaver, Jimmy Bushy; Second Row L-R Bobby Thompson, Bobby "Coon" Hightower, Myron Carter, Jerry Green

Johnnie Simmons 1969

1965 Dodgers

Earl Wesson, Jr., CHS Class of 1972

That was my first year with the Dodgers. Mr. Tubbs "picked" me up from Farm League. I was only 10 years old. I thought he was the closest thing to a pro coach in Childersburg.

Coach Billingsly with the
9th Grade Talladega County chamions.
Front row: Fray Flemming, Rod Bowlng, Russell Justice, Chris Peterson, Johnny Camp; Back Row: Coach Billingsly, Slim Milam, Steve Bartlet, Dwight Hillman, Don Baker, Larry Gardner.

Chapter 14

Childersburg High School

Childersburg High School Alma Matre

School Song

On our city's eastern border
Reared against the sky
Proudly stands our Alma Matre
As the years go by
Forward ever be our watch word
Conquer and prevail
Hail to thee our Alma Matre
CHS all hail

James Morris' Doomsday Dog Tag

Dooms Day

Beverly Rogers-Dixon Poellnitz, *CHS Class of 1959*

I remember wearing dog tags with our names and parents'
names and addresses? I still have mine.

Marsha Dillard, *CHS Class of 1970*

Remember those films they made us watch in PE about how
to protect and take care of you after the bomb went off. That
scared me to death.

Peter Wallenfang, *CHS Class of 1972*

My dad built a fallout shelter. I found not long ago the Life
Magazine where President Kennedy was telling Americans to
build fallout shelters and detailed instructions how to stock
them.

Classes, Community Leaders, and Favorites

There was no Mr. CHS before 1958

CHS Class of 1953

Year Book	The Treasure Chest
Principal	A. H. Watwood
Number One Song	"Vaya con Dios"
Number One TV Show	*I Love Lucy*
Number One Movie	*The Robe*
Miss CHS	Betty Bell
Mayor	Earle A. Rainwater
Chief of Police	J. L. Jinright

CHS Class of 1954

Year Book	The Treasure Chest
Principal	A. H. Watwood
Number One Song	"Little Things Mean a Lot"
Number One TV Show	*I Love Lucy*
Number One Movie	*White Christmas*
Miss CHS	Carolyn Lucas
Mayor	Earle A. Rainwater
Chief of Police	J.L. Jinright

CHS Class of 1955

Year Book	The Treasure Chest
Principal	A. H. Watwood
Number One Song	"Cherry Pink"
Number One TV Show	*The $64,000 Question*
Number One Movie	*Cinerama Holiday*
Miss CHS	Frances Bennett
Mayor	Earle A. Rainwater
Chief of Police	J. L. Jinright

CHS Class of 1956

Year Book	Tiger Tracks
Principal	A. H. Watwood
Number One Song	"Hound Dog"
Number One TV Show"	*I Love Lucy*
Number One Movie	*The Ten Commandments*
Miss CHS	Dorothy Cleckler
Mayor	Earle A. Rainwater
Chief of Police	J. L. Jinright

CHS Class of 1957

Year Book	Tiger Tracks
Principal	George Layton
Number One Song	"Jail House Rock" Elvis
Number One TV Show	*Gun Smoke*
Number One Movie	*the Bridge on the River Kwai*
Miss CHS	Ann Stone
Mayor	Earle A. Rainwater
Chief of Police	J. L. Jinright

CHS Class of 1958

Year Book	Tiger Tracks
Principal	George Layton
Number One Song	"Volare"
Number One TV Show	*Gun Smoke*
Number One Movie	*South Pacific*
Mr. CHS	Ronnie Hudson
Miss CHS	Mary Ann McCall
Mayor	Earle A. Rainwater
Chief of Police	J. L. Jinright

CHS Class of 1959

Year Book	Tiger Tracks
Principal	George Layton
Number One Song	"Mack the Knife"
Number One TV Show	*Gun Smoke*
Number One Movie	*Ben-Hur*
Mr. CHS	Fill Bush
Miss CHS	Barbara McCain
Mayor	Earle A. Rainwater
Chief of Police	J. L. Jinright

CHS Class of 1960

Year Book	Tiger Tracks
Principal	Charles Boozer
Number One Song	"Theme from 'A Summer Place'"
Number One TV Show	*Gun Smoke*
Number One Movie	*Spartacus*
Mr. CHS	Wayne Barnett
Miss CHS	Jeanie Wilson
Mayor	Earle A. Rainwater
Chief of Police	J. L. Jinright

CHS Class of 1961

Year Book	Tiger Tracks
Principal	Erskine Murray
Number One Song	"Tossing and Turning"
Number One TV Show	*Wagon Train*
Number One Movie	*West Side Story*
Mr. CHS	Robert Burdick
Miss CHS	Janice Giddens
Mayor	Earle A. Rainwater
Chief of Police	J. L. Jinright

CHS Class of 1962

Year Book	Tiger Tracks
Principal	Erskine Murray
Number One Song	"I Can't Stop Loving You"
Number One TV Show	*the Beverly Hillbillies*
Number One Movie	*Lawrence of Arabia*
Mr. CHS	Michael Braswell
Miss CHS	Carolyn Giddens
Mayor	Robert Limbaugh
Chief of Police	J. L. Jinright

CHS Class of 1963

Year Book	Tiger Tracks
Principal	Erskine Murray
Number One Song	"Sugar Shack"
Number One TV Show	*the Beverly Hillbillies*
Number One Movie	*Cleopatra*
Mr. CHS	Tommy Daniels
Miss CHS	Mary Walden Boaz
Mayor	Robert Limbaugh
Chief of Police	J. L. Jinright

CHS Class of 1964

Year Book	Tiger Tracks
Principal	James Williams
Number One Song	"I Wanna Hold Your Hand"
Number One TV Show	*Bonanza*
Number One Movie	*Gold Finger*
Mr. CHS	Joey Fisher
Miss CHS	Opal Johnson
Mayor	Robert Limbaugh
Chief of Police	J. L. Jinright

CHS Class of 1965

Year Book	Tiger Tracks
Principal	James Williams
Number One Song	"Yesterday"
Number One TV Show	*Bonanza*
Number One Movie	*the Sound of Music*
Mr. CHS	Ronnie Webster
Miss CHS	Ann Forrister
Mayor	Robert Limbaugh
Chief of Police	J.L. Jinright / C. L. Goodwin

CHS Class of 1966

Year Book	Tiger Tracks
Principal	Joseph Kelley
Number One Song	"Battle of the Green Berets"
Number One TV Show	*Bonanza*
Number One Movie	the *Bible: In the Beginning*
Mr. CHS	Bobby Middlebrooks
Miss CHS	Sharron Beasley
Mayor	Robert Limbaugh
Chief of Police	J.L. Jinright / C. L. Goodwin

CHS Class of 1967

Year Book	Tiger Tracks
Principal	Joseph Kelley
Number One Song	"I'm a Believer"
Number One TV Show	*the Andy Griffith Show*
Number One Movie	*The Graduate*
Mr. CHS	Guy Veazy
Miss CHS	Joyce Champion
Mayor	Robert Limbaugh
Chief of Police	C. L. Goodwin

CHS Class of 1968

Year Book	Tiger Tracks
Principal	Joseph Kelly
Number One Song	"Hey Jude"
Number One TV Show	*Rowan and Martin's Laugh-In*
Number One Movie	*2001: A Space Odyssey*
Mr. CHS	Charles Aki
Miss CHS	Sherry Lightsey
Mayor	Robert Limbaugh
Chief of Police	C. L. Goodwin

CHS Class of 1969

Year Book	Tiger Tracks
Principal	John Cox (acting) Christie Summers
Number One Song	"Sugar, Sugar"
Number One TV Show	*Rowan and Martin's Laugh-In*
Number One Movie	*Butch Cassidy and the Sundance Kid*
Mr. CHS	Merle Sanders
Miss CHS	Kaye Elliott
Mayor	Robert Limbaugh
Chief of Police	C. L. Goodwin

CHS Class of 1970

Year Book	Tiger Tracks
Principal	Christie Summers
Number One Song	"Bridge over Troubled Water"
Number One TV Show	*Marcus Welby, MD*
Number One Movie	*Love Story*
Mr. CHS	Frank Harkins
Miss CHS	Carol Hagan
Mayor	Robert Limbaugh
Chief of Police	C. L. Goodwin

CHS Class of 1971

Year Book	Tiger Tracks
Principal	Christie Summers
Number one song	"Joy to the World"
Number One TV Show	*All in the Family*
Number One Movie	*Fiddler on the Roof*
Mr. CHS	Mike Allen
Miss CHS	Cathi Graham
Mayor	Robert Limbaugh
Chief of Police	C. L. Goodwin

CHS Class of 1972

Year book	Tiger Tracks
Principal	Christie Summers
Number One Song	"The First Time I Saw Your Face"
Number One TV Show	*All in the Family*
Number One Movie	*The Godfather*
Mr. CHS	Stewart Smith
Miss CHS	Lynn Limbaugh
Mayor	Robert Limbaugh
Chief of Police	C. L. Goodwin

The Lunch Room Ladies

Mike Headley, *CHS Class of 1962*

Before Mrs. Giddens we had Mrs. Riddle in the lunch room. If God ever created two sweeter ladies, I have yet to meet them.

Malcolm Bates, *CHS Class of 1983*

Do you remember Mrs. Giddens that punched our lunch tickets?

Jill Duvall Stubblefield, *CHS Class of 1983*

I still have some of my lunch tickets. Mrs. Giddens was a precious person.

Ed Castleberry *CHS Class of 1965*

Back in the 1960s a lunch ticket cost $1.25 per week.

Buckwheat Finn, *CHS Class of 1979*

I use to lose my lunch ticket and Mrs. Giddens would say Tim go ahead and get your lunch. I'll take care of it this week. She was a great lady.

Donna Carroll Ward, *CHS Class of 1 977*

I loved Mrs. Giddens. She was the sweetest and most pleasant person to all of us kids!

Chapter 15

The Colored People, Needmore, and Glenn "Boots" Wilson

Needmore

Mike Headley, *CHS Class of 1962*

Needmore was the name the people of Childersburg called "the Colored" section during the period of time this memoir covers. As I approached the writing of this chapter I realized I also had a story to tell of what I as well as my family called the Colored people. To my knowledge Black people during that time period were never referred to as Black. Needmore was located on the west side of US Highway 280.

Two Schools

J. D. Warren, *CHS Class of 1961*

There were actually two schools in Childersburg in 1949 because there was a separate Negro or colored school (Phyllis Wheatley) — this was a different era!

A Friend of the Colored Barbers and Beauticians in Needmore

Dr. Richard (Dickey) Bean, *CHS Class of 1962*

The thing I remember the most about my father and his Barber Shop was he believed that all men were created equal in the eyes of God. Braxton Bean was not highly educated nor was he rich, but a great man of integrity and kindness. He loved Childersburg and her people.

A fond memory of my father was that dad purchased his barber supplies from a company in Birmingham who refused to sell supplies to the black barbers and black beauty shops in Childersburg. My father, being a Christian man, showed no discrimination to blacks or any minorities. Dad agreed to order all the barber supplies for the black barber and beauty shops — a service he quietly provided for at least 20 years.

I would usually go with my father and play football with the young Colored kids in Needmore who were always near the Colored barber shop when I was younger.

Carolyn Reynolds was the co-owner of the beauty shop with her husband, Walter, the barber shop owner. Carolyn was elected the "Childersburg Citizen of the Year" more than 30 years later. Carolyn stated, because of Braxton Bean, she and Walter survived financially in the Beauty and Barber business with my father's help.

Braxton Bean learned from his father, John Henry Martin Bean, who allowed a black family of poachers to live on his farm and raise crops to live and even feed themselves when the man was sick and could not farm for six months.

Fishing on the Coosa River

Charles "Turkey" Burke, *CHS Class of 1962,*

The Central of Georgia Rail Road trestle spanning the Coosa River remains as a symbol of my past as I look from my right car window traveling north into Shelby County, Alabama almost the same view as in the 1950s. For me, this view was my playground and opportunity to have fun.

Living by the Coosa River and having the freedom to fish, hunt and roam the banks was my passion. John Howard Henry, a black boy about my age, was one of my fishing buddies. Without giving any thought to danger, John

Howard would follow me from one adventure to the next — not always in his best interest. We used limb-set hooks to catch catfish, drum and logger head turtles. We would climb the slippery, bent over, hanging trees to retrieve our catch. We caught Long nose Spotted Gar with rods and reels near the train trestle's stone pillows, fishing from the bank. However, being children we soon bored with this type of fishing. The "big ones' were out in the middle of the Coosa River as we could see them swirl and splash.

We packed and carried our gear walking on the railroad bridge venturing to the middle of the trestle. Man, what a spot, sixty feet above the water teaming with big gar and catfish. We had a .22 rifle to shoot the gar before hoisting them up on to the train trestle.

We "kind of" knew the train schedule so the risk of a train hitting us was, well — low. We were perched on the pillow tops away from the rails. We did enjoy a few passing freight trains as they thundered by, vibrating and causing us to lose concentration on our fishing/shooting activities.

One trip, I hooked a big blue catfish. Looking at that fish's size, we decided that this was no match for our twelve pound fishing line. We had only one rod and reel and John Howard had to carry the rifle. I told John Howard to hold on to the fishing rod while I ran home to get an outfit with a braded line. On my return I lowered the line, hook and sinker combo. Managing to get this rig into the gaping cat's mouth and together we hoisted the catfish up to the railroad bridge. We were happy with that days catch as we walked the tracks back to the Southside of the Coosa River, and home. Our "polluted waters" catch were a hit at the Camp Childersburg Prison kitchen. The cook was happy to receive any fresh fish taking them with a big smile.

The Coosa Theater

Mike Headley, *CHS Class of 1962*

Childersburg was segregated in the 1950s and until the late 1960s. There was a door on the south side of the theater so that whites did not have to share a line with the colored people.

Coloreds were only served when whites did not want service. There was a set of stairs (inside) up the south side of the building to the second floor there the coloreds sat in the balcony, to watch the movie. I was told that sometimes a colored person would spit over the rail down on the white people, but I never saw that kind of behavior.

Betty Jenkins Breedlove, *CHS Class of 1962*

In the 1950s the theater was segregated as was every public building in the South. The white section was downstairs. It had stairs going up to another section for colored people. It was about a third the size of the downstairs seating. A projection room and a wall separated the only section that blacks were allowed to occupy. The black section did not even have a restroom. A door by the box office opened to the section that was designated for the blacks to buy tickets and a window for the concession stand and a water fountain.

Judy Brown, our maid

Mike Headley, *CHS Class of 1962*

This story must start with Edith Ellen Dudney Headley, my mother. My father, Samuel Alton Headley, was, no more prejudiced than most southern white men. However, in his later years he became more amenable to black people. I learned my tolerance of all peoples from my mother. Mother grew up in a southern family where I am sure the treatment of Colored people was the same as most southern families. I would challenge anyone who might think they have some idea as to what Childersburg was like in the day-to-day treatment of the Colored people. I will assure you it was nothing like what would be depicted in the Main Stream Media of today. The Blacks I knew were treated fairly.

My mother had a maid, as most of my aunts and their friends. The lady's name was Judy Brown. Judy lived for a number of years near our home in a rundown shack with two sisters, their mother Etta, along with many children of various ages and sexes. Whether Judy and her sisters were ever married to the colored men who seem too came in and out of their lives I have no idea. To my knowledge mother never inquired.

When I reached the ripe old age of 15 Judy had moved about a mile and a half away right off county road 95 known today as Meadow Circle. This gave me the opportunity to drive Judy home in the afternoons after work. The fact that I did not have a driver's license did not figure into the equation in Talladega County in the late 1950s. Judy needed to get home, I was available to drive, problem solved.

Judy came to work in our home must have been around 1950. She had little, if any, education. My mother taught Judy to use an electric stove, vacuum cleaner, toaster, iron, and clothes washer, not to mention a fan. Mother taught Judy to cook, and also taught her personal hygiene, among other things. Mother, for years, made sure that Judy had bathing soap, clothes, and shoes by providing Judy with many personal hygiene items on a regular basis. This generosity extended to her mother, sisters and their children on many occasions all the years Judy worked for my mother.

If Judy or any of her family were ever in need of medical care, it was my mother who would drive them to Sylacauga to the doctor then to the pharmacy for whatever medicines the doctor proscribed. It was all paid for by my father.

When Christmas arrived it was my mother who made sure every child in the Brown family got a gift from Santa Clause. That included the adult women; plus mother made sure the family had money to buy a special meal at Thanksgiving and Christmas.

Around 1960 the US Government, through the Department of Agriculture, started to distribute peanut butter, cheese, and butter. Later other products were added. Yep you can imagine who was driving the car to the government warehouse in Childersburg to get what in those days was called commodities.

Granted, you could make the case that if my mother had paid Judy Brown more than the going rate for a maid during those days Judy would have had no need for the assistance my family provided. $5.00 a day was considered the standard in the 1950s for a maid. I am sure that amount increased over the years until the government made welfare the standard, which stopped maids in the south, except for the very wealthy.

Aunt Mary Taylor

Brenda Solley Brown, *CHS Class of 1960*

I grew up knowing what it meant to be kind to your neighbors. Mamma's sister, Vee Lee, lived nearby and Old Aunt Mary Taylor, a black lady, helped her and Mamma with the chores. God made us all, regardless of skin color. When Aunt Mary Taylor died, she had as many white people at her funeral as she did black people. She was well loved.

Selling Possums on Saturday

Mike Headley, *CHS Class of 1962*

I did not date much until I was in the later part of my senior year at CHS. The main reason was that I did not have much extra money, and, well, girls cost money. Besides I enjoyed hunting with my male friends. In the late fall when the persimmons were ripe, right after the first frost, Ray Williams and I would head to the woods with his best opossum dog. This usually occurred on a Friday evening. We would stop at "That Curb Market" for Swisher Sweets cigars, a large 24 oz. coke each and some gas, at least 75¢ worth. We spent the better part of a Friday night in the cool autumn woods of Talladega County allowing the dog to run while we sat in the woods smoking our cigars drinking our cokes and listening to Rays dog run. The sound a dog makes when a possum is treed is different from when the dog is still hunting.

We usually caught at least six opossums on Friday evening, carrying them in a burlap sack. By the end of the night with a sack holding six or seven possums the sack became heavy, maybe 40 pounds, so as we tramped through woods we had to take turns carrying the sack.

Because we were always short of funds we would sell the opossum to the people living in Needmore. It rarely took more than 30 minutes on Saturday morning to sell all of our possums

We would drive to the center of Needmore get out and tell the first person we saw we had possums for sale. The Colored people would bargain hard but would usually pay 25¢ for a small opossum and up to 50¢ for large one. On a good Saturday morning we would make $2.25 which would pay for our cigars, cokes, and gas. All in all not a bad morning, besides the opossum season was short.

Glenn "Boots" Wilson the CHS Janitor

Dwain Adams, *CHS Class of 1962*

For as long back as I can remember Boots was the janitor at the Childersburg School. I loved talking with him, as most of the kids did, and I saw Boots almost every day after school. I felt like I could talk to him about any and everything and I asked Boots a tons of questions. He was always honest and good-natured.

At one time Boots drove an older model Cadillac. One day Boots told me he had gotten stopped for speeding. The policeman questioned him closely and asked him where he worked. He said, "I'm the janitor at Childersburg School." The policeman said, "I see you drive a Cadillac." Boots answered, "Yes, sir, I do." "Then what does the principal drive?" asked the policeman. Boots paused a bit, and then responded with a little chuckle, "He drives an ole beat up Ford." We both thought that was pretty funny. Boots did not mean to be disrespectful or condescending. He was just honest, and I always valued that about him.

Mike Headley, *CHS Class of 1962*

If I remember anything about Glenn "Boots" Wilson it was his attitude. Here was a black man who did not act like most black people that I knew in the 1950s. Glenn was different; he would look you in the eye. He was very happy with himself. He seemed to know what he wanted in life. He always had a better car than most people, black or white. I later learned that Glenn was a car enthusiast.

Linda Maddox Jinks, *CHS Class of 1967*

Boots was always very nice to me. Also Sara Miles was the female attendant. She was always a sweet lady — and still is.

Colored Kids Were My Playmates

Mike Headley, *CHS Class of 1962*

I had mostly Colored friends to play with — this was true for two reasons; number one; my mother taught me and my sisters that all people were God's children and deserved respect. Number two; I lived in an area where the closest children were black. I am not going to tell you I always treated every person I met in those years as I should have, and that includes some white people. However, I tried.

The black children I played with were my friends, most were boys, some were older some younger. We ate together we played together. I never gave it any thought. Willie Charles Brown was one of my best friends growing up.

An Old Black Man

Vicki Dobbs Southern, *CHS Class of 1972*

In the woods behind Pinewood Terrace on the back alley an old black man lived up there and had a horse and wagon. He would come down that back alley and would always let us kids hitch a ride in his wagon.

Patsy Cobb Willis Jones, CHS Class of 1971

Yes, we would sneak up to his house from the river, hide and watch then run when we saw anybody.

Two Water Fountains
Randall Fields, *CHS Class of 1967*

The school buses did not run through our neighborhood. My family and I along with others who lived on 13th street SW had to walk out to the Highway US 280 to catch the bus. We caught the bus next to Steve's old Dairy Queen when it was across from Lynn Motel. One morning everyone was in line to get water from one of the two Dairy Queen fountains on the side of the store. I walked over to the water fountain no one was using and got a drink.

Everyone started laughing at me. When I looked around I noticed that the water fountains were labeled "Colored only" and "White only" and I had drank from the one marked "Colored." I did not care. I had water and everyone else was still standing in line.

James Morris, *CHS Class of 1965*

One summer day my family was at the Quick-Check grocery. I thought getting ice water from a machine was the next best thing to a free coke besides the building was air-conditioned. We always raced to see who would be first at the water fountains." Everyone who saw me drinking from the "Colored only" fountain laughed. My siblings went to the fountain marked "Whites only." I thought, they didn't see the other one and I hollered I won, as I gulped the ice cold water. That's just the way things were back then.

Nelson

Sherry Machen Atkinson, *CHS Class of 1962*

My grandmother had a large home in Childersburg where the First National Bank and the A & P Store were built. Nanny owned the two-story house in the middle of the three homes that once stood there. Nelson Keith was an elderly Colored man when he came to live in Nanny's back yard. She cooked every meal for him and supplied him a place to live. He would not come in the big house to eat. He would only come to the back door and get his meals. He would tell Nanny it was best he ate his meals at his place.

He had a one room home made of wood with a tin roof. Inside his house there was a wood burning stove, a bed, table and chairs, and a huge wool rug on his floor. There was no electricity in Nelsons house he burned kerosene in his lantern. Nelson gathered eggs and did yard chores for my grandmother. Nelson did allow us kids to come in his small house. He wore overalls and a brown felt hat. And sometimes he would sit on a log in the back yard and tell my cousin Bill McSween and me stories.

Nelson got us good one day when we laughed at him for eating an orange, peeling and all. He told me and Bill that Mr. Oscar's (our grandfather) HAINT (ghost) was going to get us! Scared the living daylights out of us! We never laughed about anything Nelson did again. He had a daughter and a grandson that would come and visit. We liked for his daughter to visit and bring her young son. We got to play games with him. Nelson began to age and got sick. Nanny took care of him for a while. His daughter moved him to her home to take care of him. Those were very simple and happy times in my life. I will never forget these wonderful people that were a part of our lives.

The Lizard in My Garden

Mike Headley, CHS Class of 1962

The lizard that lives in my flower garden, oh if he would only beg my pardon.

What friends we might be if he could only see.

The fright he has given to others and me.

I am sure most busy is he looking for lunch, you see.

How pleasant he might be if his presence I could beforehand see.

He scampers no doubt which he has given little thought about.

His view from afar is more pleasant by far which I prefer to see.

Of the calamity he brings as he moves about.

Oh that we may share the garden a mutual existence I plea.

Has made me more conscious that the garden must have flowers plus a place where other creatures including the lizard may be.

M. Alton Headley

Chapter 16

Flagpole Mountain

GPS 33-13.638N 86-21.598 W

A View from the Fire Tower

Jullia Brunfeldt, *CHS Class of 1972*

How many spent time atop of Flagpole Mountain at the fire tower, looking over Childersburg. Neva Bowling, Wendy Harris, and I spent many evenings up there!

I Was Scared

Glendean Fields Ogle, *CHS Class of 1961*

My dad would take my family up to the top of Flagpole Mountain. My older sister and I would be sitting in the back seat. Daddy would back the car up close to the edge and then he would tell us to look out the back window. We would scream and say we were about to go off the edge. It would scare the begeebers out of us.

We Lived on the Kahatchee Side of the Mountain

Brenda Solley Brown, *CHS Class of 1960*

I was born in 1941 on Deloach Road known today as the Childersburg-Fayetteville Highway. I remember when daddy would take us up the mountain and parked so we could pick wild flowers in the spring, honeysuckles, sweet shrubs, and violets. We also picked huckleberries, and blueberries. We sometimes went all the way to the fire tower on top of Flagpole Mountain.

As you go down the west side of Flagpole Mountain toward Kahatchee there is a hill called "Thrill Hill". Daddy was full of mischief and people called him "Monk" (short for Monkey). One Sunday the car was full of my relatives, dressed in their Sunday best all holding dishes and desserts they were taking to a luncheon. You guessed it; daddy took them over "Thrill Hill" and one of his cousins ended up with the pie she was holding hitting her in the face.

Who is Dropping Watermelon Rinds?

J. D. Warren, *CHS Class of 1961*

One summer evening four of us guys were "hanging out." It must have been a dull night at the Dairy Queen and somebody said "let's go to the top of Flagpole Mountain." So we did.

It was getting dark, so we picked up a watermelon on the way. When we got to the top of Flagpole Mountain we found an eight-foot-high fence around the fire tower. Somebody said "let's climb the tower." So we scaled the fence and proceeded up the steps, carrying the watermelon.

We reached the platform at the top, but there wasn't much of a view. Too Dark! Somebody had a knife and we finished our first slice, and when the car's owner wasn't looking, somebody tossed a piece of watermelon rind over the side. Ker-plunk! It hit the car below! The driver said "What was that? Is something messing with my car?" As he peered down below we all looked down but, of course, couldn't see anyone. We had another round of watermelon and in a little while the same thing happened again. Ker-plunk! The driver said I know somebody is throwing watermelon rinds on my car.

After that it wasn't fun any longer, we proceeded back down to the ground and back over the fence. The driver inspected his car and found it was unharmed, so we drove back to the Dairy Queen. Once we got there we may have ordered a pizza. The Dairy Queen was the first place in town to offer pizzas. We had only learned what a pizza was on our senior trip to New York City! As we were finishing up, the driver said, "All right — who was dropping that watermelon on my car?" We all said, "Not me!"

A Trip to Flagpole Mountain

Mike Headley, *CHS Class of 1962*

Some of my first trips to the base of Flagpole Mountain started in 1954 when I would ride my bike over to Tommy Golden's house.

In those days County Road 92 was a dirt road. If you headed west you would start to climb what was called the Kahatchee hump. Reaching the top of the hump you had a choice. You could continue west and down into the Kahatchee community, or you could turn left (south) and continue your climb to the top of Flagpole Mountain.

When I was 13 I got my black 1957 Cushman Eagle motor scooter. That Cushman was no speedster with a seven horsepower flat head motor and two speed transmission, however, it got me to the top of the mountain many times.

Once you reached the top of Flagpole Mountain you had a great view of the surrounding land especially if you climbed the fire tower. The tower in the early years did not have a cyclone fence around it.

When you arrived at the fire tower house you had to push up a part of the floor. Looking out the windows on a clear day you could see Cheaha Mountain to the North East; looking northwest you could see the Wilsonville Steam Plant, and finally Fayetteville and the Coosa River to the South West.

A White Sea of Clouds, "Breathtaking"

Mickey Donahoo, *CHS Class of 1961*

Flagpole Mountain was a familiar sight in our neck of the woods with its fire observation tower rising high into the sky. I don't know if it were ever officially manned in our era; however, it was often "manned" by the local kids out for some adventure.

If you were inclined, you could sneak over the chain-link fence and climb the tower with ease. Ease is a relative term and takes on a different meaning with some people. J.D. Warren chose to climb the tower without using the steps. J.D. and normal did not always go together as exemplified by his climbing the tower via the structural framework. The rest of us considered ourselves dare-devils but even this was out of our comfort zone.

The gravel road going up the mountain to the tower was also a source of fun. With its many switch-backs, it was somewhat of a challenge to drive up and down. However, as the saying goes, "familiarity breeds contempt" and we were soon using the road up and down as a race track. Of course, the road being very narrow you couldn't pass anyone, so we would make a run against the clock. Needless to say this was a stupid venture (but we weren't always smart). Our fun ceased one night when our car stopped with the front end hanging over the side of Flagpole Mountain. I'm still not sure how we got the car back onto the road.

Flagpole was a great place to go "parking," if your date didn't mind the bumpy ride up and down the mountain. You would be presented with outstanding views, if you happened to be there on a cloudy night when the upper level of the clouds was below your parking spot and the moon was full. The white sea of clouds illuminated by the bright moon was breathtaking.

Chapter 17

Bean's Barbershop
Braxton Bean, Owner

Mr. and Mrs. Braxton Bean 1930

The Bean Family Story

Dr. Richard (Dickey) Bean, *CHS Class of 1962*

My great-grandfather's name was Mickleberry Bean; my grandfather was John Henry Martin Bean. The Clan MacBean has the oldest Family Tree in the US according to the Dissertation that was done some years ago in Cut & Shoot, Texas by a Bean. It goes back to the 1st MacBean in Scotland around 1,068 AD when there was only one MacBean. We were Bean Farmers and what the Scots called Low-Landers (people who lived in the Valley or Coast) as opposed to Highlanders who were goat & sheep herders in the mountains of Scotland. In Colonial Days, Scot's were all titled "Mac" which means "son of."

My father was born in 1919 and mother was born in 1922. They were married in 1939. Both my parents were born in Randolph County near Delta, Alabama. They married when dad was 20 and mother was 17.

During World War II dad was decorated with 27 medals for his service during combat. He went to the Armies' Barber School right after the war. In 1949 dad received an offer to work at a barber shop in Childersburg. Dad went to work in Childersburg and owned the business for 30 years. I started working in dad's shop the year it opened at the ripe old age of 5, shining shoes. A vocation I kept until I was 12.

Dad also upgraded his skills at the Roffler Hairstyling School of Atlanta, Georgia. In 1964 dad won first Place in the South East US for hairstyling at the Regional Men's Hairstyling Forum in Atlanta.

Braxton Bean was not highly educated nor a rich man, but a great man of integrity and kindness. The thing I remember most about my father was he was a Christian and showed no prejudice toward others. We were very close, and he was a great Father to my sister and me. As adults, my Father and I never had a cross word. I loved him dearly and miss him since his death. Both of my parents loved the people of Childersburg and lived there until they moved to a retirement home in Sylacauga for their final years. Mother died at 83, daddy died in 2005 at 87 years old. They were married 66 years.

Working for Mr. Bean

Ollie Pardue, *CHS Class of 1966*

Shortly after my mother and dad divorced, we moved to Childersburg. If I said we were poor that would be an understatement. If I got to enjoy anything other than the bare necessities, I had to find a way to make that happen.

I would collect bottles from the side of the road and sell them to the grocery stores. I could make a few cents per bottle and eventually get enough money to go to the movie theater. At age 13 I went to the movie for the first time in my life. Needless to say, I was amazed.

One of my older brothers, Don who was already working for a living, would always get his haircut at Bean's Barber Shop. Don was a smart guy and, though he had very little education, he really had a way with people. He was very popular with everyone he came in contact with. I know that Mr. Bean liked him. Don asked Mr. Bean if I could shine shoes in his shop and Mr. Bean said "yes."

I would walk from our house near highway 280 to downtown. It seemed like a long way at the time but was really less than a mile. Mr. Bean made a deal with me. He said "Ollie, if you will keep my shoes shined, I will keep your hair cut". Obviously I thought that was a good deal, since I was getting 25¢ for shining a pair of shoes for his customers. Most folks did not get a shine, but some did. Looking back, some of

217

them did not need their shoes shined, but now I know they did it just for me. Most folks just paid the 25¢, but a few of them tipped. I do remember one person giving me a dollar. In 1959 a dollar to a 13 year old poor kid was awesome. I still remember the guy that gave me that tip and I still appreciate it.

One day Mr. Bean showed me a pair of shoes that he said had been left at his shop to be shined and the customer never returned to get them. He asked me to try them on. I did and they almost fit. He said that I could have them if I wanted them since the customer didn't seem to want them. Looking back on that seemingly uneventful situation, I now believe that those were a pair of Mr. Bean's shoes. It might not seem like a big deal to some, but it was a big deal to a kid with only one pair of shoes to his name. I remember the shoes were black, lace-ups with a pointed toe. They certainly were not stylish for a kid my age, but were very much appreciated.

I worked there for about 6 months. One day at school one kid who knew that I was shining shoes addressed me as "Hey Shine". That really did a number on my pride and that ended my days as a "shoe shine boy". But looking back on the whole situation, I know that I grew from that experience. I'll never forget that guy that tipped me a dollar and I will never forget Mr. Braxton Bean for his love and kindness and this adds to all the memories of all the good people of Childersburg that influenced me and helped me to grow as a person and become a mature adult.

As for Mr. Bean, this guy was the best barber I have ever known. He was successful at what he did because he strived to be the best. He was a great example for a young boy who knew absolutely nothing about life and how to become a man and be successful.

Mr. Bean told me a story about when he was in a training class, at barber school. The challenge for the class was to cut someone's hair and make the most positive change in that person's appearance. So he goes out and finds someone on the street that had long hair and an undesirable appearance. Needless to say, he won.

Mr. Bean was for me a very personable man. He was always quick to ask each customer what was going on in their life. He really cared about the customers and took a personal interest in each one. Mr. Bean shared stories and events regarding his family. His children seemed to be the focus of most of his conversations.

But for Mr. Bean it was his love and caring nature to all the folks in Childersburg, especially the youth, which shows what a good man he was. He was one of the biggest supporters of all the sports activities in Childersburg as long as he lived. He was a very positive role model to me.

I remember a positive role model in the town of Childersburg, who cared about the town and its people. For Braxton Bean it was all about family, and I was made to feel a part of that family. I could see Mr. Bean cared about me and wanted to be a positive influence in my life. I will always appreciate all that he did for me. Everybody that wanted a good haircut went to Mr. Bean. I got mine for free! God is good.

Trying to Sneak By

Candy Stephens, *CHS Class of 1972*

I would try to sneak by Bean's Barbershop without being seen, but I would usually have to give Mr. Bean a kiss on the cheek and get a piece of bubble gum.

Four Hair Cuts

Robbie Riddle, *CHS Class of 1975*

I don't remember much about our haircuts other than mom would take all four of us boys in to see Mr. Bean at one time on Saturdays. We would always get a piece of bubble gum when Mr. Bean finished.

The Second Barber Chair

Mike Headley, *CHS Class of 1962*

When one entered Bean's Barber Shop the first thing you noticed was that Mr. Bean occupied the second barber chair with the first chair over the years being operated at different times by Mr. Galloway (Corky and Glenda Galloway's father) or Mr. Malone(Donald Malone's father).

When Dickey, Mr. Beans son was a star running back at Childersburg High School (All American running back for CHS in the fall of 1961) Mr. Bean decorated the area around his barber chair with pictures of Dickie and his accomplishments on the football field with lots of CHS blue and white. Many people in Childersburg considered Braxton Bean the best barber in the area. I remember having to wait to get in Mr. Bean's barber chair, because he was always busy.

A Hair Style

Mike Headley, *CHS Class of 1962*

Got my hair styled this morning. The stylist and I shared the standard greetings. After the shampoo (which brings up the question) when did shampoos start to be part of the male haircut experience? I sat there and I realized I was not going anywhere for the next 30 minutes

What to do..... I have it. You know the little hair clippings that fall down the front of your cape? Yep, the one made with silk. Why not count the number of times it takes to thump/flick the hair clippings down the front of the shroud off the knee allowing them to make a landing on my shoes or the floor. I found that it takes two flicks if my hair is drier, three if the stylist had just sprayed it again.

I don't remember 20 years ago of anyone asking if I would like my ears, nose and eyebrows trimmed. It appears as I age I am growing hair at prodigious levels, in unrelated places, not seen in the previous years. Well thanks for small favors.

Haircuts have changed a great deal over the last 60 years. I can remember when I was 12, my haircuts always occurred on a Saturday morning at Bean's Barbershop, lasting no more than fifteen minutes. This ritual occurred every two weeks. I have no idea what Mr. Bean did the other five days a week because everyone I knew got their haircut on Saturday. Yes, I am aware that adds up to six, not seven, days. You see people in those days went to church on Sunday, thus the reason for my reference to six days.

I left Bean's Barbershop with a light sweet hair tonic fragrance wafting on the breeze. There never seemed to be a shortage of the tonic which always dripped on my neck and shirt as I sauntered down the street. I hardly noticed since I was chewing on a mouth full of pink Double Bubble

221

bubblegum which Mr. Bean had given me. The entire experience in the 1950s had cost a quarter, which Mother gave me.

Not sure when those red, white and blue turning poles started to go away. Must have been during the 1970s when the razor cut first came along. I jumped on the razor-cut band wagon along with most of the younger men of that time. That was the first time I remember a hair blower being used in the process of my hair cut. Around that time I think the old timey barber shop started its demise. I remember those sights, sounds, and smells which emanated from Bean's Barbershop that are simply not found in today's salon — sad really.

Perhaps that's why I have started to count the clippings — because I know there will be no Double Bubble bubblegum when that silk cape is slipped from my shoulders.

Chapter 18

A Man Named Rosie

Franklin D. Burton

Parts of this chapter were written by
Joy Burton Lawson, *CHS Class of 1972*
David Burton, *CHS Class of 1975*
Mike Headley, *CHS Class of 1962*

How does a Son of the South gain the moniker "Rosie?"

Rosie was named by his mother — naming him after the 32nd president of the United States. The Burtons were a family of nine. Father Jim, mother Ella, along with four brothers Ed, Ellis, Earnest and Rosie, plus three sisters Evelyn, Estelle and Sis. Rosie, the youngest son, was born near the base of Flagpole Mountain four miles Southwest of Childersburg. Ironically, Rosie died in the house in which he was born. In the next few pages we hope to share with you Franklin D. (Rosie) Burton.

Rosie was a quiet, simple-living, hardworking man which some might have missed. Rosie grew up attending the Childersburg school system. He worked as a trash, utility and bush man for the city of Childersburg providing many years of loyal service. This was the only job Rosie ever held. Many from my generation remember Rosie as "the trash man."

Rosie was an avid player of several musical instruments including the Banjo, Harmonica, and Guitar. On occasions you would see Rosie playing music around Childersburg, Sylacauga, and Birmingham. Rosie loved to entertain. I'm not sure where he learned to play — I assume he was self-taught.

Rosie was not the mayor nor a council person, but perhaps an ambassador of the regular people, the ones who get up every morning and go to work quietly going about their lives. A quiet, smart man who did not let others see just how really smart he was. Rosie never married — living with his mother, Ella, until her death. Always the gentleman, I always remember Rosie tipping his hat to a lady, no matter her age.

A regular at Red Hare's Pool Hall after work, Rosie was always wearing his overalls with a small spiral-bound pad and a #2 pencil in his pocket to record the debts of those who might find themselves short on cash. Rosie, for all practical purposes, ran a Pay-Day loan service long before Pay-Day loans were popular. Because I never asked for a loan myself I cannot attest to the level of service from Rosie's Pay-Day loan company. However, others have told me that Rosie was the man to see when you found yourself a bit short on cash. Especially after one found they had lost several rounds of pool. Rosie's bank was always open. For the regular's at Red's, Rosie was a welcome sight.

Rosie walked much of the time when he was going from place to place. However, many people would recognize Rosie and pick him up to help him on his way. Rosie was taught to drive by Faye Crow, only getting his driver's license after he was 40 years old.

Rosie never went anywhere without his trusty Smith & Wesson® 38 Limon Squeezer (pistol). Many may not know but he raised chickens, ducks, turkeys, and pigeons at his home almost out of the city limits at the very end of Ninth Avenue west of CACC. Rosie only added indoor plumbing because the city made him do so. Before that, Rosie used an outhouse and drawing his home water from a well with a hand crank rope, bucket, and dipper.

Rosie: A Character

Earl Wesson, Jr., *CHS Class of 1972*

Rosie was one of those "characters" many small towns had and everyone knew him. He may have not been one of the most prominent or from high-society, but I think everyone had/has their own Rosie Burton stories and memories. Cowboy hat, cigar and a guitar or banjo was part of his Saturday night wardrobe. I remember Rosie playing at a talent show at the Armory in Childersburg many years ago. Rosie brought the crowd up with his rendition of a song he says was called "Run N-word, Run."

Christmas with Uncle Rosie

Joy Burton Lawson, *CHS Class of 1972*

A character is right, but Rosie had a heart of gold. If we didn't get a Christmas present from anybody else, Uncle Rosie would show up at our house on Christmas morning with a gift for all five of us kids. He was kind of like Santa Clause to us; Rosie would deliver our gifts and leave. Usually walking, maybe headed to Birmingham. I guess somebody picked him up and gave him a ride; because he always made it back home to Childersburg. We would see him walking toward home on Sunday afternoon always with his banjo and his pistol on his hip.

Rosie at the River View Curb Market

James Morris, *CHS Class of 1967*

The time was 12:30am on a Sunday morning. I'd had just taken my date home before her appointed time. This lady loved to eat Mexican food at a restaurant in Birmingham called Uncle Julio's Hacienda Bar & Grill. I liked aged skirt steak and other sides mostly of beans and very hot peppers, but I should never ask or get them too hot.

My date liked the 'little bit of everything' plate, and we both drank Margaritas swirled with frozen sangria. But as usual I could not help myself from eating the peppers, beans and Mexican hot spices; despite the fact this meal would fill me with large amounts of gas. This was the reason I had to get my date home. I needed help so I stopped at Coleman's River View Curve Market to get some relief.

As I passed Rosie at the cash register we nodded, and I received the usual "How You Doing Hoss" as I walk by. I quickly moved over to the medicine aisle looking for some anything to help. There it was an anti-gas but didn't say anything about pressure reliever, or anti-stink, but read 'extra strength.' The bloated feeling was on the edge of no return as I leaned over and let a silent whoosh go free.

I needed more of the same quickly and a cure. The smell while invisible came in contact with my surroundings. It was gagging me and I had created it! So holding my breath and with watery eyes I turned heading for the cash register. As I looked up from reading the tiny words "RELIEVES GAS FAST" there blocking the aisle was Rosie. As usual Rosie was all smiles and ready to talk about anything, and for as long as I would stay. New pressure was reaching the release point; which affected my judgment so I panicked. As I slowed to say hi to Rosie gas was escaping reaching just above Rosie's moon-pie chewing mouth.

Suddenly Rosie said "GOD ALMIGHTY, HOSS!" as the odor reached his nose. Poor Rosie's eyes were watering and his nose wrinkled up. Both eyes where squinted shut and both eyebrows now down on his nose. With his hands flying and trying to cover his mouth, a mixture of sweet milk and Moon Pie spewed from both Rosie's nostrils like a just opened can of hot beer that had just been dropped.

Rosie's mouth being close tightly only increased the pressurized sweet milk and Moon-Pie mixtures spewing a great distance. This involuntary reaction on Rosie's part created the need for my hasty retreat. Rosie opened his watery eyes saying "God Almighty HOSS!" "What's wrong with you?"

As I hurried past Rosie splattered with the Moon Pie and warm milk mixture I headed for the cash register. Old man Coleman was crying from laughter and begging for Rosie to stop, until the odiferous cloud reached his nose. I was famous for a time. However, Coleman and Rosie never trusted me after that night, always checking the air upon my arrival.

Rosie the Trash Man

Tom Herndon, *ISHS Class of 1971*

I would wait for Rosie to come by my house (on his trash run) through Pine Crest. In the summer I would have a cool drink of iced tea, RC, or lemonade ready for Rosie and we would talk. I was nine years old and I told everyone who would listen "I wanted to be a trash man," just like Rosie when I grew up. I am now retired from the Nevada Nuclear Test Site & Nellis AFB, and live in Utah.

Rosie around Childersburg

Earl Wesson, Jr., *CHS Class of 1972*

Rosie could be seen many times on the weekend walking and hitch-hiking. Other times you might see him downtown Childersburg or Sylacauga entertaining people with his banjo. Rosie never played for money, although people did chip in a little sometimes. He loved entertaining people, or maybe showing off a bit. Rosie worked in the street and sanitation department and there were restrictions on city employees going into yards, behind houses, etc., to collect limbs, trash and debris. Rosie would; especially if the homeowner was disabled. Rosie lived a simple life and probably gave away far more of his money than he spent on himself because as Joy Burton Lawson said, "Rosie made sure kids had Christmas."

"HOW YOU DOING HOSS?"

ROSIE

Known by most, seen by all, who was this Renaissance man
of Childersburg for 69 years?
Was there more to this son of the south, perhaps something
some may have missed?
A working man through the week, his overalls he wore,
often soiled by his day's work, he quietly bore.
Robust of chest, yet regular of height, many would say he was strong,
and sometimes quiet.
Rosie's greeting passes through my mind, and rings in my ear,
60 years later clamorous and clear.
When on the street, Rosie's way of making a friend was his greeting.
Males both young and old were acknowledged as Rosie passed
with "How You Doing Hoss?"
With a tip of his cowboy hat to ladies young and old
was Rosie's way of displaying his courtesy to ladies all.
It was of little importance if a person was tall or small
to Rosie all were the same.
Rosie's lit pipe, a smoke he did enjoy, or at other times a good cigar.
On weekends Rosie wore different attire, moving among us
in his cowboy hat and boots polished to a shine, his cowboy belt
and black bolo tie a western figure never one to opine.
At Red Hare's Pool Hall ever ready with cash for a small usury fee,
reminding those who were short of funds, the loan was not free.
On his hip his trusty S&W 38 lemon squeezer ever near,
with overalls for his workday were his standard ware.
Whether on a fall Friday night or during the winter
when round ball was played, our CHS boys and girls Rosie
support was assured because he was there the Tigers to cheer.
That old green Dodge truck around town was often seen.
A quiet ambassador walking amongst us, some chose not to see.
We remember, and salute Franklin D. Burton, this renaissance man of
Childersburg, Alabama all knew simply as, Rosie.

M. Alton Headley

My last thoughts on Rosie

Mike Headley, *CHS Class of 1962*

Franklin Delano (Rosie) Burton lived a quite simple life, and often spent money on others, especially children; Rosie left this world making sure he was not a financial burden to any man, which included his family. Thinking about that situation makes you realize that's what Roosevelt D. (Rosie) Burton had done his entire life. The town of Childersburg salutes you. Rest well Rosie, rest well.

Chapter 19

CHILDERSBURG-SYLACAUGA CRUISING

Mrs. Peter Wallenfang at the Childersburg Dairy Queen

The Dairy Queen / Tastyee-Freez Loop

Mike Headley, *CHS Class of 1962*

It's hard today to express the car culture which enveloped the United States during the 1950s and 1960s. It was a heady time. Driving the loop from the Dairy Queen's parking lot south exit, you would turn left (burning a little rubber) heading north past Grove Park, up Highway US 280/231 north toward the main red light in Childersburg with the water tower on the hill. Next we would travel through the red light, crossing State Highway 76, then across the bridge over the train tracks, and down the hill past Wilson Brothers Construction. We would make a quick check to see if anyone was at "That Curb Market," then drive on north by Marie Taylor's restaurant. After passing Taylor's you took a quick left into the Tastyee-Freez parking lot. Driving through the parking lot around back of the Tastee-Freez we could see the cars lined up side-by-side and rear-to-rear with the cars facing out. In those days we always backed in when parking behind the Tastyee-Freez. I suppose so that we could make a quick getaway. I have no idea why because we really had nowhere to go.

When leaving the Tastyee-Freez to complete the loop you passed Marie Taylor's back to highway US 280 and then took a quick right, hit the gas, D1, shift, D2, and then shift to Drive. Yes, it was a three speed automatic in Dad's Coup Deville. Most automatics were two speeds in those days. Then it was time to check the red light at the top of the hill which would be coming up quickly. If the light was green that meant you put the pedal to the metal ... meaning you were in for a fast trip back to the Dairy Queen ... a total distance of less than a mile. In the late 50s and early 60s we called this "The Loop."

The odyssey continued as you checked the scene to see who was in the parking lot at the DQ. We were always on the alert for strangers from faraway places like Harpersville, Vincent, or (God forbid) Sylacauga. For the most part the kids from other towns did not come around much especially to the Dairy Queen. They understood the Dairy Queen was our place. Yes, the property deed was in Steven Garrett Stephens' name, but that mattered little to us.

The White Midget Loop, Sylacauga

Mike Headley, *CHS Class of 1962*

The old White Midget in Sylacauga was located on the south side of Fort Williams Street near downtown. The new White Midget Restaurant opened in 1955 and closed around the end of 1960 and was located on what is today Talladega County

Road 511, just south of Tar Water Branch in the northern part of Sylacauga, Alabama.

My first visit to the White Midget must have been about 1956 when I had reached the ripe old age of 12. I could not drive, so my cousin, Frank Russell (who was three years older), would do the honors.

I would ask Daddy on Friday or Saturday evening if we could use his 1956 Chevrolet Bel-Air 2 door hard top convertible. It had a two tone paint job Indian Ivory on the top, and Roman Red on the bottom, and continental kit and fender shirts complete with twin aerials on the rear fenders. It also had a 265 cubic inch small block (bowtie) Chevy V8 motor with a four barrel carburetor and power pack producing 205 horsepower, complete with a three-on-the-tree shifter.

Frank would drive us south down US Highway 280 about a mile and a quarter to his uncle's Gulf Gas station and restaurant, which was known in those days as "Johnnies." At Johnnies we would fill the tank with what was sold as super premium 104 octane gasoline — Gulf Crown in the purple pump.

Daddy had credit with Johnnie Russell's Gulf gas station, restaurant and garage. It was common in those days to have accounts with several gas stations and food stores in the area. Another was at Casey Holt's store where Casey pumped Standard Oil products at Holt's Cross Roads one mile north of our house on US Highway 280.

Some weekends I would drive to Sylacauga and back but due to the price of gas at 35¢ a gallon I had to watch my money. If someone wanted to go to Sylacauga to the White Midget for a hamburger they would have to pitch in at least a quarter. If I had car gas or a friend with seventy five cents (which was rare), or three friends with a quarter each we could get enough gas to drive over to Sylacauga a round trip of twenty two miles.

Cars in those days did not get more than about 12 miles per gallon. We made that trip no more than two times a week, mostly on the weekends.

If we headed to Sylacauga, a trip to the White Midget was in order. The White Midget was a one story building kind of low slung with a red band around a flat roof with lots of glass on the front and a large parking lot with a big sign out front. The White Midget had a dining room inside, but for some reason it was remodeled a few years later allowing cars to drive in the south end, place and pick up your order then proceed out the north end. I don't remember any one being asphyxiated from the car fumes even burning leaded gasoline as we drove through. The new location was ¾ of a mile north of downtown Sylacauga, a town at that time of about 12,000 people. We felt fairly safe going to the White Midget because it was on the north edge of town. For the most part the kids from Sylacauga did not come to Childersburg, and the Childersburg kids did not go to Sylacauga.

The White Midget had car hops so you pulled in facing the restaurant and when everyone had decided what to order the car lights were flashed to let the girl inside know we were ready to place our order. Quickly the girl would come out; however, they were not on roller skates. The regular menu was burgers, cheeseburgers, French fries, hotdogs, milk shakes, and malts. Speaking of malts what happened to malts? I don't see them anymore. Sitting at the White Midget gave me my first experience hearing a D. J. on an AM radio in Dad's 1956 Chevy. The music came from a Chicago, Illinois station. Rock and Roll here we come.

The Comet Drive Inn

Mike Headley, *CHS Class of 1962*

On your Childersburg-to-Sylacauga-and-back-to-Childersburg loop you would pass the Comet Drive In on your left three miles north of Sylacauga, Alabama.

Sixteen Fathoms Deep was the movie opening night July 1st 1949.

1950s Drive Inn Car Speakers

Did you ever pull away from the speaker post and forget to hang up your speaker?

Cruising

Earl Wesson Jr., *CHS Class of 1972*

One of my favorite times growing up in Childersburg involved getting a driver's license and gaining the independence that only the open road can give you. My first car however, left a good deal to be desired as it was not what you would call highly desirable by a 16-year-old boy trying to impress the ladies.

It was a 1962 Ford Falcon Station Wagon with the fake woodgrain on the sides; "Squire" was what they called this thing. It had a luggage rack on top, factory under dash air conditioner that sort of worked sometimes, but robbed too many ponies from the mostly dead "6 banger" under the hood, "Three on the tree" transmission, and all sitting on recap tires. Of course it was bought brand new at the Childersburg Ford dealership owned/operated by L.V. Poole.

Recaps were $15 a pop and I threw those recaps off at least six times before I was able to buy decent tires. The recaps seemed to fly off mysteriously at about 90 mph. Most of the time that Ford was kept at a respectable speed to conserve gas; which I bought myself since I worked at the A&P grocery afternoons and Saturdays. The A&P was closed on Sundays.

I could ride to Putman's Gas Station and put in $3.00 of their regular gas at 29.9¢ per gallon and ride to school, work, and date until the next Friday night when I got paid. When I was lucky, the gas stations had a "gas war" going and I could sometimes get gas for as low as 27.9¢ a gallon.

If you had a car with some horsepower ... the customary burnout was in order. That way the crowd in the parking lot at the Dairy Queen could see you as you turned left on to Highway 280 heading north to the red light near downtown, Childersburg.... life in a small southern town.

Dairy Queen®, Tastee-Freez, and Taylor's

Mickey Donahoo, *CHS Class of 1961*

The Dairy Queen, Tastee-Freez, and Taylors were the social center of Childersburg's young people, especially on Friday and Saturday nights. The activities generally consisted of "cruising" from one end to the other and making a "circle" around the parking lots. This allowed you to "see" who was out-and-about and who was with whom. It was a good time.

If you happened to have a car that would "burn rubber" you were in the elite and expected to show off a little for the rest of us. Most of us were unable to perform this feat due to sheer power from the engine, so we would have to improvise. One form of the improvising was in down shifting a stick shift so that the tires "barked." This was nowhere at the level of "smoking" but at least gained a little attention.

Growing Older

Mike Headley CHS Class of 1962

Now that I am in the winter years of my life

The older I have grown time has taught, life comes with strife.

Will this condition continue to be?

Will there be additional turmoil for me?

Where have the years gone, it seems they were not mine to own?

From childhood thru high school on to college I grew.

Military, marriage, children, and grandchildren came through.

When does this odyssey cease to be, as a traveler I cannot see?

The gait slows and the grandchildren grow.

The shoulders stoop and the eyelids droop.

The skin has additional spots and hair with color is not.

Nor does this time frighten me, for these eyes have seen much you see.

My makers open arms are now in view, a promise he has made for me, and you.

Which is a comfort to me, for my sins are great,

And them I often contemplate.

M. Alton Headley

Chapter 20

Camp Childersburg (the Prison)

My Dad the Warden

Carolyn Green Price, *CCHS Class of 1965*

Quinton Green, born January 15 1919, was the superintendent of Camp Childersburg from 1955 thru 1960. The Alabama prison system transferred Quinton from Camp Auburn located in Auburn, Alabama to Childersburg. Quinton and Lois Green moved their family, including 4 children: James, Dennis, Donald and Carolyn, to Childersburg in the summer of 1955. Camp Childersburg housed only Colored (black) prisoners, as they were called during that period. Camp Childersburg was what would today be considered a minimum security facility.

Some Camp Childersburg prisoners were incarcerated for major offences, including murder and burglary while others had shorter sentences. Some were in for life. My family and I went about the prison unmolested spending time with the dangerous prisoners as well as the not-so-dangerous.

Sundays the prisoners would play ball with us for hours behind a ten foot tall fence. The prisoners lived in one story white buildings with a tin roof. The supper time meal most days was some kind of beans (pintos, butterbeans, or great northern) with cornbread and potatoes. The prisoners usually had milk to drink with their meals. They grew a huge garden and sugar cane.

I can remember one incident where one of the prisoners got out or escaped and Daddy found him in a ditch close by, very drunk. My brother Donald was bad to run away from home when he was three years old. It took the rest of us to watch him when he was outside. Many times we would find him in the prison lying up with the night cook on his cot and they would both be sound asleep. We didn't see anything to be afraid of. We didn't think anything of it and Daddy trusted the prisoners with us.

We lived in a house right across the street from the Camp. Sandy Maddox and I played on the big gravel piles a lot. We would get us a piece of tin and ride it from the top of the gravel pile to the bottom as we called it back then.

My parents would go to town every week to buy groceries. They took us with them most of the time but we had to sit in the car while they went in the Jitney Jungle. I always wanted to go to the dime store and get new jack stone or coloring book and crayons. I could spend a quarter and get those things.

The first family I met after moving to Childersburg was the Maddox family, Charles, Lynese, Billy (Peanut), Don, Delores, Sandy, Linda and Mike. I spent almost every other night at the Maddox house. There were eight of them so Mr. and Mrs. Maddox didn't think one more child made much difference. They treated me just like I was one of their own. I loved them just like they were my brothers and sisters.

Sandy Maddox and I were the same age and we were together from sun up to sun down most every day. We played Jack stones and hopscotch all day in our yard. I was the only girl in my family of 4 children so the Maddox girls were like sisters to me. When I spent the night with Sandy there would be 4 girls in one bed; two at the head of the bed and two at the foot of the bed. We laughed and giggled until Mr. or Mrs. Maddox would holler for us to go to sleep. Sandy Maddox and I were close; Sandy was my partner in crime.

In the summer of 1960 we moved from Childersburg to Heflin, Alabama. My Dad was transferred to the Heflin Prison Camp which later changed the name to Camp Hollis because they built a new prison about 10 miles from Heflin.

Camp Childersburg continued to operate for several years after dad was transferred to Camp Heflin.

After we moved to Heflin, Sandy Maddox and I thought the world had come to an end. We thought we couldn't make it without each other. But as time went on we did. I have kept in touch with Sandy Maddox Giddens all these years. She and I are still best friends.

I started to Cleburne County High School the 59-60 school year. Starting the 7th grade and graduated there, as did my brothers. I married Glenn Price the year after I graduated and we still live in Cleburne County.

My dad retired from the State of Alabama penal system at Camp Hollis in Heflin, Alabama with more than 35 years of service, and died in April 1988. At this writing his wife Lois lives in a nursing home.

Growing up near Camp Childersburg

Charles "Turkey" Burke, *CHS Class of 1962*

The trail to the Prison Camp was a short trip from our family café, Morgan Bridge Inn. Just cut through the trailer park pass the Warden's House and you were at the front gate. Looking left and right are the four guard towers staffed with uniformed rifle-carrying guards in the towers. The Prison had an alabaster hue, everything was white, buildings, post, uniforms everything a striking contrast to the "white clad" black occupants of the camp. Every hour, each of the four guards in the towers would "ring out" a signal cadence, "all clear — everything is OK". Not too often, usually at night, the siren would sound; an alarm went out — "prisoner escaped".

It was easy to enter the camp grounds and the prison interior. During week days the camp's occupants were out with sling blades grass cutting, picking up litter and other highway maintenance jobs. Usually the warden's children were my

241

play mates which made getting into the prison quite easy. All of the prisoners were friendly and welcomed the opportunity to talk and tell their stories. The entire prison was very clean and orderly inside. All of the cots were lined up and the kitchen shelves were neatly stocked. Each of the white dining hall tables had salt, pepper, pepper sauce and a quart mason jar of ribbon cane syrup in the center. From the kitchen area was the smell of butter beans and cornbread. The row of large aluminum pots on the stove revealed a hefty cloud of steam with fatback aroma. Most of the cooks were fat. The camp had a huge garden, where the prisoners grew vegetables and sugar cane. The prisoners made their own syrup. Also, the prison raised hogs.

On week-ends the situation changed as the inmates were all inside the compound. As you approached the grounds a loud African accented chatter could be heard. Many would be out of the barracks and pitching baseballs. This was my first exposure to some hearty cursing punctuated with lots of "MFs." Some of our friends, including the Maddox boys, were allowed to use the prison baseball field.

We thought our group was pretty good. On a few Sunday afternoons we "white boys" would play a game with the inmates. We did not stand a chance and were soundly beaten every time.

I always enjoyed a visit to the blood hound pens. Some of the trustees would pretend to escapee so that the hounds could be trained. The whole exercise would be completed with the sounds of baying blood hounds. Most of the time this was training exercises, but not always.

My almost daily visit to the camp included time at the maintenance shop. My favorite hangout was with Pete, the black trustee maintenance helper. I enjoyed seeing him weld, repair gear boxes as a skilled maintenance tradesman. He would tell me about "camp secrets."

242

Inmates would steal ribbon cane syrup, sugar, and yeast from the kitchen. They would mix these components and cut a plug out of a pumpkin in the garden, pack in the compound and wait for the natural fermentation to occur. After a few days, Pumpkin Beer was the reward. Also, a quick brew was made in a quart mason jar and stashed outside in the highway sign materials storage area. I would find the hiding places for this "stash".

One day Pete made me an offer; He would produce two large shop-made "Bowie Knives" for $1.50 each. I was so excited, I immediately went to the café and talked daddy out of three dollars. Pete and I completed the transaction and I was the proud owner of two Bowie knives. I started throwing the knives, and one broke at the brazed joint of the handle. I took the broken halves back to Pete, however, Pete explained there was no warranty. Pete said, "They are not throwing knives."

Pete also explained the reason for the every other Sunday visit from women. It was an opportunity for wives, girlfriends, and others to visit, telling me this was a way to have intercourse, which was most helpful in keeping the inmates calm, and from attempting an escape from the prison.

Sometimes my friends and I would use set hooks or limb hooks to catch fish on the banks of the Coosa River below my home. The catfish and drum had to be released because the river was polluted from the paper mills chemical discharges. One day we caught a 20 pound logger head turtle. After a discussion of "what to do with it' and watching it bite finger sized sticks in two; we decide to take it to the Prison kitchen where we were offered 50 cents for our prize turtle, and we quickly accepted. After that we brought several long-nose Gar, free of charge, for the prisoners' dining pleasure.

243

The Dairy Queen at the Prison

Tony Butts, CHS Class of 1960

I worked at the Dairy Queen, driving a three-wheeled Cushman Truckster scooter for Steve. When I drove by Camp Childersburg located about a half mile south of the Coosa River. I would stop and spend some time with the prisoners, and some evenings I would stay for dinner, eating with the prisoners. The cook served the best corn bread in Childersburg. I was the Dairy Queen ice cream piper for the children and, yes, even the prisoners of Camp Childersburg for several years.

A Motorcycle Gang Came to Talladega County

Sherry Machen Atkinson, CHS Class of 1962

In September 1971 a few years after the Talladega Speedway opened the Talladega County Sheriff arrested a large motorcycle gang who had come to the Talladega International Speed Way, but were creating problems. Because of the large number of men arrested the Sheriff decided to send the prisoners to Camp Childersburg prison.

Billy and I were returning from a trip to Prattville when we saw a black fellow that worked for the city by the name of Nelson standing on the street by Cliett's Hardware Store carrying a sawed off shotgun. We stopped and Billy asked "what was going on?" Nelson told us "Hells Angels were coming from California to shoot up Childersburg, and bust their buddies out of the prison." The entire matter was well — funny.

James Morris, CHS Class of 1967

The Outlaws Motorcycle gang had gotten out of hand at the Talladega International Raceway and after a dawn raid

244

which took place on a September Sunday morning. "This is the Talladega, Alabama Race Track and y'all will behave!" said Sheriff Luke Brewer.

J.D. Pricket and I were standing downtown Childersburg on the Monday night of September 6, 1971. This was night the Outlaws motorcycle gang was to seek revenge on Childersburg because the Talladega County Sheriff had placed 200 of their friends in jail. The Outlaws gang passed on threats of revenge for holding their buddies at the Childersburg Prison Camp.

Some people thought it was the way the Sheriff treated their bikes that angered the Outlaws so badly. All of their Harleys were loaded into an 18-wheel dump truck trailer. At the prison their bikes were unloaded like a load of coal into a big pile out in front of the prison. In plain view of the 200 bikers who were watching from behind the prison fence.

The Outlaws were upset about their pile of bikes and more so about the way they had to work to untangle the pile when they wanted to leave town. All 200 were made to leave quietly one bike at a time.

The Outlaws said, "We'll be back." So, late on Monday night after the biker threats, a group of armed men formed on Main Street in Childersburg. J.D. and I were among the group. Shadows of armed men could be seen on the roof tops standing guard with their deer rifles reflecting in the street lights.

All of us standing on the street that night knew the loaded guns on the roof tops where no joke. All were happy to see dawn come. That angry crowd had turned into a sleepy, tired group. So, the Childersburg defenders loaded up and drove to DoDo's restaurant for hot coffee and a great breakfast. We were all happy the Outlaws gang never came through Childersburg that night.

A Voice of Reason

James Morris, *CHS Class of 1967*

The September night in 1971 we thought The Outlaws biker gang was coming to take their revenged out on Childersburg for holding their buddies at the prison; talk on the streets was getting ugly. Threats and let's listen to reason facts were shared. Then from the back of the crowd we heard a familiar voice speaking over the crowd. It was Glenn "Boots" Wilson the Childersburg High School janitor. Glenn was trying to be heard over the noise of the crowd, as the group turned to hear what Boots had to say. Boots said "the longer I stands here the meaner I gets!" The crowd exploded in laughter.

We Were Accepted

Mickey Donahoo, CHS Class of 1961

If you honed your baseball skills to an acceptable level, you might get invited to Camp Childersburg (the prison) to play the black prisoners. The prison always had a good team. We were well accepted and it was great fun.

Chapter 21

Cars and Cruising

Muscle Cars Because No Kid Ever Grew Up With A Poster of a Honda Civic On His Wall!

The 1964 Chevy (foreground) was owned by Peter Wallenfang. The light blue with a white top 1962 Corvette convertible (back ground) was owned by Charles (Beatle) Bailey.

The Beast

Earl Wesson, Jr., *Class of 1972*

Life for male teenagers in Childersburg during the old days involved cruising around the Dairy Queen. One of my old time buds, Peter Wallenfang, was our group "gear head" and always had some sort of mechanical venture going on. Peter and I shared many hours together riding, cruising, loafing, and tinkering with cars.

Peter Wallenfang bought a 1964 Chevrolet Impala 2-door hardtop and dressed it up with chrome rims and white lettered tires. Peter thought up ways to make the paint shine like it was wet. Our cars were our identity and we did not want to pass another that looked like the one we drove. How young guys today can live with a 4 door Camry that looks like 50 million other Hondas, Mazda's, and Toyotas — it is heart breaking.

Wallenfang decided one day that the 283 cubic inch engine and automatic transmission in the Impala just didn't put air in his long hair. So he purchased a 396 cubic inch big bloc Chevy engine and a four speed M-21 Rock Crusher transmission. We then proceeded to install that big block in Peter's 64 Chevy Impala.

Getting anxious to ride in this beast, Peter got it to the point where the engine and tranny were in the car and hooked up with the exception of the shifter for the transmission, however, the hood and mufflers were missing. We were not sure if the distributor was set with the proper degrees so it could have been out of time, however, we wanted to start the motor. So we fired that 396cubic inch big block Chevy up (no pun intended).

Peter was positioned in the driver's seat, ready to turn the key, while I assumed my position sitting on the fender well inside the engine compartment (remember no hood). I had one leg extending over the engine to the other fender to brace myself. The distributor was behind the carburetor so I was leaning over the engine and carburetor to turn the distributor back and forth to see if we could get the distributor to the sweet spot and make the engine start.

Peter turned the key and as luck would have it, the timing was 180 degrees out; the engine backfired through that Holly double pumper carburetor which sent flames shooting straight up and taking both of my eyebrows off and singeing my beloved sideburns, which I had been trying to grow for 3 years. However, my semi-afro hairdo somehow didn't go up in flames. Later, corrections to the distributor position enabled the engine to start and we rattled most of the windows in Grove Park when that beast busted off.

We had not gotten around to installing the transmission linkage so my job was to crawl under the car and move the transmission linkage to reverse. Peter backed that Impala out of the drive and once again I crawled under the car (with the engine running) and shifted into second gear. — VOILA! We were in business, driving through Grove Park, and you guessed it, we headed straight for the Dairy Queen. Proud peacocks we were cruising through Childersburg in that Beast. It's all about the illusion.

An Accident

Marilyn Alexander Primero, *CHS Class of 1963*

I was 14 and it was Thanksgiving weekend. My dad, who was kind of a backyard mechanic, sent me to Limbaugh's hardware store to get some bolts. He was working on the seat of a 54 Ford pickup truck he had bought for me to learn how to drive a stick shift on the floor

The seat had to be adjusted for my 5 foot tall stature! Daddy told me to go straight to Limbaugh Hardware and come back right away. Being the know-it-all that I was, I knew I had time to pick up my BFF, Mary Nell. So I picked Mary Nell up and off we went! I was barefooted of course, my dad taught me to drive by the time I was 12 so at 14 I was an accomplished driver ... or so I thought!

As I turned toward Limbaugh's, Mary Nell said, "Look, there's Wayne Dobbs in his Santa suit." I was looking to my left at Santa and rear ended Gary Frank's dad who was driving a dry cleaning van! He was stopped at the light in front of Limbaugh's! OMG!

Mr. Franks jumped out of that truck so fast! Mary Nell took her shoes off for me to wear because it was against the law to drive barefooted! Never mind that I did not have a driver's license! Her shoes were at least two sizes too big! Anyway, Mr. Franks came over to me and hugged my neck, he was so happy! He said I was the best chiropractor around, he'd had a crick in his neck and couldn't turn his head for weeks, and I knocked it out!

The police called daddy to come downtown. Needless to say, daddy was not happy! He had the seat out of the truck waiting on me and the bolts to come back to the house! So he improvised a seat by using a chair from our kitchen, and drove downtown. Daddy came driving up and boy I knew I was in big trouble from the look on his face. I can't begin to tell you how mad he was!

We Weren't Tough

Mike Headley, *CHS Class of 1962*

In the late 1950s and early 1960s there were movies and magazines which depicted black leather jacket toughs and car gangs which we would love to have been a part of, but the whole thing was more want-to-be than anything close to reality for us. The truth was we were part of a small southern town. Yeah, we had car clubs (two) with tags identifying our clubs but that was about it. We did wear black leather jackets and black motorcycle boots from time to time — mostly to show off and be seen.

Old Mild Hogs

Earl Wesson Jr., *CHS Class of 1972*

"The Mild Hogs" as we named ourselves, took a road trip to Orlando Florida to visit Disney World also taking a "day trip" to Daytona Beach while we were in the neighborhood.

I was barely 17 years old and surprised when my dad let me go on the Orlando/Daytona trip. We were accompanied by one of the 'hogs" parents that drove their car so they could go visit relatives in Orlando and give us our space. Their son drove the family truck with camper on it and some slept in it and others of us slept in a tent.

The original "hogs" involved in this trip besides me were, Edward Davis, whose parents went with us and supplied the camper, Donnie Smitherman, the local Methodist preacher's son, Joe Johnson, Jack Washam. Peter Wallenfang, our favorite hippie, and Ferron Mayfield. Donnie and I went together because we were going to come home a little earlier (we were in love but not with each other) and couldn't stay too long away from our girlfriends.

Over the years our "hog" group has expanded somewhat and we continue to take trips together. Jimmy (Red) Harkins couldn't go on the original trip, Stewart Smith was most likely training for some sporting event and his dad wouldn't let him go, Roger Littleton, who somehow got lost in the 60s, and recently we added Jim Frinak, our class "brainiac" — we thought that would help the IQ quotient of our group — but as it turns out he is quite the party animal. The "Hogs" planned a surprise visit with Ferron Mayfield a few years back.

Ferron has homesteaded in the wilds of Oregon and is a rafting guide on the Rogue River in Merlin, Oregon. Joe rode down from Washington on the bus, Jack flew in from Chicago, Edward from Memphis, and Roger, Peter, and myself from Birmingham.

The next trip brought Ferron from Oregon in his rafting company's 9 passenger van, Stewart and Red joined the group and we met in Vegas and set out on the road for the Grand Canyon via the Hoover Dam. We rode Route 66 a great deal and saw several states. Most of the ramblings here have nothing to do with Childersburg — oh but it does — friendships made and cherished for 60 years lives on in each one of us Hogs. The morals we learned from our parents, lessons we learned in school where we got our butts busted when we misbehaved, all the days and nights we thought were "oh so boring" when we lived them, well, those memories and the new ones we make every time we are together go on and on. Our children get involved in our exploits and mine can't wait to hear of our new tales of adventure. My oldest daughter Brandy sees herself as part of this group because she has spent lots of time in their company. My youngest daughter Darby is fascinated to get to go to our reunions and laughs at our stupid antics as if she were there when it first happened. Life in a small town — maybe John Mellencamp will write a song about it someday.

An "R Code" Ford

Mike Headley, *CHS Class of 1962*

Ford had been making the Galaxie 500 XL for a number of years in both hard tops and convertible models. In the spring of 1963 Ford came out with what was referred to as a 1963 ½ Hatch Back Galaxie two door. This peculiar rust-colored Ford purchased from the Coosa Motor Company in Childersburg came with an "R Code" engine. In simple terms it was a high-performance 427 cubic inch dual 4 barrel carbureted special cam with 425 Horsepower pulling 480 foot pounds of torque at 6,000 RPM. This car could be bought from any Ford dealer in America as long as you had two things — lots of money, and extra time.

Most Ford dealers did not carry this car in stock. It was called a Police Interceptor Special — a fast car, you bet. For a loaded Galaxie in 1963 a person might spend around $3,000.00. This car with all the bells and whistles required for the "R Code" FE engine priced out north of $4,500.00. A princely sum to pay for a Ford in the 1960's.

There was a guy from Shelby County who ordered this particular rust colored R code Ford from Coosa Motor Company. The car was often seen parked at the Dairy Queen on weekend nights during the mid-60s. His name fails me but he had a flat top and smoked a smaller type of cigar. I remember him as a nice fellow, kinda quiet.

Driving to Birmingham on US Highway 280

Vicki Dobbs Southern, *CHS Class of 1972*

I remember having to go to Birmingham through the Narrows and Highway US 280 was a 2-lane road then, having to follow a semi-truck over Double Oak Mountain it took forever to get to the south side of Birmingham.

A 1968 Buick Wildcat

Linda Joyce Seay Williams, *CHS Class of 1969*

Mike was driving a '68 Buick Wildcat and that Buick would run! It had 405 horsepower 430 cubic inch engine. When Mike "kicked it" your head would snatch back. In 1972 Daddy had a heart attack and we were home on Lakeside drive. Mother decided that we should drive Daddy to the hospital in Sylacauga. So, Mother, Daddy, Jo Ann (my sister), Mike and I all climbed in that Buick. Mother and Daddy were in the back seat — Mike driving — and me in the middle with Jo Ann riding shotgun.

When Mike started the car, Jo Ann said, "Mike, will this Buick run?" He nodded "yes" and Jo Ann said "don't spare the horses." I thought "Oh, my!!" Mike waited till we got on Highway 280 and then slowly but steadily sped up to 120 MPH. That was as high as the speedometer would show, but he was going faster. We were in the passing lane with the flashers on and blinking headlights as we passed every car on 280 heading to Sylacauga. It was a very smooth ride. Unless you looked at the speed odometer you would have thought you were going 70 MPH. Only the three of us in the front seat knew how fast Mike was really going.

As we entered Sylacauga, Mike slowed down to go through town. When making a turn we went just a little fast and we all felt the turn. Daddy spoke up and said "alright now, Mike, we don't need to be in that big of a hurry." The whole front seat cracked up laughing because if Daddy had only known how fast that Buick had been going, we would have gotten in trouble. That was one fast trip to Sylacauga.

Wyatt's Lake/Lake View Race Track

Mike Headley, *CHS Class of 1962*

The race track at Wyatt's Lake was located west of the swimming hole. To say this facility had any remote resemblance to a NASCAR race facility would be a complete misstatement. As I remember, it had a slight banking so that you had a very small amount of help to counter the centrifugal force which was trying to make the driver ride shotgun on those bench seats. By the time bucket seats were coming along we were on to other interests.

The distance around the track was a quarter mile. For some reason we never seemed to drive that oval during daylight hours. Nope, we decided to have a go of it in total darkness except for those Delco-Remy seal beam T-3 head lamps which had the projection distance of about two hundred feet. Doing up to 40 MPH on the straits made for a fun trip around that track when I was 16.

A 1953 Plymouth Cranbrook

Earl Wesson Jr., *CHS Class of 1972*

In 1972, a friend and I bought a 1953 Plymouth Cranbrook car together as a joke. It had a sun visor over the windshield and we felt it was the perfect attention getter to have fun with. We were 16 and I had a "real car" but this was for pure fun. We each paid $50 and towed the ugly thing home. We purchased a six volt battery from Britches Miller at the Western Auto and fired the old tank up then went riding around town. Wasn't long until the battery died and we towed it to Felix Crocker's Garage that was in the rear of Veazy Auto Parts.

Mr. Crocker was quite the jokester himself and told me he wasn't going to fix it — I was. "Anybody stupid enough to put a battery in backwards in a Plymouth or Dodge car needs to fix it himself." I knew that Chrysler Corp. built cars were "positive" grounded and GM and Ford were "negative" ground. I had forgotten about the reverse polarity of the Chrysler products. That fact had completely slipped my mind in the excitement to get the new battery in and ride around Childersburg; I had ended up burning up the generator.

Checking at every auto parts business in town; no one had a generator for a 1953 Plymouth. All cars built in the last ten years had come with an alternator. In desperation and a last ditch effort, I went to the Western Auto and wouldn't you know it, Mr. Miller had one in stock and we were running before dark.

We drove this old Plymouth to the Jr. College in Alex City to save putting miles on my good ride. Of course we did go by Halls TV shop first and pick up an old metal Zenith TV cabinet and cut the sides out to weld into the rear floor boards of that Plymouth (it seems the rear floor boards had rusted out) so our rear passengers would have somewhere to rest their feet, plus keep water, mud and dirt from flying into the rear seat.

Fast Cars

Mike Headley, *CHS Class of 1962*

There were some super-fast cars in Childersburg especially during the mid-1960s. I had a fast car but not a super-fast one.

Corky Galloway's older brother Sam had a 1964 maroon with cream top Chevrolet Impala SS convertible with a 4-speed transmission and fender skirts. That was a fast car. That Chevy came with a 409 cubic inch 425 horse power engine with dual 4 barrel carburetors and a special cam. Chevrolet referred to this engine as a Super Turbo Fire. While this was one fast car, it was hamstrung to some degree by the additional 150 pounds because it was a convertible.

Another was Roger Gambrell's white 1964 Plymouth Fury with black bucket seats and a 383 cubic inch 330 Horse Power Super Commando engine. Rogers's car came with a four speed transmission, fender skirts and a black interior. Fast car ...you bet. I remember one evening coming back from Sylacauga we were going about 90 miles an hour when Roger dropped off the hill north of my home on US 280 putting the pedal to the metal in that Plymouth Fury. We passed Casey Holts' store at Holts Cross Roads doing about 130 miles per hour. Was I scared? You bet! As I recall, Roger let up as we passed his parents' house on the west side of Highway 280. It did not take long to get back to Childersburg from Sylacauga that night.

1966 Chevy Impala

Earl Wesson Jr., *CHS Class of 1972*

The car was a 1966 Impala SS bright red with black bucket seats, and an AM radio that I tuned to WLS 890 AM out of Chicago at nights to hear the best rock and roll. Daytime I listened to WVOK690 AM or WSGN 610 AM out of Birmingham.

That Chevy was my pride and joy. I paid $1,099.00 for that car at the Chevy dealer in Sylacauga using the money I made working for A&P after school and on Saturdays. The car was a trade in so the transmission had to be rebuilt. Joiner's garage rebuilt the transmission and installed a "shift kit" so it would bark the tires — claimed he knew what us young boys wanted.

Soon after buying that 1966 Chevy, I installed the first of many 8 track tape I said many tape decks because I kept blowing them up trying to get more and more sound out of them. My old 8 track tape box sits on a shelf in my garage today with The Grassroots, Steppenwolf, Neil Diamond, Rolling Stones, and Carpenters (parking and smooching music) still locked in time on those tapes decks with the latest and greatest speakers.

My First Car

James Phelps, *CHS Class of 1965*

The first car I owned was well......full of holes. I had a 1953 Chevrolet from above the Mason Dixon Line, with all the obligatory rust holes, which really made it lighter, that way it would run a bit faster. My dad had the exhaust pipes split so dual glass packs were under the floor boards. This Chevy was so loud it rattled the windows in downtown Childersburg when I passed.

I did race it sometimes on the Plant Road Saturday nights. I thought I had one of the fastest cars around. The one race I remember best was the night I raced Jimmy Williams, Jimmy had 1953 Mercury with a V-8 engine. I beat him and he was so mad he wouldn't speak to me anymore.

Buddy Rowland sold me a carb set-up that I knew would make my car one of the fastest around. The 1/4 mile run was recorded at a blistering 60 miles an hour, with a time of one minute flat. WOW, talk about speed!

That Chevy had holes in both front floor boards that made it handy for dumping ash trays and empty beer cans on the road as I went on my way. I remember running over the rail road tracks one afternoon and most of the right front fender fell off. It was my first car which cost me a $100 bill. A fair amount of money in those days, I remember working all summer to pay for that car.

A Drag Racing Challenge

Mickey Donahoo, *CHS Class of 1961*

If the right cars showed up at the same time at the Dairy Queen or Tastee Freeze a drag racing challenge would be given and accepted. The two cars would proceed to the Plant road, Winterboro Highway, or to the Tree Farm in Shelby County.

The group along with a flagman would assemble for the race. There would be several cars of spectators to witness this exciting activity. Everyone except the flagman and the drivers would assemble a quarter mile down the road to determine the winner.

A Shelby Country Drag Race

Mike Headley, *CHS Class of 1962*

In the late spring of 1964, I was home from Auburn University for the weekend. Standing in the parking lot of the Dairy Queen (minding my own business) when a conversation started between several guys as to who had the fastest car. This occurred from time to time when two or more very fast cars showed up in the Dairy Queen parking lot. It was not long until a challenge was laid down and accepted.

While there was a drag strip near Sylacauga in those days it was not open at 2 o'clock on a Sunday morning. Well that only left the racers one choice. There was a piece of straight road — State Highway 76 — which today is referred to as Kline road in Shelby County. Our readymade drag strip passed what was in those days was known as the Tree Farm.

We used this road from time to time as our drag strip. So off the two cars go toward Shelby County. One was an "R Code" 1963½ Hatch Back Ford, the other a 1964 Plymouth Hemi Cuda, both extremely fast cars. As you might expect three of us jumped in Ray Williams' 1954 four-door Ford and headed off to Shelby County.

A group of maybe six cars with 20 guys total — I mean what would go wrong, RIGHT? The Ford and Plymouth lined up on the road, ready to race, looking down the road in an easterly direction. Then wouldn't you know it here came a car. I mean 2:30 on a Sunday morning, really! So the cars had to get out of the road then reassemble for the drag race. The racers made two passes with each winning a round so it's obvious a third run would have to be made. I suppose none of us ever thought, due to the inordinate amount of noise two cars with squalling tires and racing engines might make, that we might be possibly maybe disturbing someone's Saturday night's sleep.

Long story short, someone must have called the Shelby County Sheriff's office. After the third run the Sheriff was waiting when the racers finished their run, arresting the racers on the spot. Since the guys did not return after the last run we became curious. So we decided to drive down to see just what might have happened. Before we could get in the cars and drive down to where the cars were stopped, an Alabama Highway patrol car drove by us slowly looking around.

Not wanting to drive 70 miles out of our way to get back to the Dairy Queen we decided we would just drive by the cops like we were heading to an early Sunday morning church service. Just as we were driving by, the Alabama Highway patrol officer shouted "stop those cars!" They could not arrest us for drag racing so we all got a ticket for disturbing the peace.

Well great, I was not about to tell Mother or Daddy. So Sunday afternoon when Daddy gave me the money to pay my meal ticket for the month of April at Auburn University I took it, of course. Not knowing what the ticket would cost I ate little for two weeks. Two weeks later I drove up to Columbiana Courthouse in Shelby County to pay the fine. That fine took most of my meal money for the entire month of April. I almost starved that month, but Mother and Daddy did not find out for 25 years. When I told them 25 years later we had a good laugh.

A Car Wash at the Powder Plant

Danny Wiginton, *CHS Class of 1965*

In the summer of 1958 the old part of CHS burned and we were sent to the vacant Ordinance Works buildings on the plant road. This was part of the vast network of buildings used to produce powder for the World War II industries. Looking back, we were probably exposed to all kinds of environmental hazards. No one thought it was much of an issue in those days.

There was an old car wash in the complex which was used to wash residue from your car. The spray would come on when a cars weight was applied as the car pass through. One day I left class on an errand and I decided to run though the car wash. I could get all the way through before the spray came on. I did this several times, and then went on my way. But someone in another class saw me and I was turned into the principal at that time, Mr. A.H. Watwood.

I can't remember my exact punishment, but principal Watwood was not too hard on me. I have laughed at this over the years. I was probably the only student at CHS ever sent to the Principal's office for running through a car wash during school.

A Saturday Night Car Swap

Robert E. Burdick, *CHS Class of 1961*

On a Friday evening during the summer of 1961 due to a set of straight pipes on Billy Hall's 1955 light blue Ford, Billy swapped cars with Phillip Payne, who had a black 1960 Ford convertible. The reason for the swap was Billy had a date with a girl from Sylacauga and did not want to be hassled by Officer Shell of the Alabama Highway Patrol which happened well ... a lot

There were two Shell brothers who were highway patrolman in the area. The Shell brother I am talking about was the one most people remember as the highway patrolman who chased the 1955 Chevy through town going north on US 280 through Childersburg, blowing a left front tire, losing control going down the hill from the main red light at the top of the hill, hitting the gas pumps at "That Curb Market" and killing several young people.

Phillip and Billy swap cars at the Dairy Queen in Childersburg. Phillip Payne, Edward Brown, and Phillip Stevens and I had the fun of driving Billy's 1955 Ford with a Police Interceptor engine, that evening. We did the normal loops of the Childersburg Dairy Queen and Tasty Freeze and then it was time to make the other loop which included the White Midget and Tasty Freeze in Sylacauga. I suppose we thought because Billy was not driving his car we would not be stopped by Officer Shell. Looking back at that thinking today well...we probably were not thinking.

We made the trip to Sylacauga taking care to see, and be seen. All was going well as we headed north back to Childersburg on Highway US 280. As was the case Officer Shell of the Alabama Highway Patrol was on duty that evening. Understand the eleven miles between Childersburg and Sylacauga on highway US 280 was Officer Shell's domain.

Phillip Stephens wanted to drive on the trip back to Childersburg so he and Phillip Payne swapped seats. Officer Shell fell in behind us as we started up Merkle Mountain. Payne said "Hit it! Hit it!" Stephens pressed the accelerator and that big Ford interceptor engine answered with a surge. As we topped Merkle Mountain Stephens told Payne he didn't want a ticket and he could swap driving if he wanted to try and outrun the Alabama Highway Patrol.

So they switched seats while still traveling at a very high rate of speed. Payne floor boarded Billy's Ford. Merkle Mountain and Officer Shell were getting farther and farther behind us as we sped north on US highway 280. By the time we got to Casey Holt's store the Highway Patrol was a distant speck. And this is when the fun begins. As we headed back to Childersburg we had no idea we would be going by way of Flagpole Mountain.

By the time we got to Holt's Cross Roads we were so far ahead of the Highway Patrol I don't know why we didn't just go on into Childersburg and split up. But by then the whole thing had turned into a big thrill, besides we were young. So we turned left at Casey's store and floored that Ford heading west on Talladega County Road 94. In those days the road was dirt and full of pot holes. If you were traveling at a normal rate of speed it would feel like riding over a scrub board. At our speed it felt like we were touching the road only once in a while.

By the time we reached the four-way stop at the Mountain View community the road began to smooth just a bit and we could see Officer Shell had made the turn just as we had. We could see his flashing lights bobbing around like a small boat in rough weather. So Phillip floored it and we were off again. That road is hilly and crooked and after going up Ghost Hill the road continued to rise until we got to the turnoff to go to the Flagpole Mountain fire tower.

If you'd don't take the left turn up to the tower the road goes on to Fayetteville through Kahatchee. We were going too fast to even consider turning toward the tower so on west we went. The lights behind us were far enough behind we should have slowed a bit, but in the heat of the moment four young men don't think about the logical thing to do. We came over a hill that curved slightly to the left going down the other side, then it quickly swerved back to the right, and that is where our trip came to an abrupt halt.

We came to a stop with the right front of Billy's Ford in a ditch. You could tell by how quickly we jumped out of that Ford that no one was hurt. We took cover in the thick bushes on each side of the road. Don't remember which direction the two Phillips went, but Ed, with me carrying the guitar, hit the woods on the left side of the road. We were lying low. It was not long until the Highway Patrol arrived and started shinning his spotlight into the woods. Officer Shell shouted that we may as well come out because he knew who we were.

We remembered from all the cops and robbers movies we had seen that you don't give up that easy. So we laid low. The police finally left, but we could see headlights coming and going up and down the road. Ed and I decided to head back toward Childersburg, but away from the road where we were convinced there was dozens of cops looking for us.

In the dark Edward and I got separated from the two Phillips who made their way back to the Dairy Queen that night because someone gave them a ride. Edward and I did not fare as well. On our way to Mountain View Cross Roads we fell down a bank about 15 feet. Edward hurt his ribs so I ended up carrying his guitar.

Edward had a girlfriend in the area so we decided to go to her house and make a call so someone would come pick us up. When we arrived at the house his girlfriend's dad had a bunch of hounds which were making so much noise we did not stop. Down the road we found an old hay barn where we laid down for a few hours to sleep. When we woke up the sun was shining. We headed to Childersburg (walking). I got home to Minor Terrace and got my dad's car and drove back to get Ed's guitar at the hay barn.

Officer Shell told Chief Jinright to tell Phillip Payne that his ticket was waiting at the Childersburg Police station.

Learning to Drive

Mickey Donahoo, *CHS Class of 1961*

I don't know if this were standard procedure, but my second "official" driving education with my father was on Flagpole Mountain. I thought my first test on a dark night with a torrential downpour was going a little too far but it paled in comparison to the mountain. I supposed we were just taking a family outing until my dad stopped the car on a steep uphill incline put the car in neutral, set the parking brake and told me to take over.

The average (or above average for that matter) teenager does not have enough foot and hand co-ordination to get the standard shift automobile into gear, release the parking brake, step on the gas and let out the clutch without backing over the side of Flagpole Mountain. Somehow I was able to pull it off and, after that learning to drive was relatively easy until it came time for the license examination.

Of course the highway patrolman excluded rainy night and driving on the mountain, but just the thought of taking a driver's test while sitting beside an armed official who could put you in jail was, to say the least, daunting. However, not all of my driver's training was supervised as shown by the following.

I went home one summer afternoon to mow our 500-acre yard when I suddenly realized that I needed to hone my driving skills. I hopped in our 1930' era white Plymouth pickup and proceeded to drive around the block. Everything went well until I met the Chief of Police going downhill around a curve. During the ensuing panic, all thought of brakes totally escaped my mind. Due to defensive driving skills, Chief Jinright wound up in the ditch and I hurriedly made my escape back the house where I hid and acted as if no one were home.

A couple of facts, however, were working against my flight from the law. First, this was the only 1930 white Plymouth pick-up probably in the entire state of Alabama. Second, but not least, you could see our house and the white pick-up in the yard from where the chief was in the ditch. Due to his extensive background in detective work, I was shortly in the back of the police car headed to jail. I will never forget the words he said to my father on the phone—"I have your son in jail and you can come get him, if you want to."

Of course, most of us learned to drive on the many back roads around Childersburg with a parent or older sibling. This freedom has mostly passed and kids today are sent to driving school. Which is pretty mundane and unless, the school was conducted by.....NASCAR.

Childersburg High School Bus Drivers

Daniel Lee, *CHS Class of 1984*

I remember riding the school bus home, when it was hot and raining, with the windows up, and the exhaust fumes where so strong you fell asleep, but once you got off the bus you were wide awake again, but had a headache. Oh, the good old days. I remember bus 16. Coach Walker was our bus driver for years. When I got expelled off the bus, they did not take my bus drivers licenses--I could not ride on the bus, but I could still drive it!

Peter Wallenfang, *CHS Class of 1972*

My brother, Butch Wallenfang, drove a school bus. Butch has some great stories about taking the governor off the school bus engine. There is a great story which took place in front of Hassel's Grocery. It was drag race between two school busses. Pure legend, I'm sure. Butch drove bus #90, Buddy Hobbs drove bus #76 and Ed McDonald drove Bus #3, and Mr. Green drove bus #5. Now the story of the drag racing busses has faded in Butch's memory. Not sure, but I think he is in denial.

Thomas Douglas Herndon, *IHSH Class of 1971*

I remember catching the school bus in Pine Crest. The bus made its last stop at Wilson's store between Coosa Court and the school so we could spend our lunch money on stuff in Wallace's store and the driver could have a quick smoke. The buses were driven by senior boys and you always had the same bus and driver, so they were allowed to take the buses home.

No Tires, Rims Only

Joe Peerson, *CHS Class of 1968*

In 1967 a pair of brothers, JB and Mike Sandifer, from Winterboro decided to drive to Childersburg in a 1954 green and white Chevrolet on the rims with no tires. They drove down the Southern Rail Road tracks west toward Childersburg until they reached the Forest Hills rail crossing then preceded down the highway driving into Childersburg. There were grooves in the road all the way past the Economy

Gas Company on the east side of downtown at which point Childersburg's finest stopped their progress. I personally saw the tracks and the car.

Peter Wallenfang's 1966 and
Gary Bowen's 1967 GTOs

Chapter 22

Lowell Ray Williams, Jr.

CHS Class of 1962

"It is one of the blessings of old friends that you can afford to be stupid with them." - Ralph Waldo Emerson

Lowell Ray Williams was born in Alabama in 1942 and passed from this life in Virginia in 2013 in his 72nd year.

Mike Headley, *CHS Class of 1962*

There are many classmates and friends who shared fond memories with Ray. I tried to include the best stories. There were just too many to print.

Water Skiing on Land

Mike Headley, *CHS Class of 1962*

During the summer of 1961, Ray and I were enjoying a weekend of camping and water skiing at Wind Creek in what would be called today a male-bonding experience. Ray enjoyed water skiing as much as anyone I knew, and that included me. We got to Wind Creek on a Friday afternoon around 6:00 pm. First, unload the camping gear, set up camp and then — launch the boat. A fair amount of work needed to be done before the fun of water skiing could begin.

OK, first of all, it was my boat. And yes, it was my responsibility to get the boat launched. However, you must understand, Ray had driven that boat almost as many water miles as I had. He had certainly had the pleasure of skiing behind my boat as many miles as I.

269

Trying to be a good friend I allowed Ray to ski first. After Ray had skied a good 15 minutes, I, the boat owner, decided it was my turn. I signaled to Ray that I was bringing him around for a drop off. That way Ray, as an experienced skier, could turn loose and glide to the shore, no problem right?

As we came around the lake I made a nice turn and lined Ray up for a good exit. One problem — he decided he was having far too much fun to stop skiing. As I steered the boat back across the lake for a return trip I anticipated Ray letting go of the rope so that I too could have the same pleasure that he had enjoyed for more than 20 minutes. Remember we had arrived for a weekend of mutual boating and skiing. As we headed for the shore I signaled to Ray "GET OFF," In return, Ray gave me a pronounced head signal that indicated that he did not wish to "GET OFF."

My patience at this point had had it with my waterskiing buddy. I decided that if Ray would not let go of the rope I would force him to do so. On the next pass I increased the boats speed so that upon Ray's arrival at the beach he would be traveling at a very high rate of speed. Ha, this will show him! I drove in "with the pedal to the metal". At the last moment I turn the boat hard to the right, making Ray swing wide at a much increased speed.

My calculation for the arch and the length of rope was off by ... well ... a few feet. When Ray sung wide I felt sure he would simply let go of the rope and come to a nice stop, in maybe, six inches of water.

Instead of letting go of the rope, Ray hung on as the water became shallower ... and shallower. Since Ray was at the end of the arch he figured, if he could hang on he would again reach the water. At this point I witnessed, to the best of my knowledge, the very first human being to water ski on dry land.

It was amazing, first water was flying then the next thing I knew, sand was flying. Ray was actually water skiing on dry land.

Ray had the biggest grin a person could imagine plastered on his face. Well, why not? The man had just entered the Guinness Book of World Records without even trying. At his point even I was pulling for Ray to ski back to the middle of the lake.

Unfortunately this was not to be. While Ray had managed to ski on dry land and had managed to reenter shallow water there was just one problem. A bush was quickly looming in Ray's path. The bush was around five feet high. As fate would have it Ray was not successful in his attempt to get over or by that bush. Yes, the entire scene was spectacular as Ray cart wheeled thru the air. At this point Ray had decided he no longer needed the ski rope. Ray released the ski rope, which, if one recalls, was the reason for the whole unfortunate matter in the first place.

No longer having a water skier attached I wheeled the boat around hard to the left and headed to shore as fast as I could. I drove the boat into the sand jumping out of the boat ASAP to check on Ray's condition. Ray was lying on his back in about four inches of water making some rather unpleasant remarks as to my boating abilities.

I don't remember where the water skis went, but when I arrived Ray had apparently lost them while becoming up close and personal with that bush. After a few minutes, Ray was almost back to his old self, somewhat sore and without too many skinned places. We finished our weekend at Wind Creek with no additional problems. Ray and I skied many times in the future and when asked to give up the ski rope he did so without complaint. Rest well old friend you are missed.

3 Guys, Rang, and a Skunk

Paul Dillard, *CHS Class of 1961*

One day, in the fall of 1959, Ray Reeves, Ray Williams and I, decided to get a little squirrel hunting in before our dates that night. Ray R. and I loaded our guns into Dad's brand new 1960 Pontiac and headed over to pick up Ray W. When we got to Ray W's house, we not only picked up Ray, but also his hunting dog, Rang. Ray W said "Rang was the best squirrel dog anywhere!" So off we went.

The three of us headed out Talladega County Road 180, turned onto Grist Mill Road and headed to the Hubbard farm close to Alpine to start our hunt. It wasn't long before Rang treed some squirrels and the hunt was on! We got in a few shots and Rang took off after what they thought, was a squirrel that was getting away. So off we go following Rang. When we caught up with Rang, he was in a tussle down in a small ditch. Well, it didn't take long until we realized Rang had a SKUNK!!

Ray W called Rang off the skunk and everyone headed to the car. Yes, that brand new 1960 Maroon Bonneville Pontiac! On the way back to the car we were choking from that skunk smell and trying to decide what we were going to do with Rang.

I told the two Rays "that stinking dog could NOT get in Dad's new Pontiac Bonneville." So, they decide to put Rang in the trunk. We were in a hurry because I had a date with Joyce Latta that night and I knew he was going to be late.

As we drove toward Childersburg, that skunk smell was mighty powerful. I dropped off Ray W and Rang, then dropped off Ray R and headed home to get cleaned up for my date with Joyce that evening.

As soon as I stepped in the house, Mama smelled me and stopped me at the door with an "Uh, uh, get on out of here! "So, I took my clothes off outside the house and hung them on the clothes line. Then I went in the house to bathe and scrubbed and scrubbed, then put on clean clothes and LOTS of cologne, I was ready!

When I got in the car, that smell hit me hard, so I figured the Pontiac needed some cologne too. Surely Joyce wouldn't notice. An hour and a half late I arrived at Joyce Latta's house. I had some explaining to do. Upon entering Joyce's house, Mr. Latta says "I smell a skunk!"

Riding a Pine Tree

Mike Headley, *CHS Class of 1962*

The amount of entertainment available in 1957 for a boy living in the country four miles south of Childersburg was ... limited. We had no I Phones, I Pads or other electronic games which kids enjoy today. With that in mind I think you can see how the following accident might have occurred. It was a Sunday afternoon and, as Sundays go, not a bad day. If my memory services me correctly it was June and the weather was not too dry. The time of year, as well as the amount of humidity in the air, you will learn later is important to the outcome of this story.

My best friend Ray Williams and I would meet at the old Church of Christ on the corner of 8th Ave. SW and 2 Street S.W. in downtown Childersburg on Sunday mornings. Together we would attend Sunday school then sit with each other during church trying (unsuccessfully) not to get in trouble. After church most Sundays we would take turns spending the afternoon at each other's house. It was understood both families would be back for Sunday evening church services. That way we could go home with each other on Sunday afternoons and then return to church Sunday evening.

This particular Sunday was the day to go to my house. After church my family headed for the standard Sunday after church meal at Marie Taylor's restaurant. It was important that the preacher not drone on too long, because it was understood that we had to beat the Baptists to Taylor's. My family won most Sundays.

Upon our arrival at my house that Sunday afternoon Ray and I quickly changed clothes and went looking for our next great adventure. The week before Ray came over I had been having a great deal of fun doing what we called riding trees. But I'm sure an explanation is in order.

Riding trees is not in itself inherently dangerous. The trick is finding the right tree. The absolute best were Sweet Gum. Oak would do if you had ridden all the Sweet Gum's down. Allow me to explain what the term "riding a tree down" means. If a tree is full of sap and the weather has not been too dry, you find a tree maybe eight or ten inches at the base and climb close to the top, maybe 25 feet up. Get that tree swinging back and forth, then at the right moment swing out and allow gravity to take you on a great ride to the ground.

Depending on the size of the tree if you got one too big (at the base) you might find your feet dangling a few feet above the ground. That tree was just not going to bend anymore. At that point you had to make a decision either drop to the ground maybe five feet. If you got one too big (which would not bend) you just had to climb it again. So you see, tree selection had become a study of great importance to this 12-year-old mind, and I thought I had mastered the art of tree sizing and riding.

Now, my previous trips to the woods that week had left the available crop of riding trees a bit well ... limited. You must understand, most trees would recover from my rather juvenile adventures. Depending on the time of year, and the amount of moisture in the tree, most would recover in two weeks because of that stuff which makes trees look up to the sun. Chlorophyll, yeah, that's the stuff. I never said I made wonderful grades in biology.

What was a fellow to do? Here I had invited my best friend over for an afternoon of tree riding and the crop (due to my exuberance) was limited. At this point we had ridden a number of oaks down, because the Sweet Gums were somewhat horizontal.

Ray had just ridden an oak, and I did not see any suitable riders except a few pines which were still vertical. I picked out a nice 40 foot pine and started to climb.

Not having had the benefit of studying biology since I was only in the sixth grade I had no idea as to the cellular nature of the American Southern Short Leaf Pine. As we usually did, one of us would stand and watch while the other rode a tree to the ground.

I was up maybe thirty feet and had that Pine going back and forth. Things were going well. One more rather large swing and I decided it was time to ride that puppy to the ground.

At just the right moment out I swung. Almost immediately I heard what sounded like a loud cracking sound. At that point I was far too busy to notice that while I was still holding on to that pine top I was headed to the ground at an unusually high rate of speed. It seems that the pine had broken right below my grip, which meant I had all six feet of the top of that pine in my grasp. One thing I noticed as I came down was the abnormal number of pine tree limbs I seemed to be removing from that pine's trunk as I descended.

When I hit the ground, the impact knocked all the air I would ever breathe in my entire, limited lifetime out of my lungs. As I lay on the ground gasping for any breath, I could not help but notice Ray's uncontrolled laughter. Here I am dying and Ray was laughing his head off.

After a few minutes of Ray's hysteria, I realized I could not get up and would require medical help. We were a half mile from my house. I could not walk and I was too big for Ray to carry. Ray decided he could drag me, under fences and over rocks. At this point I decided if I was going to live I had better attempt to walk. With Ray's help I managed to walk, stumble, crawl and be dragged the half mile home.

Long story short, I spent three day in the Sylacauga Hospital with bruised kidneys and a compressed spine. Until the day Ray died he could not tell that story without breaking out laughing. I suppose if I had been the one standing on the ground looking up as I trashed those Southern Short Leaf Pine limbs, I would have laughed too. Rest well, old friend. You are missed.

A Penny Collection

Paul Dillard, *CHS Class of 1961*

By the middle 1960s, I started a Lincoln penny collection. This was the type of penny collection book with a slot for dates and mint marks. I had almost filled the collection with the easy to find pennies. I mentioned it to Ray and he said "I have a glass piggy that I have had since I was a kid." Ray brought that piggy bank to my house. I did not want to break the bank so I got a table knife and slid all those still bright pennies out one by one. I filled that coin collection book. Ray even had the World War II wartime steel pennies plus pennies with hard-to-find dates. We replaced the others with bright new pennies. I still have that collection today. I wish I had kept all the steel ones but I let Ray Reeves have those and he still has them.

A Kahatchee Camping Trip

Jimmy Ray Williams, *CHS Class of 1963*

The year was 1960 and the location was the west side of
Flagpole Mountain better known as Kahatchee, Alabama.

The instigators of this fiasco were none other than Lowell
Ray Williams, Jr. and Michael Alton Headley, myself being so
much younger and innocent (pure as the driven snow
according to my dear departed mother) than either of these
hoodlums, they forced me to accompany them. I was then, as
now, a sweet, innocent young man.

Ray's dad loaned us a one axel homemade utility trailer so we
would have a covered shelter to sleep in and store our gear.
Mr. Williams towed the trailer along with us and our stuff
out to Kahatchee, leaving the trailer and us alone in the wilds
of west Flagpole Mountain with NO transportation.

So off we go with enough food, clothing and other stuff to
last about two months. We certainly had more than enough
for three days! Not much happened on the first day. We did
hunt (we called ourselves Deer Hunters) a little that
afternoon. Then we carried on normal (for us) stuff for a
while then went to sleep after dinner because the sun had
gone down and we, obviously, had limited lighting.

Day two started a little early. We had breakfast and went off
into the woods. We found a couple of game trails the first
day, so we spread out near some of the trails. I found a nice
comfortable tree to lean against and sat there watching for
the deer to come jump in the boat. Those of you that know
me know that a comfortable tree and me "hunting" means I
promptly went to sleep.

When we returned to "camp" that afternoon, Ray was just a
little upset with me. Said he sighted a buck and as he was

about to aim, I started snoring. Ray, still kinda upset, walked up the hill to just wander around and "commune with nature."

About then, Mike had a "GREAT" idea. Hiding behind the trailer when Ray came within range on the top of that hill, I pointed my gun at Ray and Mike fired off a shot with his 22 rifle. We took three or four shots at Ray then stopped shooting. It took Ray about a half hour to work up the courage to come down the hill to camp. At that point, Ray was NOT a HAPPY CAMPER. As I mentioned before, being just a young innocent child, these two delinquents forced me into these shenanigans!

I don't remember much about the last day in the Kahatchee wilds except we ran low on food (someone ate all of the Georgia Hash). I suppose I must have slept through most of it

A Hunting Trip

Jimmy Ray Williams, *CHS Class of 1963*

There was this time Ray Williams, Paul Dillard, and I were hunting near the Coosa River News Print paper mill. Ray had one of the best squirrel dogs I have ever had the pleasure of hunting with. I have quite a few Ray/Rang stories. Anyway, the three of us were hunting uhh down uuhh up, uuuuhhhh in the woods. I am sure we were in the woods!

Rang treed a squirrel, so the three of us ran about a mile to catch up to Rang (a small exaggeration). When we caught our breath, one of us (I don't remember which) spotted the squirrel. Shot it and the squirrel fell out of the tree.

Rang had a bad habit of grabbing the squirrel and running off with it. Well, the squirrel was not dead! Rang put his nose down on the squirrel and the squirrel bit Rang on the nose and sunk his teeth in like a snapping turtle.

Have you ever seen a dog playing with a ball in a sock? He'll grab the top of the sock and shake it side to side with the ball hitting him every time he shakes it. Then he'll drop it and look at it and pick it up and do it again.

Rang did not have the option of dropping the squirrel. None of us could help Rang because we were on the ground laughing. I finally was able to catch Rang. I had to choke the poor squirrel to death before we could get it off of Rang's nose. The dog's nose swelled up like a tennis ball. Needless to say that day's hunting was over.

A Poem for My Best Friend

Mike Headley, *CHS Class of 1962*

When I became aware that my best friend of more than 60 years Ray Williams had a terminal illness I immediately sat at my computer and attempted to share my feelings with him.

I wrote this poem in two hours with a very heavy heart. Yes, I cried, and, yes, I beat on that table as I was writing this poem. I hope I was able to convey to Ray the love two men can and did share from childhood.

Ray Williams was able to read this poem two weeks before he died.

Ray

Old friend, when this journey began.
We did not know, we could not see.
Where it would lead or what the times would be.
But through them all we have gone, you and me.
We have done it standing with each other
back to back, no matter the score.
We have been there for each other when the distance was great.
Most could never have forged the bond we made.
A bond none were able to derail.
Together we have gone where many have failed.
Now you tell me our time is short.
My mind says, this is not right, this cannot be.
No one can share the laughter the good times of you and me.
The phone will no longer ring on New Year's Day.
When the voice on the phone would say "Hey, it's Ray."
Three score plus was the time we shared, you and me.
So many memories our older minds now see.
Memories rich with recollections of things only we two know.
The friendship we have known will now us flee.
A journey neither of us wanted the end to be.
Just a little more time is my plea.
Please, oh please, Ray wait for me.
The stories we know now others will see.
For a chapter in a community memoir you will be.
We will again laugh and share, that day we will surely see.
The odyssey we shared must now end, as it must be.
This odyssey we started many years ago at the Childersburg
C of C.

M. Alton Headley

Chapter 23

Poems, Remnants, and Recipes

Childersburg

Your teaching, as a young man, my eyes could not see
the hopes and dreams I had you set in place for me.
Your warmth was always there to see.
A place my mind's eye goes often for me.
It is time; yea long past,
to express what you have done for others, and me.
You were the whisperer
who told me I could be whatever I wished to be.
You set me free to see the potential I knew could be there for
me.
You taught me I could be what I dreamed I would someday
be.
Could it be the quality of those who came before others and
me?
I admit somewhat nostalgic I am for thee.
Why after so many years I with you wish to be.
Some stayed to make Childersburg a better place for others
to see.
No longer my home, but in my heart you will always be.
Why after so many years I with you wish to be.
I cherish the memories for it may not always be mine to see.
To you I will return if only in my dreams I plea.
Best wishes to you the CHS family.

M. Alton Headley

HIGHBURG Explained

It is your vision that allows poetry be digested
for pleasure or not at all.
This is my shared imagery of Childersburg High School
through this monocle.

War Child

We all were given life in the fury of the horrible rage
of World War II as a backdrop.
The road sign: "Welcome to Childersburg"
"Home of Buck Thompson,"
"Boomers" are coming from "The Greatest Generation."
Some of our mates were raised fatherless.

Faired haired and full
Many smooth haired, Anglo Saxon
with heavy Irish and English linage.

Mild in Complexion, Strong in Competition
Light skinned, alabaster hue blended with a summer,
no shirt, tan. Strictly Caucasian.
All competing for attention and approval.

Red, Blond, Coal, and Sandy
Scanning the classroom with heads on top of the desk for a
nap. Open one eye to view a patchwork of inherited "mops".

Cotton, Silk and Flower Sack Panties
First Grade after lunch was nap time.
Boys were on the floor
and girls were sitting in the straight chairs at the tables.
Looking up, "risking one eye" only,
an inquiring, innocent, six year old boy
could view up the dangling legs leading up to "underwear
land"
and the variety of materials in this diverse display of bottoms.
You begin to realize early, silence is a virtue.
You could get in trouble fast
and lose your spot on the floor
and get your own bottom "worn out."

Patton Browns and Barefoot Minnie
The variety of footwear
represented a diverse social economic class

from the one strap "Mary Janes"
to the "Black and White" oxfords.
Slaves to conformity.
In class, off came the shoes,
for some, revealing an unwelcome odor.
A few miles away at Phyllis Wheatley
some attended barefooted.
Minnie was my barefoot nanny.

Shuffle across the oiled floor
The smell of sweeping compound
was shared in the dark halls
of the old fourth-grade class area.
As one period begin and ended with a shuffle,
a classic dance.

Ring that Bell
Ring the bell
as Mr. A. H. Watwood stood watch
as we changed classes
or, as we said, "Rooms".
No opportunity for mischief here;
"Not in my hall, Mr. Man."

Baby make it last
That smile, that image of the girl you liked,
takes this emotion to the next level
and into the next class room. T
his is "yours" to keep.

English is next
Not necessarily everyone's favorite class.
I vote this as the most valuable player
and very under-appreciated.
Not paying attention is a lifelong cost.

Smell the sour milk, with light beams pushing
Descending the stairs to the basement lunchroom,
you can smell the aroma of sour milk.
Spent milk cartons were allowed to collect

just outside the bottom of the stairs.
The sunlight would heat the drums
and release the pungent smell.
The thick glass blocks allowed an opaque illumination
to guide us down the stairs.
Waiting, staring into this column of oblivion,
quite mesmerized.

Foolish thoughts are plenty
Waiting in line for lunch,
next to your buddies
allowed ample time to discuss stupid subject matter
and check the label in their shirt to see it was a "McGregor."
An opportunity to show off
those new red or chartreuse pants
with the buckle in the back from Sonny Salaway's store.

Butterbean Sandwich, an Orange Jell-O Stare
Not all of the mates could afford the quarter for lunch.
One of my buddies would bring a sandwich
consisting of cooked dried butterbeans
on a white bread shroud.
He would apply the free ketchup to add flavor.
I had an extra nickel to buy him a carton of milk.
We had red, green or orange Jell-O variety
"nervous pudding" served frequently.
Looking into the congealed mass, one could see
a distorted reflection of other mates waiting in line to be fed.

Boy what a figure
We were served before upper class mates,
Looking up from the bench.
I could view the good looking older girls,

11th graders.
Picking out the ones that had been associated
with promiscuous reputations.
They were the most attractive to the underclass eye.

Always, the one you could not have,
the one that would not give you "the time of day."

That makes me jitter
The age of puberty
in combination with shyness
can create an inner behavioral thought process
that carries the full range of emotions for a boy.
If one of those good looking
upper class girls looked my way
or even smiled at me,
I could not handle this.
I would start shaking,
turn bright red
and be so withdrawn.
Like, "The turtle going back into his shell."

Lights are out
Fast forward to May, 1962
"Graduation Night".
A storm, with lighting, hit the transformer
and the main electrical feed
supplying power to the school
as we "The Elite Class of Sixty Two"
were preparing for this most momentous climax
to our twelve year association.
Several gifted, knowledgeable fathers
tried to trouble shoot and find a solution
so we could exercise this "Right of Passage".
This was a long delay as we waited
"close quarter" in the hall.

Ok, Mates .... Let's do it
Being 18, grouped in the pitch darkness
and waiting for the lights,
primed with estrogen and testosterone
is a combination for "risky behavior".
Who cares anyway?
We are about to do this thing,

separate and "move on."
Let's use this moment
to reflect our love and care for each other.
No matter what happens,
they can't take away this moment away.
This is the last time we will share this closeness,
this inanimate body
of companionship and comradery.

So, why not? Come on. "Let's do it".
Now and forever.
Save these words for the marriage vows.
Everything is for "Now",
this impulsive moment.
Forever is such a long incomprehensible concept.
Nothing is forever.
Or at least,
I think not, forever.

A kiss, a touch, looking good now
Total darkness allows the hands to roam,
an impulsive moment
to express your feelings with an innocent kiss.
Of course, we were all looking good, glamorous, handsome,
a striking pose.

Smile and Laughter
Coleman Lanterns
brought forward and lit
and the procession to the auditorium began
with all smiles and laughter.
Smiles reflected by the lantern glare.

Come on CHS
To you, Childersburg High School,
addressing the body of knowledge,
the collection of many classes
from 1953 through 1972
and beyond.

We are just better!
This is not "bull."
This is an undisputed fact:
The Class of 1962 was and remains the best.
A non‑narcissistic view of this body
as evidenced by the continuous association of mates.
Communicating, socializing and exchanging
once per month over wine and dinner
like no other class.
This group has earned the respect and right to be

"The Best"
We have chosen to communicate our memories
and share our values
as evidence by this collection of stories.
This is a tribute to that work.

Charles "Turkey" Burke

Yesterday

Did I misplace yesterday?
It was here what only a day ago.
As a young man only ten swimming, or riding my bike,
a meal with family, or friends.
Off to college I go, with the Army along the way
it all seems, well.....Yesterday.
A failed marriage but onward I go,
a divided family my greatest blow.
Have I learned my lessons well?
Have I given enough, only time will tell?
Did any yesterday's slip thru my hands?
Did I throw them in the sand?
Where did they go?
I am sure; they were here not long ago.
Oh now I remember what happened to yesterday?

It is what I called my life.
Mostly good, a little...... well not so good,
all in all not a bad day.
Yesterday.

M. Alton Headley

Torturing a Seven-Year-Old Boy

Mike Headley, *CHS Class of 1962*

Who came up with one of the most unpleasant rules ever to torture a seven year old boy? That would be the Wiseinstine that said "you had to wait one hour after eating before going swimming." I can assure you my mother and aunts thought that law was created in heaven. On numerous occasions there I sat wasting my life away and longing to be swimming and playing in the water. I was not allowed as much as a toe to enter. Friends, that gave a new meaning to the term "Water Torture."

I know my older sisters; Bettye, Sandra and cousins, Robert, and Frank Russell, plus my cousin, Brenda Dudney, would sneak off and swim before the hour was up; leaving cousins Mary Joe Russell Guy, and Marie Dudney Stewart and myself at the water's edge alone. How could I see these things? When you're seven years old you have X-Ray eyes, which I received from watching Flash Gordon on TV.

Sharing a Family Meal

Judy Elliott McGee, *CHS Class of 1964*

I remember one of the best things when we were growing up was having my family sitting down together, having a prayer of thanksgiving, eating the good meal Mama put on the table for us, and then actually talking about our day, kidding each other a little, laughing a lot, and appreciating that we had a comfortable home, food to eat, clothes to wear, and a family that was built on so much love. I miss those days a lot.

Future Homemakers of America Spring 1962

OFFICERS IN F. H. A. CHILDERSBURG HIGH SCHOOL — From left to right Miss Edna Alexander, Shirley Trucks, Marilyn Alexander, Deloris Maddox. Sitting are Gayle Simpson, Betty Lawrence.

Recipes

Fighting Cake: Graham Cracker Torte

Betty Lawrence Jones, *CHS Class of 1962*

22	crushed graham crackers
1½ tsp.	Baking powder
1/2 cup	chopped nuts (I use pecans)
1/4 cup	shortening (I use butter flavored Crisco)
3/4 cup	sugar
1	egg
3/4 cup	milk

- Mix crackers, baking powder and nuts and set aside.
- Cream shortening and sugar until light and fluffy then add egg, milk and vanilla mix well.
- Add this mixture to the crackers and stir well.
- Bake in   a greased 8 x 8 or 9 x 9 glass Pyrex dish at 400 degrees for approximately 20 minutes.
- This cake is best served warm topped with hard sauce.
- If I bake it ahead of time, I warm each piece in the microwave before adding hard sauce.

Hard sauce for fighting cake

1/3 cup	oleo
1 cup	powdered sugar
2/3 tsp	Vanilla flavoring

Mix well.   Leftovers should go into the refrigerator.

Sour Cream Pound Cake

Betty Lawrence Jones, *CHS Class of 1962*

3 cups	sugar
2 sticks	oleo
2 tsp.	Vanilla flavoring
2 tsp.	Lemon flavoring
1 tsp.	Almond flavoring
6	eggs
3 1/4 cups	cake flour - sift twice before measuring
1/4 tsp	Baking soda
Scant 1 tsp.	Salt
1/2 pint	sour cream

- Place eggs in warm water a few minutes ahead of time to bring them to room temperature.
- Cream oleo, salt and sugar well then add eggs one at a time, beating well after each addition.
- Add flavorings and beat well.

- Add flour sifted with soda alternately with sour cream. Mix well.
- Bake in a large greased and floured tube pan at 325 degrees for approximately 90 minutes. Ovens vary, so keep watch on it after about 75 minutes.

School Soup

Vicki Helms Smith, *CHS Class of 1962*

I remember it from school. It was always served with a sandwich made from white bread and what must have been a mixture of government peanut butter and honey.

1 48 oz. can	tomato juice
1 lb.	Fresh lean ground beef
1 bag	frozen mixed vegetables
1 8.5 oz. can	lima beans
1 14-oz can	whole peeled tomatoes, mashed and with juice
2	potatoes, diced
2	med. onions, diced
2 tsp	salt
1 tsp	pepper
1 tsp	Worcestershire sauce

- Bring tomato juice to a boil.
- Slowly add crumbled ground beef.
- Cook until beef is separated.
- Add onions, mixed vegetables, potatoes, salt and Worcestershire sauce.
- Cook over medium heat until vegetables are tender, stirring occasionally.
- Add more salt if desired.

Stuffed Cabbage Rolls (Mike's Favorite)

Bettye Headley Donahoo, *CHS Class of 1954*

2 heads large	Cabbage
2 medium cans	canned tomatoes
2 medium cans	Sauerkraut
1 ½ pounds	Hamburger meat
One	Onion, large (white) chopped
2/3 cup	Rice

- Steam cabbage until you can separate leaves.
- Brown hamburger meat and onions.
- Boil rice until fluffy.
- Mix meat, rice, chopped onion and just a bit of tomato juice to make stuffing.
- Be sure to salt and pepper meat mixture remembering kraut is salty so adjust as needed.
- Roll some meat/rice mixture in a cabbage leaf and secure with tooth pick.
- Continue until all meat is used.
- Place half sauerkraut and half of the tomatoes in bottom of the pot.
- Next place all stuff cabbage rolls on top of ½ the kraut, and tomatoes.
- Add remainder of kraut and tomatoes on top the cabbage rolls.
- Cover pot and cook on simmer for 2 hours.
- If too dry, add a little water along.
- Some poppy seeds can be sprinkled on top if desired.

Makes 15 cabbage rolls

Chapter 24

The Headleys, Dudneys, And barely do

The Headleys

Samuel Alton Headley

Mike Headley, *CHS Class of 1962*

Samuel Alton Headleys family for the most part is English decent. The Headleys first settled in South Carolina having arrived by ship from England in the middle part of the 18th century. In the 19th century, the Headleys relocated to the Clanton, Alabama area. They have for the most part lived either in Chilton county or the greater Birmingham area most of the last 150 years.

Research has shown that the name Pinckney was a prominent one in the beginning of our country. Charles Pinckney, a distant relative, was a signer of the U. S. Constitution from South Carolina. I have an uncle named James Pinckney and a great-grandfather named Charles; therefore, the names Pinckney and Charles have been sprinkled throughout the male side of the Headley family for generations.

Samuel Alton Headley met Edith Ellen Dudney in Birmingham, Alabama in the early 1930s. Birmingham was much larger, and while only one hour away in the 1950s, unless you encountered a semi on your trip over Double Oak Mountain, then it turned into a one and a half hour trip. Remember "The Narrows?" In the 1950s those trips were mostly to visit my Headley grandparents in North Birmingham, however, sometime we would see uncles, aunts, or cousins. They were spread from Hueytown to North Birmingham.

In 1948, Samuel Alton Headley (usually referred to as Alton), built my mother, two sisters, and me a new brick home next door to my Dudney grandparents. We moved from our house in Minor Terrace to our new home. This was my home for the next 14 years, on the west side of US 280/231 one mile south of Holt's crossroad. I lived next door to my grandparents, Bennett and Annie Dudney, until leaving for college in the fall of 1962.

Sandra Headley Limbaugh, *SHS Class of 1957*

When daddy built our new house we could look out across the backfield at a beautiful view of Flag Pole Mountain. I missed living in town and walking almost everywhere but the mountain was beautiful with a white blanket of dogwood in spring and the most amazing reds, yellows and oranges of the leaves in the fall. We truly were "free range" children. I look back with fond memories of both the times and the special friends.

Bettye Headley Donahoo, *CHS Class of 1954*

Our Headley grandparents had 5 children, 4 boys and 1 girl. The girl was our Aunt Ruby. On occasion in the summer, my sister, Sandra, and I would be put on the Trailways bus to visit our Headley relatives in Birmingham. Our grandmother Headley's name was China Leona, called Chinee. Our Aunt Ruby worried that her nieces and nephew would never know anything of the world while living in Childersburg.

When we went to visit the Headleys in Birmingham they would try to see that we saw and did different things. Aunt Ruby was unmarried at the time and the height of sophistication in my eyes. She was tall and slim and dressed beautifully. I did not know any woman who went out to work, but Aunt Ruby worked as a secretary in a law firm. I would watch her getting ready for work and would be in awe.

She wore business suits with silk blouses, usually with a big bow at the neck. She wore very high heels, and stockings with seams. Her hair nails and cosmetics were perfection. To top it all off, she smoked and had a large gold cigarette case with cigarettes on one side and a gold lighter on the other.

Aunt Ruby was very kind to me and spent time making sure I learned a lot. She always wore red nail polish and showed me how to polish my nails. She told me to always apply polish to the tips of the nail first. To this day, I follow her advice when doing my nails. I felt then that Aunt Ruby was the most beautiful and sophisticated woman in the world, and, though I have been and lived many places, and have seen many attractive people, Aunt Ruby still holds that title.

The Dudneys

Edith Ellen Dudney Headley

Mike Headley, *CHS Class of 1962*

Our mother's side of the family is of English-Dutch descendant. The Dudneys lived in middle Tennessee (White House) for at least seven generations until our grandfather William Bennett Dudney killed his brother-in-law. Great-uncle Bob and our grandfather had adjoining land. A dispute arose over a boundary line. Uncle Bob said he was going to kill grandfather. One day Uncle Bob marched up the field with a shot gun. Because of grandfathers pacifist religious beliefs he was not going to fight. Grandmother pleaded with grandfather to protect himself and not leave her a widow.

Finally grandfather relented and got his pistol. He tried to change Uncle Bob's mind. However, Uncle Bob started shooting through the front door. Grandfather shot back and killed his brother-in-law. He was arrested and then released - it was declared he acted in self-defense.

Sometime after the shooting grandfather hitched his two mules to the family wagon loaded our grandmother and their children including our mother, Edith, along with their belongings, and leaving behind their first born child, a son buried in the local cemetery. The family headed south toward Alabama hoping for a new start and a better life. Grandfather Dudney settled his family in Huntsville for a few years.

At each town the family lived in on their odyssey moving south toward Childersburg, the older Dudney daughters found husbands in Huntsville, Alabama. In the early 1930s the Dudney family which at that time still included our mother moved to Birmingham for a short sojourn where our parents met. Our mother, along with her parents and siblings, moved again to Sylacauga, Alabama. A short time later grandpa Dudney built a white wood framed house on Meadow View Lane near the base of Flagpole Mountain. Around that time our totally smitten father quickly left Birmingham, Alabama moving to the, Sylacauga area.

Around 1946, grandfather Dudney built a white block home on the west side of the new two-lane U S Highway 280 known in those days as the "Florida Short Route."

Grandfather Dudney

Bettye Headley Donahoo, *CHS Class of 1954*

William Bennett Dudney was a different personality from his wife. While grandmother was kind, but stoic and unsmiling, Pa Dudney was full of fun. He could make almost any situation fun so, of course, his grandchildren loved being with him. I never recall him being grouchy or not having time for all of his grandchildren.

Though his life was hard, he never complained He was a rather small man with dark coloring, and beautiful black, curly hair. I have wonderful memories of him sitting on his front porch reading the Bible and smoking his pipe. He always had a Bible story to share, and could tell it in a way that even the smallest of us could find interesting.

Pa Dudney had only a fourth grade education because he had to leave school to help his family on their farm. He was mostly self-educated and quite knowledgeable. Often times his only source for education was his Bible and encyclopedia. He read and studied both constantly.

Grandpa's flowers were so outstanding that it was not uncommon for complete strangers to pull off Highway US 280 into his driveway to admire his yard. His roses were his pride.

He had fruit trees, and various types of grape vines, which he turned into various wines. His vegetable gardens were large, and beautiful. One of granddad's greatest joys was sharing all his crops with family and friends. Nothing suited him better than a barbecue with his extended family, the more the merrier.

Grandfather had a unique way of naming dogs. After a great deal of thought grandfather offered up names such as Blunderbuss, Twasee and Four Square. I have absolutely no explanation for such names. No new animal was ever named until Pa Dudney took days or even weeks to observe the animal, then coming up with the proper name. We children would continually urge him to pronounce the name, but he advised patience. He said the animal's character and personality had to be closely studied before a name could be found. The names were always unique and fitted perfectly.

He never missed going to the Old Church of Christ downtown Childersburg. At the end of most church service granddad would signal the preacher that he had a few words of "exhortation to share with the congregation." The "few words" would usually take 15 to 20 minutes. I have learned that this was known as "Exhorting the Congregation" and was quite common in small southern churches in earlier years.

In a letter grandfather wrote to me filled with wisdom and love he wrote. *If a man's memories are not happy ones, that man is to be pitied.* This was written near the end of his life, and I believe he felt his life had been blessed indeed.

Grandmother Dudney

Bettye Headley Donahoo, *CHS Class of 1954*

Our Grandmother Dudney was a small, dark skin woman. She wore her gray hair pulled back in a bun and wearing cotton "house dresses," and unless she was going to church or town, she always wore an apron. Her clothes were immaculate, washed, starched and ironed. She didn't wear make-up except for a little powder. Her modest home was also always immaculate, and she prepared large sumptuous meals using the bounty of her and granddaddy's vegetable garden.

Grandmother was a stoic woman, not given to laughter, and I seldom saw her smile. She did not share her feelings and rarely cried. She did not complain or indicate that she was tired. She did not portray that she was anything except contented with "her life." I only realized as an adult that there were tragedies in her life which would have shaken a lesser woman.

Grandmother spent much of her time working and cleaning her house, but also took an interest in the yard. She had many blooming flowers and plants, including a plant called Elephant Ear which was poisonous. One day our grandfather decided to trim some leaves and stalks from the Elephant Ear plant. My brother, Mike, was six years old, and walked by the stalks and decided to eat some because someone had told him they were the sugar cane he had eaten a few days before. He became quite ill with swelling and inflammation in his mouth. There was quite a to-do for he was screaming and crying. Grandmother used butter to treat him by swabbing his mouth.

She did not play with her grandchildren or teach the girls to cook, etc., but I never felt anything except comfortable and loved in her presence. We knew we were always welcome at grandmother Dudney's, as our yards connected; we were in her home almost as much as our own. She never missed a Sunday at the Church Of Christ in Childersburg.

Barely Do (My Play Place)

Mike Headley, *CHS Class of 1962*

I asked my grandfather William Bennett Dudney why the place we lived was named "Barley Do". He looked at me and said "Son, because this place will barely do."

To the west I could look up to see the fire tower on Flagpole Mountain standing against the clouds on the horizon. The smell of Honey Suckle, Pine, Sweet Gum, and Oak trees in the spring mixed with cotton poison in the summer were forever on the breeze, my mind remembers these things well.

The 14 acres between US Highway 280 on the east and the old Sylacauga Highway on the west one mile south of Casey Holt's store was my territory to explore. I roamed those woods and fields as my private hunting grounds, with my trusty BB gun always at the ready. Hiding in the ravines and woods was my cover from the bad guys or Indians, whichever might attack.

In the summer I ate blackberries ripe from the bushes in the brambles also there was a small gurgling brook in the spring to drink from. I had May Pops to stomp, and Black Eyed Susans in the fields to see. By July grandpa Dudney's watermelons were ready. Just sit down in the field and cut a big red one open with my knife. I had no napkin with which to wipe my mouth because I only wore shirts to church on Sunday. Remember it was summer time. However, I could spit a water melon seed quite a distance.

In late summer there were Cattails to burst and watch the fuzz fly.
In the fall if my Uncle John, whose orchards was on the adjoining farm to my south was not looking, a trip to his peach orchard was in order for a fresh peach or two right off the tree.

As I remember those days, it was truly a beautiful yet simpler time.

Mike Headley, 1961

The End

Final Thoughts

"There is no real ending.
It's just the place where you stop the story."
Frank Herbert (author of *Dune)*

Mike Headley, *CHS Class of 1962*

As I look back at the creation of this community memoir I see what the writer Frank Herbert was trying to tell us. The story of Childersburg continues, as it should. We, the authors, just stopped our story.

From the Authors

It is the hope of all 92 authors of this memoir that you, the reader, have enjoyed these vignettes, pictures, and stories from a different time in Childersburg, Alabama.

From the Editor/Publisher, Mike Headley

I read the book "Images of Childersburg" by Leigh Mathis Downs which showed me what Childersburg was like from its beginnings. This memoir is an attempt to cover some of the events which occurred in Childersburg between the years from 1953 through 1982, through the eyes of the people who lived there.

The following list identifies the people and/or families who have joined me in the writing of this memoir providing stories, vignettes, blurbs, and pictures. Without their help this memoir would have not been possible, and I thank every one of them.

Contributors

Roscoe Limbaugh	CHS Class of 1953
Bettye Headley Donahoo	CHS Class of 1954
Jane Watwood Gibbs	CHS Class of 1958
Beverly Rogers-Dixon Poellnitz	CHS Class of 1959
Charles (Beatle) Bailey	CHS Class of 1959
Brenda Solley Brown	CHS Class of 1960
Tony Butts	CHS Class of 1960
Ken Herndon	CHS Class of 1960
George Gilbert	CHS Class of 1961
Sue Ellison McDuffie	CHS Class of 1961
Glenden Fields Ogle	CHS Class of 1961
Robert E. Burdick	CHS Class of 1961
Paul Dillard	CHS Class of 1961
Mickey Donahoo	CHS Class of 1961
JD Warren	CHS Class of 1961
Joyce Mayfield Allen	CHS Class of 1962
Sherry Machen Atkinson	CHS Class of 1962
Betty Jenkins Breedlove	CHS Class of 1962
Betty Lawrence Jones (deceased)	CHS Class of 1962
Vicki Helms Smith	CHS Class of 1962
Linda Justice Simpson	CHS Class of 1962
Patsy Rich Weaver	CHS Class of 1962
Dwain Adams	CHS Class of 1962
Dr. Richard (Dickey) Bean	CHS Class of 1962
Charles "Turkey" Burke	CHS Class of 1962
Billy Hall	CHS Class of 1962
Mike Headley	CHS Class of 1962
Sue Brannon	CHS Class of 1963
Marilyn Alexander Primero	CHS Class of 1963
Jimmy Ray Williams	CHS Class of 1963
Judy Elliott McGee	CHS Class of 1964
Elaine M Greer	CHS Class of 1965
Martha Denton Webb	CHS Class of 1965
Ed Castleberry	CHS Class of 1965
Danny Wiginton	CHS Class of 1965
James Phelps	CHS Class of 1965

Contributors (cont.)

Nancy Pressley Beckham	CHS Class of 1966
Ollie Pardue	CHS Class of 1966
Mark Riddle	CHS Class of 1966
Brenda Williamson	CHS Class of 1966
Linda Maddox Jinks	CHS Class of 1967
June Melton Lassiter	CHS Class of 1967
Jan Machen Minor	CHS Class of 1967
Randall Fields	CHS Class of 1967
Billy (Mike) Miller	CHS Class of 1967
James Morris	CHS Class of 1967
Jimmy Owens	CHS Class of 1967
Joe Peerson	CHS Class of 1968
Linda Joyce Seay Williams	CHS Class of 1969
Brian Miller Sr.	CHS Class of 1969
Marsha Dillard	CHS Class of 1970
Marilyn Brown Lawson	CHS Class of 1970
Patsy Cobb Wills Jones	CHS Class of 1971
Jullia Brunfeldt	CHS Class of 1972
Dianne Fuller Harrelson	CHS Class of 1972
Judy J. Headrick	CHS Class of 1972
Dianne Hillman Prisoc	CHS Class of 1972
Candy Stephens	CHS Class of 1972
Vicki Dobbs Southern	CHS Class of 1972
Joy Burton Lawson	CHS Class of 1972
Joey Ratliff	CHS Class of 1972
David Swanger	CHS Class of 1972
Peter Wallenfang	CHS Class of 1972
Earl Wesson Jr	CHS Class of 1972
Gary Bowen	CHS Class of 1973
Herb Haynes	CHS Class of 1973
Chuck McMillian	CHS Class of 1974
David Burton	CHS Class of 1975
Jim Redder	CHS Class of 1975
Robbie Riddle	CHS Class of 1975
Peter Storey	CHS Class of 1975

Contributors (cont.)

Donna Carroll Ward	CHS Class of 1977
Steve Hindman	CHS Class of 1977
Buckwheat Finn	CHS Class of 1979
Jennifer Trucks Botta	CHS Class of 1980
Phyllis Jinks Boyett	CHS Class of 1980
Jackie Morris-Cates	CHS Class of 1980
John Madison (Johnny) Giddens Jr.	CHS Class of 1980
Denise Crawford Maul	CHS Class of 1982
Jill Duvall Stubblefield	CHS Class of 1983
Malcolm Bates	CHS Class of 1983
Dlaine Pogue	CHS Class of 1984
Daniel Lee	CHS Class of 1984

Contributors who graduated from schools other than CHS

Sandra Headley Limbaugh	SHS Class of 1957
Bubba Cleckler	ISHS Class of 1958
Carolyn Green Price	CCHS Class of 1965
Ron Poole	THS Class of 1968
Linda Johnston Wallenfang	UHS Class of 1969
Tom Herndon	ISHS Class of 1971
Cynthia Summers	PHS Class of 1977
Allison Teague Bell	TCHS Class of 1983

And

The Family of Leslie McInnish

29845299R00204

Made in the USA
Middletown, DE
04 March 2016